ISBN 978-0-259-94672-4
PIBN 10829547

1 MONTH OF
FREE
READING

at

www.ForgottenBooks.com

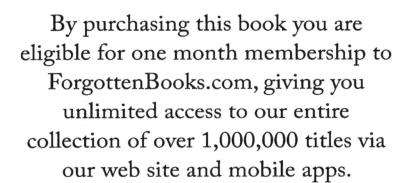

By purchasing this book you are eligible for one month membership to ForgottenBooks.com, giving you unlimited access to our entire collection of over 1,000,000 titles via our web site and mobile apps.

To claim your free month visit:

www.forgottenbooks.com/free829547

THE

GARDEN COMPANION,

And Florists' Guide:

BY

ARTHUR HENFREY, F.R.S., F.L.S.,

VICE-PRESIDENT OF THE BOTANICAL SOCIETY, AND LECTURER ON BOTANY AT ST. GEORGE'S HOSPITAL ;

THOMAS MOORE, F.L.S., &c.,

CURATOR OF THE BOTANIC GARDEN, CHELSEA, *Conductor ;*

WILLIAM P. AYRES, C.M.H.S.,

BROOKLANDS, BLACKHEATH, KENT ;

AND OTHER PRACTICAL CULTIVATORS.

JANUARY TO OCTOBER, 1852.

LONDON:

WILLIAM S. ORR AND CO., AMEN CORNER,

PATERNOSTER ROW.

MDCCCLII.

Eng
G - 3.1

LIST OF PLANTS DESCRIBED, FIGURED, OR SPECIALLY NOTICED.

₊ d. described ; f. figured.

INDEX OF ILLUSTRATIONS.

COLOURED FIGURES.

FLOWERS.

ILLUSTRATIVE WOOD ENGRAVINGS.

PLANTS.

The Garden Companion

AND FLORISTS' GUIDE.

NEW HYBRID HEATHS.

BEAUTIFUL as are many, very many, of the shrubs of the Heath family, which have come to our gardens from the land of their nativity, the Cape of Good Hope, and varied as are the forms and colours they present, yet it must be confessed that objects still more beautiful and varied, and often more useful, because more cultivable, have been produced from them by the skill and perseverance of the hybridizer. In this, as in other instances, the hand of art, guided by science, has succeeded in elaborating the most lovely combinations of form and colouring from the exquisite "raw material" of nature. Some of the results of this triple combination—of art and science with nature—we present in the accompanying plate, on which are representations of two hybridized Heaths,* which have been produced, along with many others of great merit, by Mr. A. Turnbull, gardener at Bothwell Castle, to the noble representative of the name of Douglas. Bothwell Castle has long been famous for its Hybrid Heaths, and those now represented will take a place among the best of its productions of this class.

Erica Thomsonii is the offspring of *E. aristata*, crossed with *E. cerinthoides*. It is of rather more vigorous growth than the former, but bears a greater resemblance to that species in its habit and mode of flowering, than it does to its other parent, from which it has derived something in colour, and in the slight glandular hairiness which occurs towards the upper part of the tube of the corolla. The colour is crimson, brighter along the exposed side, and deepening about the throat, the under side being much paler; on each flower are eight ribs, which are deeper coloured than the rest of the flower; the limb has a slight coppery tinge. It is a very striking Heath, and quite distinct, and has been named in compliment to Mr. Thomson of Glasgow.

Erica Mooreana has been bred from *E. retorta major*, crossed by *E. Linnæoides*. In its general appearance, it partakes more of the latter than the former, but is much dwarfer, and more branching in its growth, and a remarkably free bloomer. It will no doubt become a popular Heath, from its being a plant of free growth, and blowing profusely in autumn and in the early part of winter; in fact, con-

* *Erica Thomsonii*, Turnbull MS. (hyb : ♀ aristata, ♂ cerinthoides).—Leaves five in a whorl, numerous linear-lanceolate ciliate aristate recurved, flowers in a terminal spreading umbellate head, pedicels bracteate near the calyx, and as well as it, glandular-hairy, corolla oblong inflated, slightly glandular hairy on the outside towards the neck, limb short erect, anthers mutic, and as well as the stigma enclosed.—M.

Erica Mooreana, Turnbull MS. (hyb : ♀ retorta major, ♂ Linnæoides).—Leaves four in a whorl, linear recurved hairy, flowers very shortly pedicellate, in fours terminating the small branches, corollas oblong inflated slightly hairy, limb spreading, anthers mutic, the style sub-exserted.—M.

tinuing to blossom until *E. hiemalis* comes into flower. The colour is a lovely purplish rose, tipped with white.

The specimens from which the plate has been prepared were communicated by Mr. Turnbull in October last.—M.

Among the originators of new Heaths, Mr. Turnbull, must be considered one of the most fortunate; for, unlike most raisers, Mr. Turnbull gets strength of constitution as well as beauty of flower, and hence at the same time attains two very important advantages. Mr. Turnbull's may be considered wild crosses, his object being to get fine flowers upon strong and robust growing plants. Most of the raisers in this country breed from the rare and choice kinds, and hence the plants are very delicate, and rarely grow with freedom; Mr. Turnbull, on the contrary, would wish to transfer the lovely flowers of *E. splendens* to the constitution of *E. hiemalis*, and the flowers of *E. aristata*, *Aitoniana* and *obbata* to the rude growth of *E. ventricosa*, and the like; in fact, he wishes to get the splendid flowers of the hard-wooded species and varieties upon the strong constitution of the soft-wooded kinds, by which means he would secure plants of easy propagation, strong growth, and great freedom of flowering.

As one of the principal objects of the conductors of this work is to record, pictorially when necessary, the results emanating from the labours of the hybridizer and cross-breeder, whether his object is to improve those kinds already considered Florists' Flowers, or by assiduous crossing to elevate many of our commoner plants to the rank of Florists' Flowers, we shall always be glad to receive specimens from our friends, and, when worthy, give them such notice as may render them of permanent interest to cultivators. From the wild Pansy of our corn-fields, the splendid varieties which decorate our gardens and exhibition tables in early spring, have been originated. From the almost petal-less wild Pelargoniums of the Cape, the gorgeous broad-petaled brilliant-coloured flowers which make our gardens and greenhouses a blaze of bloom for many months in the year, have come. The single thin petaled Rose, or more poetic " Eglantine," of our lanes and hedge-rows, is the foster parent of the queen of flowers; and even La Reine, Géant des Batailles, Coup d'Hebe, and equally magnificent kinds, must own such humble origin. The gorgeous Azalea, the stately Rhododendron, the magnificent Hollyhock, the lovely Picotee, Pink, and Carnation, all acknowledge similar humble parentage; indeed though plants were perfect when originated, it is man's mission upon earth to beautify it, and to render flowers and trees, and all living things, what they ought to be. A glorious mission it is, and, so far as our own peculiar duty is concerned, none but those who have tasted the sweets can appreciate the delightful allurements of cross-breeding and improving flowers.

There is yet a vast field unexplored, the little that has been attained is nothing as compared with what is to come. Every tribe of plants which has the primary colours, or an approximation to them presented in its flowers, is susceptible of immense improvement, not only in form of flower but also in colour and constitution of plant, and there is no reason why our Lilacs and Laburnums, and other gay shrubs, trees, and herbaceous plants, should not present a more gay and varied aspect, if an effort to improve them was rightly directed and followed up. But we are writing a dissertation on cross-breeding instead of Heath-growing, and hence must return to our subject.

Now, it may be laid down as an indisputable truism at starting, that more Heaths are annually killed by kindness than by neglect; and hence the amateur cannot do better than dismiss from his mind all idea that they will turn sickly if they get a drop too much water, or die outright should they ever know the want of a sufficient quantity. We have seen plants in rude health with their pots covered with mosses and lichens, and almost lost amid weeds, and where they were watered broadcast with a coarse rose, and with no more care than a bed of cabbage plants; and we have seen one of the largest collections in England, in a house which cost thousands of pounds, attended with the most assiduous care, and scrupulously clean, almost every plant with death written on its long lank lean visage,—and all because some great gardener, in a neighbourhood remarkable for the humidity of the atmosphere, had said or written that Heaths must have the collar of the plant elevated above the rim of the pot, or, in other words, have in more arid situations, their balls or roots hung up to dry.

Hence, after a general shifting, came, as a natural consequence, a funeral, and for a few dozens, scores or hundreds of plants (according to the stock), to be committed "to the tomb of all the Capulets" was no unusual thing; indeed, it was not until the discussion consequent on the promulgation of the large-shift system took place that the philosophy of the practice was explained, and the absurdity eradicated. The mistake was that of elevating the collar of the plant *above* the level of the rim of the pot;—to elevate, or round up the ball *below* the rim of the pot, is an allowable practice at the present time, if the surface roots are not too much exposed. Now, the three great requisites in the successful management of Heaths are good peat, good water, and good air. The first can only be obtained from upland situations, or from places where it is not covered with water for the greater part of the year. Peat may be described as decayed vegetable matter, the accumulation of ages, which has become thoroughly disintegrated, and consisting principally of natural carbon. That kind which is very turfy and closely compressed, rather than soft and spongy, is the best; and this, when thoroughly aërated by exposure to the weather for a few months, is the sort of thing to use. In collecting it, take care only to cut the thickness of the very turfy part, and if any of the sand adheres to it, cut it off before it is laid by to rot. The soft peat may be used, well mixed with sand, while the plants are small and in free growth; but, in large quantities, it is liable to become sodden and water-logged, and hence the plants, though they grow rapidly at first, soon turn sickly and die.

In using peat, it should be carefully picked over, removing all the parts which look likely to become sodden. Then break it all up and pass it through a sieve with a half-inch mesh, making the entire quantity to pass through by breaking or chopping it until it is sufficiently reduced, as it is upon an intimate admixture of the larger vegetable parts of the mass that the soil must, to some extent, depend for its porosity. To soil so prepared, add a good quantity of sharp silver sand, potsherds, and charcoal broken small, in sufficient quantity to make the whole mass light and porous. It is now fit for use, and fit for hard-wooded Heaths; but, if you are going to pot the soft and free growing kinds, one-third of the soft peat and a proportionate quantity of sand may be added to it. Water and *air* such as the locality afford must be used, but hard water should always be avoided, and care should be taken to keep the air of the house in which the plants grow as free from smoke and all impurities as possible. The next point is to procure your plants, and for this purpose it is neither worth your time to raise plants from seed (except for originating new kinds), nor to strike them by cuttings; therefore, either throw yourself upon the nearest practical cultivator to select for you, or go to a respectable nurseryman and trust to his honour and honesty to supply you with suitable plants. As general rules, however, take care that the plants are dwarf and healthy, with plenty of vigorous roots, and quite green to the extreme points. Such plants, if they, according to the kinds and size of the plant, have stems as strong as the "gray goose quill," we are writing with, must be regarded as promising plants, and such as will, under proper management, make specimens equal to the finest in cultivation. Too much attention cannot be devoted to securing young plants such as we have described here, for it is upon a thorough good start that you must depend for a good specimen in a short time. This is the hinging point of success with the metropolitan exhibitors; they have a chance of selecting plants which a country gardener, except in special localities, cannot have, and hence in a great measure the marvellous specimens they produce.

We now come to the potting; and presuming that the plants have been selected, and the soil prepared as above directed, the next point is the pots; and these, if not new, should be thoroughly washed, and be made as clean as possible. Then take and drain them properly, that is, if the pots to be used are those called four or six inch, place a piece of flat crock over the orifice at the bottom, and over that from half an inch to an inch in depth of potsherds and charcoal, of the same size as that used for mixing with the soil. Over the drainage, to prevent the soil getting into it, some persons put a small quantity of moss—but that we do not approve of; for if the roots get into it, and it gets dry, it is difficult to moisten again; and hence the plants receive a severe check by the injury the roots receive. We therefore prefer to cover the drainage with some of the coarser parts of the peat, filling up with the finer material. In turning the plants out of the old pot, take care the ball is in a uniform state as to moisture; and if the roots are much matted, pick them out a little with a sharp pointed stick, so as to give them a chance of entering at once into the new soil. In potting, press the soil, especially if dry, very firmly; so firmly that the thumb, if pressed upon it, after watering, will scarcely leave an impression. The sticklers for porosity, mechanical action, and so forth, may object to this firm potting; and indeed the plants will not grow so rapidly in it as in porous potting; but they will make more healthy growth, and live a much longer time. After the plants are potted, place them in a frame or pit, water occasionally as required, until the whole mass of soil is moistened, and keep them tolerably close, and the atmosphere moist, until the plants get into free growth, when abundance of air must be admitted. The plants must now be considered as fairly started, and their subsequent treatment must form the subject of another paper.—A.

ON THE PERIODICAL EMISSION OF THE ODOURS OF PLANTS.

IT is a well-known fact that many plants give off the most powerful perfume in the evening and night-time. This phenomenon has been attributed to various physical causes, arising out of peculiar conditions of the atmosphere, &c.; but little is known on the subject, and some observations, published several years ago by Professor Morren, seem strongly opposed to any physical explanation of the facts. It had been supposed that flowers merely gave out the more powerful odour at night on account of the volatile perfume being less quickly dissipated at that time than when the sun was above the horizon. It was also a question whether the condensation of the atmosphere during the night might not be the cause of the increased power of the scent. *Orchis bifolia* occurs abundantly about Liege in spring, and its white flowers, which are quite scentless during the day, give out a pleasant, penetrating aroma in the evening, and especially about eleven o'clock at night. Professor Morren convinced himself by five days' observation that the perfume began to be manifested at twilight, exhibited the greatest energy at the time when the darkness of night prevailed, and decreased with the dawn. Two spikes of flowers of this *Orchis* were placed in two cylindrical glasses filled with water, in which the plants were totally submerged. One glass was placed so that the sun might shine upon it all day, the other was kept in the shade. Any scent emitted from these flowers could only be perceived through the water by which they were covered. As evening came on a delicious aroma became evident, and was emitted throughout the night, being lost at sunrise. This proves, says Professor Morren, that the condensation of the vapour has not the slightest influence upon the perception of the odoriferous constituents by our senses. It further proves, in regard to the plants exposed to the air, that neither the evaporation of the particles nor the accumulation of them on the parts of the plant where they have their origin, is the cause of the periodical absence and recurrence of this exhalation; so that the explanation of this phenomenon must undoubtedly be sought in physiological facts.

Professor Morren made another experiment. The blossom of *Maxillaria aromatica* is well known for its strong odour of cinnamon, so that two or three flowers will scent a whole conservatory. And it is well known that in the fertilization of the Orchideæ, the deposition of the pollen on the stigmata is effected very quickly, that the pollen-tubes elongate in less than one hour, the flowers and the perianth begin to close, and the columella shoots up. In a plant bearing many flowers, examined by Professor Morren, the scent was strong, penetrating, agreeable, and resembling fine cinnamon. The unfertilized flower retained this odour day and night, morning and evening, for eight days. Each flower that was fertilized by Professor Morren lost its odour in half-an-hour after the operation, and never gave further signs of it. This fact seems alone sufficient to prove that the emission of the odour is a vital phenomenon.

This is a subject upon which good and careful observations are still requisite.—A. H.

MR. WARINGTON'S AQUARIUM.

THE AQUATIC PLANT CASE, OR PARLOUR AQUARIUM.

NEARLY two years since, Mr. Warington communicated to the Chemical Society the following interesting paper:—

"This communication will consist of a detail of an experimental investigation, which has been carried on for nearly the last twelve months, and which appears to illustrate, in a marked degree, that beautiful and wonderful provision which we see every where displayed throughout the animal and vegetable kingdoms, whereby their continued existence and stability are so admirably sustained, and by which they are made mutually to subserve, each for the other's nutriment, and even for its indispensable wants and vital existence. The experiment has reference to the healthy life of fish preserved in a limited and confined portion of water. It was commenced in May, 1849, and the subjects chosen were two small gold fish. These were placed in a glass receiver of about twelve gallons' capacity, having a cover of thin muslin stretched over a stout copper wire, bent into a circle, placed over its mouth, so as to exclude as much as possible the sooty dust of the London atmosphere, without, at the same time, impeding the free passage of the atmospheric air. This receiver was about half filled with ordinary spring water, and supplied at the bottom with sand and mud, together with loose stones of limestone tufa from Matlock, and of sandstone; these were arranged so that the fish could get below them if they wished so to do. At the same time that the fish were placed in this miniature pond, if I may so term it, a small plant of the *Vallisneria spiralis* was introduced, its roots being inserted in the mud and sand, and covered by one of the loose stones so as to retain the plant in its position. The *Vallisneria spiralis* is one of those delicate aquatic plants generally selected by the microscopist for the exhibition of the circulation of the sap in plants; it throws out an abundance of long strap-shaped leaves of about a quarter of an inch in breadth, and from one to three feet in length. These leaves, when the sun shines on them, evolve a continued stream of oxygen gas, which rises in a current of minute bubbles, particularly from any part of the leaf which may have received an injury.

" The materials being thus arranged, all appeared to go on well for a short time, until circumstances occurred which indicated that another and very material agent was required to perfect the adjustment, and which, from my not having thought of it at the time of commencing the experiment, had not been provided against. The circumstances I allude to, arose from the decay of the leaves of the *Vallisneria*, which became yellow from having lost their vitality, and began to decompose. This, by accumulation, rendered the water turbid, and caused a growth of mucous or green slimy matter on the surface of the water, and on the sides of the receiver. If this had been allowed to increase, I conceive that the health of the fish must have suffered, and probably their vital functions have been destroyed. The removal of these decaying leaves from the water, therefore, became a point of paramount importance; and to effect this, I had recourse to a very useful little scavenger, whose beneficial functions have been too much overlooked in the economy of animal life; I mean the water snail, whose natural food is the very green slimy growth or mucus and decaying vegetable matter, which threatened to destroy the object which was wished to be obtained. Five or six of these creatures—the *Limnæa stagnalis*—were consequently introduced, and by their continued and rapid locomotion, and extraordinary voracity, they soon removed the cause of interference and restored the whole to a healthy state; thus perfecting the balance between the animal and vegetable inhabitants, and enabling both to perform their functions with health and energy.

" So luxuriant was the growth of the *Vallisneria* under these circumstances, that by the autumn the one solitary plant that had been originally introduced had thrown out very numerous offshoots and suckers, thus multiplying to the extent of upwards of thirty-five strong plants, and these threw up their long spiral flower stems in all directions, so that, at one time, more than forty blossoms were counted lying on the surface of the water.

" The fish have been lively, bright in colour, and appear very healthy ; and the snails also, judging from the enormous quantity of gelatinous masses of eggs which they have deposited on all parts of the receiver, as well as on the fragments of stone—appear to thrive wonderfully, and besides their functions in sustaining the perfect adjustment of the series, afford a large quantity of food to the fish in the form of the young snails, which are devoured as soon as they exhibit signs of vitality and locomotion, and before their shell has become hardened.

" Thus we have that admirable balance sustained between the animal and vegetable kingdoms, and that in a liquid element. The fish in its respiration consumes the oxygen held in solution by the water as atmospheric air, furnishes carbonic acid, feeds on the insects and young snails, and excretes material well adapted as a rich food to the plant, and well fitted for its luxuriant growth. The plant by its respiration consumes the carbonic acid produced by the fish, appropriating the carbon to the construction of its tissues and fibres, and liberates the oxygen in its gaseous state to sustain the healthy functions of the animal life, at the same time that it feeds on the rejected matter which has fulfilled its purposes in the nourishment of the fish and snail, and preserves the water constantly in a clean and healthy condition. While the slimy snail, finding its proper nutriment in the decomposing vegetable matter and minute confervoid growth, prevents their accumulation by removing them, and by its vital powers converts what would otherwise act as a poison into a rich and fruitful nutriment, again to constitute a pabulum for the vegetable growth, while it also acts the important part of a purveyor to its finny neighbours."

In this way is the economy of the animal and vegetable kingdoms wisely and beneficently adjusted so that the vital functions of each are permanently maintained.

The engraving represents an improvement on the original plan; for the opportunity of presenting it we are indebted to Mr. Warington, who has also kindly furnished the following additional observations founded on his now more lengthened experience:—

"Since the reading of my paper before the Chemical Society, on March 4, 1850, respecting the Miniature Aquarium (*Quarterly Journal of the Chemical Society*, iii. 52), I have continued the investigations, introducing other water plants, and also three other varieties of water snail. But the principal alteration has been the construction of a better form of vessel for holding the water, as I found that the globular form of the glass receiver, produced a distortion in the vision of the fish, besides being very inconvenient for observation. I have therefore adopted the form of vessel, of which a sketch is appended, having flat surfaces of plate-glass at the back and front, the bottom and ends being formed of slate, and supplied with a loose plate of glass at the top to keep out dust and soot. To render the whole more ornamental, as it was to stand in a sitting room, some pieces of tufa, or sandstone, were attached to the ends by means of Roman cement, so as to form ledges and slopes rising from the water line, on which mosses and ferns, such as luxuriate in an atmosphere loaded with moisture, could be grown. These materials are set in a stout angular zinc framework, and connected with a mixture of white-lead ground in oil, to which about an equal quantity of red-lead is added. This arrangement I have found to answer all my expectations, as it has been going on most flourishingly since January 1851. The plants consist chiefly of *Hymenophyllum tunbridgense*, and *H. Wilsoni*, *Trichomanes speciosum*, *Blechnum boreale*, *Adiantum Capillus-Veneris*, and several mosses. The whole of the interior can be viewed with the greatest ease, so that the natural habits of its living inhabitants can be watched and accurately noted in every particular.

"The rapid increase in the growth of the *Vallisneria* is very extraordinary. As I have before mentioned, the plants of necessity get the whole of the rejected matter from the fish and snails for their nutriment, and in consequence of this great supply of food their propagation by runners is very rapid, so that I have found it necessary to weed out this vegetable member of the series, and thus prevent it from becoming too extended, as I conceived this would interfere with the health of the fish, inasmuch as there would consequently be more decaying vegetable matter than the snails present could remove. It is true that this might be remedied by increasing the number of snails, which would no doubt effect the object, but the increase in those two members of the arrangement must in such a case be continually going on, so that the removal of the plant is the least troublesome course. Thus in the spring of 1850 *twenty-eight* healthy plants were weeded out; and in the spring of 1851 *thirty-five* more were removed. The prolific growth of this plant may be further illustrated by the observation made during the last summer, on the rapid elongation of the silky spiral flower stem, which was found by actual measurement to have increased in length *fourteen inches* during *twenty-four hours*; the total extent was five feet, and as soon as the flower expanded itself the growth of the stem ceased altogether. At present I am attempting the same kind of arrangement with a confined portion of sea water, employing some of the green sea weeds as the vegetable members of the circle, and the common winkle or whelk to represent the water snails."

THE WOODS OF COMMERCE.*

ALTHOUGH it is our intention chiefly to confine our "literary notices" to works newly issued from the press—one great object of such notices being to supply a record of progress—yet in the present instance we willingly deviate from that course, for the purpose of calling attention to a valuable work, the only one of its kind hitherto produced, and which, although published more than eight years since, is still almost quite unknown even to those botanists engaged in the investigation of the subject of which it treats. It was only by accident that we recently made acquaintance with it; Mr. Holtzapffell, its author, being an exhibitor of woods in the Great Exhibition in Hyde

* *Holtzapffell's Descriptive Catalogue of Woods, with extensive Botanical Notes by Dr. Boyle.* Holtzapffell, Charing Cross. 1843.

Park. This descriptive catalogue of the woods commonly employed in this country for the mechanical and ornamental arts, originally appeared as a portion of a much more extensive work of five volumes, entitled *Turning and Mechanical Manipulation*, which the author was led to undertake from the circumstance of there being no general treatise in the English language for the guidance of the amateur in these pursuits. The " Catalogue" is, however, very complete in itself; embracing not only a valuable and instructive account of the various woods used for useful and ornamental purposes, as well as other vegetable substances wrought by the turner, but also a valuable practical treatise on turning, containing much information on the different qualities of woods and the kinds chosen for certain purposes, their ornamental characters, and the art of combination, added to which we have a brief and important memoir on the preservation of woods, We have shortly indicated the nature of Mr. Holtz-apffel's work, with the view of making it known among those to whom it may be of service; and we know that there are many devoting attention to this subject at the present time. It only remains for us to show by an extract the manner in which the subject is treated, and we take the notice of the Mahogany as one containing many valuable and interesting observations from Dr. Royle's pen :—

" The *Swietenia Mahagoni* is a native of the West Indies and the country round the Bay of Honduras. It is said to be of rapid growth, and so large that its trunk often exceeds forty feet in length and six feet in diameter. This wood was first brought to London in the year 1724 ; its Spanish name is *Caóba*. Spanish Mahogany is imported from Cuba, Jamaica, Hispaniola, St. Domingo, and some other of the West Indian Islands, and the Spanish Main, in logs from about twenty to twenty-six inches square and ten feet long. It is close-grained, hard, sometimes strongly figured, and generally of a darker colour than Honduras; but its pores frequently appear as if chalk had been rubbed into them. Honduras Mahogany is imported in logs of a larger size than the above, that is, from two to four feet square, and twelve to eighteen feet in length; sometimes planks have been obtained six or seven feet wide. Honduras Mahogany is generally lighter than the Spanish, and also more open and irregular in the grain : many of the pieces are of a fine golden colour with showy veins and figures. The worst kinds are those the most filled with grey specks, from which the Spanish Mahogany (except the Cuba) is comparatively free. Both Spanish and Honduras Mahogany are supposed to be produced by the same tree, *Swietenia Mahagoni* of botanists; some suppose that the Honduras is the wood of a different species, but Long, in his ' History of Jamaica,' says, ' What grows on rocky grounds is of small diameter but of closer grain, heavier weight, and more beautifully grained; what is produced in low, rich, and moist land is larger in dimensions, more light and porous, and of a pale complexion. This constitutes the difference between the Jamaica wood and that which is collected from the coast of Cuba and the Spanish Main; the former is mostly found on rocky eminences, the latter is cut in swampy soils near the sea coast." African Mahogany (*Khaya senegalensis*,) from Gambia, is a more recent importation; it twists much more than either of the above, and is decidedly inferior to them in all respects except hardness. It is a good wood for mangles, curriers' tables, and other uses where a hard and cheap wood of great size is required ; it admits of being turned equally as well as the others. Mahogany shrinks but little in drying, and twists and warps less than any other wood; on account of which it is used for founders' patterns, and other works in which permanence of form is of primary importance. For the same reason, and for its comparative size, abundance, soundness, and beauty, it is the most useful of the furniture woods, and it holds the glue the best of all. Mahogany is also used for a variety of turned works, apart from upholstery and cabinet work. The Spanish Mahogany is, in general, by far the best, although some of the Honduras nearly approaches it, except in hardness and weight. The African is by no means so useful or valuable as either of the above, as it alters very much in drying. There are two other species of Swietenia, besides the Mahogany tree, which are natives of the East Indies : the one, a large tree, of which the wood is of a dull red colour, and remarkably hard and heavy ; the other is only a middle-sized tree, the wood of which is close grained, heavy, and durable, of a deep yellow colour and much resembles Box-wood; but neither of these species is in common use in this country.' (*Tredgold.*) The first of these trees was formerly referred to Swietenia, but is now *Soymida febrifuga*, the second is probably *Chloroxylon Swietenia*, which is the Satin-wood of India and Ceylon. A third species, much admired for its light colour, close grain, and being elegantly veined, is the *Chickrassee* of the natives, and *Chicrassia tabularis* of botanists: the wood is much employed in making furniture and cabinet work. The wood of the Toon tree, *Cedrela Toona*, is sometimes called Indian Mahogany.''

The investigation of the climatic influences of tropical forests, and other questions relating to their commercial importance and the means of increasing their value, has for some years engaged the attention of a Committee of the British Association; and the extensive collections of woods from different parts, which were exhibited in the Crystal Palace at Hyde Park, were instrumental in calling general attention to the riches of the indigenous arboreous vegetation of foreign lands, about which too little is known. Botanists cannot even tell by what families of plants many of the finest woods known in the arts are produced.—L.

L. J. Rosenberg, del. & lith.   Printed by G. J. Chisholm, London.

Pompone Chrysanthemums

1 Asmodie 2 Perfecta 3 La Pygmee 4 Modele 5 Sacramento

POMPONE CHRYSANTHEMUMS.

CONSIDERABLE advance has already been made in the improvement of this miniature race of Chrysanthemums. Even now, among the numerous varieties which the last two seasons have produced, are some which approach very nearly to the standard of *ideal* perfection, and in another season or two we may almost expect to see it reached. At present, the acquisition of increased firmness of texture, and the obliteration of the notches at the end of the petal-like florets, are the points at which it is most desirable to aim; fulness and breadth in the florets having been already in great measure secured.

The accompanying plate represents some of the best of the new varieties, for which we are indebted to Mr. Salter, of the Versailles Nursery, Hammersmith, and Mr. Henderson, of the Wellington Nursery, St. John's Wood.

As the Rose is the admitted queen of summer, and the Dahlia the autumn's king, so may the Chrysanthemum be ranked as the king of winter; for, coming into bloom just at the season when the autumn monarch succumbs to the terrors of the ice king, it may be said to be the floral connecting link between the old and new year, like an oasis in the desert, or a star to cheer the florist when all around is drear and dark. Unlike most other plants, the Chrysanthemum seems to delight in smoke-pent cities, for within a stone's throw of Fleet Street, in the Temple Gardens, abutting upon the Middlesex side of the river Thames, may be seen every autumn a display of this flower, which for effect rivals the American Nurseries of Bagshot, or the grand display of these plants at Chiswick and the Regent's Park. Our attention was first directed to these gardens one thick November morning, when, the fog being of true London character, we landed at Paul's Wharf, and wended our way westward through Thames Street, Whitefriars, and the Temple, where, through the aid of a sudden gleam of sunshine, we descried, amid the yellow mist, a grand display of this splendid flower. At the first sight we thought they must have been transplanted from some suburban nursery or garden, but a closer inspection satisfied us that they were the veritable productions of the place. In Lincoln's Inn Fields also the Chrysanthemum flourishes, and would do so more fully if more attention was devoted to its management; and in most of the squares a few straggling plants may be seen, amply testifying, that, if properly managed, they would make London gay even when the country is cheerless, for they are less likely to be injured by frost in London than in the suburbs.

With these facts before us, it is in the nature of things that Chrysanthemums should be rising in public favour, and the gorgeous specimens which have been produced not only of plants but of cut flowers also, at the Stoke Newington and other exhibitions, prove that the Chrysanthemum, as a Florists' Flower, will become as popular as the Rose, the Dahlia, and the Hollyhock.

Among the novelties lately brought into notice are the varieties figured upon the annexed plate, all of which belong to the class of Pompones, or small varieties which have originated from the Chusan Daisy, a variety introduced by Mr. Fortune from China, and the ordinary kinds. These varieties are specially remarkable to the hybridizer as having taken on, in crossing, the varied colours of the large kinds without increasing in size, for though some of them are larger than the Chusan Daisy, the majority scarcely exceed it in size, and some of them are even smaller. In form also several of the varieties are nearly perfect, while one of them, called La Nain Bébé, when the flowers are fresh, has the scent of Violets! The plants in habit are mostly compact and shrubby, but some of them are a little inclined to become tall. Most of the varieties flower very freely, and therefore are likely to become very useful plants for bedding out in the flower garden for a winter's display; hence we shall address ourselves to their treatment for that purpose, in the present notice, and leave the subject of their cultivation for exhibition till a more suitable time.

Premising, then, that you have supplied yourself with a stock of plants of each of the varieties which you are desirous of getting a quantity of for flower garden purposes, place them at once in a warm greenhouse or pit, at a temperature of 45° to 55°, and as fast as they produce cuttings of sufficient

c

length, take them off, and strike them in the propagating pit, or a close frame. Continue that practice until you have a sufficient number of each kind, and pot the cuttings off as they get well rooted :
but bring them up hardy, and keep them as dwarf as possible. The young plants, after they are established in small pots, may be protected under temporary frames, until they are planted out in June.
Having provided a sufficient quantity of plants, the next step will be to prepare the ground, and this
should be rather strong and well enriched, so that the plants may be taken up with good balls. Now,
if large specimens are wanted, averaging say eighteen inches in height, and the same in diameter, the
plants must be put out in rows three feet apart, the plants standing two feet apart in the row; but, if
smaller plants will suffice, then you may take the cuttings in June, and after rooting them in a close
frame, plant them out direct from the cutting pots, taking advantage of dull showery weather, and
just sticking them in with a dibble, as you would a lot of cabbage plants. These young plants
will not require so much room; and hence, if they stand eighteen inches apart each way, that will be
sufficient. As soon as they are established, and begin to grow freely, go over them, not later than the
middle of July, and stop each plant by cutting the head off within a few inches of the ground: this
will cause them to branch, and to become dwarf and very compact plants. If the larger plants are put
out, they will require the same treatment as to cutting back, or they may be allowed to grow on, and
have the points of the shoots layered the first week in August, by which means they will form very
dwarf and compact plants for potting. One thing, however, must not be forgotten, and that is, that
these small varieties must never be stopped later than July, or the probability is that they will not
flower. Through the summer and autumn, the only care the plants will require will be to keep the
ground clear from weeds, and deeply hoed occasionally; to water the plants in dry weather, giving
them, when necessary, a thorough soaking; and to protect them by timely tying, and staking from
being broken by the wind. Towards the end of August, if the plants continue to grow strongly, go
along each row on one side, and with a spade cut the roots to within three or four inches of the stem,
then in about a fortnight go along the other side, and cut the roots in the same way, and, if necessary,
a third and fourth time. This will check the growth of the plants, and by ripening the wood induce
and promote the blooming principle. Chrysanthemums, to bloom them properly, should not be planted
upon a cold soil, as the buds are found to come blind, hard-eyed, and otherwise deformed: therefore, in
cold situations, it will be found advisable to grow the plants upon a south border, or to remove them
to other situations at the end of September. They will not receive much check if they are shaded
afterwards, and receive a good drenching or two of water.

Now, the time of removing the plants to the flower garden must, of course, depend upon circumstances, but the sooner they are in the beds in which they are to bloom, after the end of September,
the better. Before moving them, take care to give the bed in which they are to bloom a good dunging;
and if fresh, so as to ferment a little after the plants are planted, it will be more beneficial to them.
After planting give a good soaking of water, and, if necessary, shade the plants in the middle of
the day. So far we have said nothing of protection; but, should the weather prove severe, a little
protection will be necessary. We should, therefore, recommend a few neat iron or hazel hoops to be
thrown over the beds, over which mats or waterproof covering could be placed at night. So
managed, we have no doubt the plants would bloom splendidly, and the beds be gay until the close of
the year,—a great point, more especially in establishments where the family is only at home in the
shooting season.

From the varieties at present in cultivation, we select the following as the most likely to be
suitable for the flower garden :—

1. Adonis; white, tipped with cherry colour.
2. Autumnum; brown, medium size.
3. Argentine; silvery white.
4. Asmodie; yellowish buff, tipped with reddish brown.
5. Bizarre; straw yellow, anemone centre, full size.
6. Cybele; yellow, medium size.
7. Daphne; reddish purple, full size.
8. D'Or; golden yellow, very fine.
9. Golden Drop; anemone flowered; guard petals numerous.
10. Henriette; pinkish lilac tipped maroon.
11. La Ruche; blush white, anemone flowered.
12. La Fiancée; pure white, rather thin.

13. La Lilliputienne ; brownish red, rather tall, very free.
14. La Pygmée ; deep yellow, tinged with buff.
15. Le Jongleur ; clear yellow, very free.
16. Madame Lemichez ; deep lilac, double.
17. Modèle ; pure white, of fine form.
18. Nini ; anemone flowered, reddish buff.
19. Poulidetto ; lilac rose, very double, free.
20. Pomponette ; bluish lilac, tinged with orange, anemone centre.
21. Sacramento ; bright orange yellow.
22. Solfaterre ; clear primrose, fine.
23. Surprise ; white tipped with rose, fine.
24. Sydonie ; pure white, semi-double.—A.

Modèle is probably the best variety which has yet been produced. Its flowers are hemispherical, about 1½ inch in diameter, very full in the centre, the florets all strap-shaped, broad, and very slightly notched : the colour is a pure white.

Sacramento is a bright yellow variety, in the same style as Modèle, and equal to it : with age a tinge of buff is acquired at the tips of the florets.

Perfectum is a variety, with broad flat entire florets, of a motley rosy-lilac ; but it has a few quilled florets in the centre, which is rather flat : it is nevertheless desirable ; the flowers are 1¾ inch in diameter.

Asmodie has copper-coloured flowers, yellow in the centre, and acquiring a deep reddish tinge on the older florets : the flowers measure 1¾ inch across, and the florets are smooth and broad, but the centre is rather flat.

La Pygmée is a small clustered-flowered kind, having the characters of the variety called La Fiancée, but the colour is deep yellow,—a very pretty variety for bouquets.

ON PHOSPHORESCENCE IN THE MOSSES.

DR. MILDE has recently made some observations on this subject, in the *Botanische Zeitung*, which are interesting in reference to the debated question of luminosity of plants. He states that he had formerly observed an emerald-green light emitted from the germinating fronds of Ferns, which were standing in a dark part of the Orchis-house of the Botanic Garden at Breslau, and this exactly resembled what he had seen on the little germinating plants of *Schistostega osmundacea* (the well-known *Catoptridium smaragdinum* of Bridel) in hollows of the cliffs at the summit of the Altvater in Bohemia, in 1848. This summer he met with the same phenomenon in another locality, perceiving the light in clefts of the rock at some distance. The rock was kept constantly moist by a shower of fine spray from a neighbouring waterfall. The light was emitted from globular bodies. On close inspection it was found that the luminous places were thickly clothed with another moss, *Mnium punctatum*, almost every leaflet of which bore a largish drop of water, and this produced the pretty light which made exactly the same impression on the eye as that of the germinating *Schistostega*. Meyen was correct in saying, that the luminosity of this latter must be struck out of the phenomena usually cited as illustrations of the evolution of light from plants ; for it is the cellules of the germinating plant of *Schistostega* swollen into little globules, and the little drops of water on the leaves of *Mnium*, which produce that glimmering by a peculiar refraction and reflection of the day-light ; and there is no true production or evolution of light from the substance of these vegetables. The light of *Schistostega* is improperly termed phosporescent, for it is of a delicate emerald green.—A. H.

New Garden Plants.

SAXE-GOTHÆA CONSPICUA, *Lindley*. Conspicuous Saxe-Gothæa. Order Pinaceæ (Conifer tribe).—This plant which has been named in honour of his Royal Highness the Prince Consort, is a very beautiful, hardy, evergreen tree, growing thirty feet high, and in its foliage and habit of growth, resembling the common yew tree. It is, in truth, intermediate between the yew tribe and the coniferous plants, having, as Dr. Lindley has remarked, the male flowers of a Podocarp, the female of a Dammar, the fruit of a Juniper, and the seed of a Dacrydium. It is described as a tree of beautiful growth, and will, no doubt, rank as one of our most highly-valued hardy evergreen trees affording also a useful timber. It inhabits the Andes of Patagonia, ascending from the summer snow-line to that of perpetual snow, and was introduced in 1849, by Messrs. Veitch, of Exeter. A very full and beautifully illustrated account of it is given in the *Journal of the Horticultural Society*, vi., 258, from which we have taken the annexed figure.

FITZ-ROYA PATAGONICA, *J. D. Hooker.* Patagonian Fitz-Roya.—Order Pinaceæ (Conifer tribe).—This is a fine hardy evergreen sub-antarctic tree, forming, when young, a graceful evergreen shrub, but growing to a magnificent size (100 feet high, and eight feet diameter) in its native regions. The leaves of young plants are spread-

1. SAXE-GOTHÆA CONSPICUA.   2. FITZ-ROYA PATAGONICA.   3. ARAUCARIA COOKII.

ing linear acute, decussate, with two glaucous lines on the under side. When they become older, the leaves have the character of triangular sessile closely imbricated scales. It is from the Andes of Patagonia, and was introduced in 1849, by Messrs. Veitch, of Exeter. Dr. Lindley remarks, that "*Saxe-Gothæa conspicua, Fitz-Roya patagonica, Libocedrus tetragona* and *Podocarpus nubicola*, are, no doubt, the four most interesting conifers for this country after *Araucaria imbricata*, which South America produces." See *Journal of Horticultural Society*, vi., 264, and *Botanical Magazine* t., 4616.

ARAUCARIA COOKII, *R. Brown*. Captain Cook's Araucaria.—Order Pinaceæ (Conifer tribe).—This is a fine evergreen greenhouse tree, with the general appearance of the well known *Araucaria excelsa*, but differing from that in having a more compact habit when old, and in being less rigid and graceful while young, in the scales of the cone having a longer and more reflexed mucro, and in their gibbous, not wedge-shaped form ; the scales moreover do not terminate in a hard woody truncated extremity, as in *A. excelsa* and *A. Cunninghami*, but are wholly surrounded by a thin wing. It is naturally a very tall-growing narrow-branched tree, and has been compared to a factory chimney. A native of New Caledonia, whence it was introduced in 1850, by Mr. C. Moore, Superintendent of the Sydney Botanic Garden, under the MS. name of *A. Simpsoni*. See the *Journal of the Horticultural Society*, vi., 267, whence our figure is taken.

PHYLLOCACTUS SPECIOSISSIMO-CRENATUS, *Lindley*. Hybrid crenate Leaf-cactus.—Order Cactaceæ (Indian fig tribe).—A very showy hybrid Cactus, with the broad crenated stems, and loose narrow petalled flowers of its mother, *Phyllocactus crenatus*, and salmony pink coloured flowers, tinged towards the centre with purple, derived from its male parent, *Cereus speciosissimus*. It has been recently raised by Mr. Gordon, in the garden of the Horticultural Society. Dr. Lindley suggests the crossing of the Mammillarias and Echinocactuses with Cereus, and Phyllocactus and the hardy Opuntias with the brilliant hothouse species, as likely to yield interesting and beautiful results. Mr. Gordon's hybrid is figured in *Paxton's Flower Garden* ii., t. 62.

PHYSOCHLAINA GRANDIFLORA, *Hooker*. Large-flowered Physochlaina.—Order Solanaceæ (Nightshade tribe). —A hardy herbaceous plant, apparently perennial, with a much branched glandular stem, and stalked ovate acute glandular alternate leaves. The flowers are drooping, and grow in leafy terminal panicles on elongated stalks. They are dingy-coloured, being like those of *Hyoscyamus*, to which indeed they are immediately allied. The corollas are an inch long, in form between bell-shaped and funnel-shaped, with a spreading mouth of short rounded lobes ; the colour is yellow-green, tinged with purple, and marked with purple veins running longitudinally, and also obliquely transverse. It blooms in summer. From the plains of Thibet, at an elevation of 15,000 feet ; it was introduced in 1850, by Lieut. Strachey, to the Royal Botanic Garden, Kew. See *Botanical Magazine*, t. 4600.

DENDROBIUM ALBO-SANGUINEUM, *Lindley*. Sanguine-spotted white Dendrobe.—Order Orchidaceæ (Orchid tribe).—A very beautiful summer-flowering stove epiphyte, with the appearance of *Dendrobium formosum*, but having more conspicuous flowers. It grows with thick erect knobby stems, bearing broad firm leaves. From the edges of the stems are produced the large showy nodding blossoms, in pairs, or, according to Mr. T. Lobb, in five or six flowered racemes. They measure three to four inches across. The sepals are linear-lanceolate, the side ones being extended into a short obtuse rounded chin ; their colour is creamy white. The petals are much broader, oblong, of nearly the same colour, and vault over the lip and column ; the lip is very large, flat, roundish-obovate, retuse and apiculate, white, with two large deep red stains at the base. It is from Moulmein, where it occurs in open forests on hills near the Atran River, and was introduced in 1851, by Mr. T. Lobb, to the nursery of Messrs. Veitch, of Exeter. See a very handsome figure in *Paxton's Flower Garden*, ii., t. 57.

NYMPHÆA ELEGANS, *Hooker*. Elegant Water-Lily.—Order Nymphæaceæ (Water-Lily tribe).—A very handsome and fragrant plant, flowering in the early part of summer. The floating leaves are nearly orbicular, measuring about six inches long by five broad, and having the margin sinuate and sub-dentate, and the sinus at the base long and narrow ; the upper surface green, the lower purple, both marked with elongated black spots. The flowers are nearly as large as those of the common white water-lily, and stand about a foot above the water. They have a calyx of four spreading oblong acuminate sepals, green, marked with dark brown streaks, and a corolla of from twelve to fourteen petals of the same form, yellowish-white, tinged with purplish blue ; the stamens are numerous, deep yellow, and in the fully expanded flower stand in radiating lines or phalanges corresponding with the number of rays of the stigma, which are about fifteen. From New Mexico. Introduced in 1850 by Dr. Wright, to the Royal Botanic Garden, Kew. Figured in *Botanical Magazine*, t. 4604.

ACACIA BOMBYCINA *Bentham*. Silky Acacia.—Order Fabaceæ § Mimoseæ (Mimosa-like Leguminous Plants).— This is the *Acacia podalyriæfolia* of the gardens, but not the true species ; it is described under the above name by Mr. Bentham ,in *Paxton's Flower Garden*, ii., 101. It is a handsome evergreen spring-flowering greenhouse bushy shrub, with sub-angular branches, having soft obovate-oblong, one-nerved phyllodes, one and a half to two and a half inches long, tapering to the base, and usually bearing a gland on the upper edge, a little below the middle. The globular flower heads grow on stalks shorter than the phyllodes, and are either single or in short racemes of from two to five, from their axils ; the flowers are bright yellow. The whole plant is densely covered with a fine silky hairiness. It is from Swan River ; and was introduced to our gardens by Mr. Drummond within the last few years.

PENTSTEMON WRIGHTII, *Hooker*. Dr. Wright's Pentstemon.—Order Scrophulariaceæ (Linariad tribe).—This plant, introduced from Texas in 1850, to the Royal Botanic Garden, Kew, is a very handsome, nearly hardy perennial herb, of erect habit, one and a half to two and a half feet high, branching from the base, and in the lower part furnished with opposite oblong-obovate glaucous leaves, which taper into a stalk, the pair at the base of the panicle being ovate and sessile. The flowers come in a narrow elongated panicle, a foot or more long, consisting of two-flowered peduncles, axillary to small opposite ovate bracts ; they are drooping, of a deep rich rose colour, with a tube an inch long, ventricose on the underside towards the mouth, and a spreading limb as much across, of five roundish nearly equal lobes. The blossoms are a good deal like those of *Achimenes rosea*, but richer coloured ; they are produced in June and July. It is beautifully figured in the *Botanical Magazine*, t. 4601.

COLLINSIA MULTICOLOR, *Lindley*. Many-coloured Collinsia.—Order Scrophulariaceæ (Linariad tribe).—A handsome hardy annual with the habit of *Collinsia bicolor*. It grows a foot and a half high, with downy stems, bearing coarsely toothed ovate-lanceolate leaves, with a cordate base ; the lower floral leaves are of the same form, the middle ones linear-entire, and the upper ones abortive, smooth on the lower side, and changing to a brownish purple. The flowers are stalked, with nearly glandless pedicels, and form whorls along the upper part of the stem. " The middle boat-shaped lobe of the lower lip of the corolla is crimson, the lower lip itself lilac, and so is the upper lip, except that there is a broad white spot in its middle, relieved by numerous sanguine speckles." *C. tinctoria* from the same country, is said to differ in having smaller flowers, which are sessile, but both these and *C. bicolor* seem very nearly allied. It is from California, and was introduced in 1850 by Messrs. Veitch of Exeter, who exhibited it at one of the Chiswick fetes. It flowers in May and June. See a figure in *Paxton's Flower Garden*, ii., t. 55.

DESFONTAINEA SPINOSA, *Ruis* and *Pavon*. Spinous Desfontainea.—Order Gentianaceæ (Gentianwort tribe).—A very handsome evergreen shrub, supposed to be hardy or nearly so, having the aspect of a common holly, though with opposite leaves. The flowers are tubular, cylindrical, almost two inches long, with a scarlet tube and a yellow border. They are produced in the greatest profusion. It seldom exceeds five feet in height, according to Mr. Lobb, who found it on the Andes of Patagonia, and sent it to Messrs. Veitch of Exeter in 1849. It has been noticed in the *Journal of the Horticultural Society*, vi., 265, and appears to have produced a flower or two at Exeter in the course of last summer.

VACCINIUM ROLLISONI, *Hooker*. Rollison's Whortleberry.—Order Vacciniaceæ (Cranberry tribe).—A charming greenhouse (or cool stove) autumn-flowering evergreen bush, with something the aspect of the Minorca Box. It grows two feet or more in height, erect, glabrous, and much branched, and is clothed by numerous obovate leaves about three-fourths of an inch long, leathery, glossy, and dark green above, paler and almost glaucous beneath. The drooping flowers grow in terminal four to six-flowered racemes ; the corollas are smooth, rich crimson, pitcher-shaped, tapering upwards, with a limb of five short reflected lobes. It is a native of Java, where it grows on the lava of the " silent volcanoes ;" it also grows on the Salak Mountain. Messrs. Rollison of Tooting introduced it in 1850, through their collector Mr. J. Henshall. It promises to be a free flowering plant, and if so, its neat habit, glossy leaves, and rich-coloured flowers, will make it a favourite in cultivation. There is a figure in the *Botanical Magazine*, t. 4612.

PLATYCODON CHINENSE, *Lindley*. Chinese Platycode.—Order Campanulaceæ (Bellwort tribe).—This plant formerly referred to *Platycodon grandiflorum*, by Dr. Lindley, and under that name pretty well known in gardens, is now supposed to differ from the plant properly so called, in having stouter stems, racemose instead of solitary flowers, and ovaries half-egg shaped instead of being of the form of an inverted cone ; very slight differences, it must be confessed, which have no doubt resulted from vigorous growth under cultivation. It is a fleshy-rooted plant, with stiff erect stems, bearing ovate nearly sessile leaves, and large blue bell-shaped flowers. Mr. Fortune introduced it from the South Coast of China, in 1845, to the garden of the Horticultural Society, and it is found to blossom towards the end of summer. A figure, under the name of *P. chinense*, is given in *Paxton's Flower Garden*, ii., t. 61.

SPIRÆA CALLOSA, *Thunberg*. Callous-toothed Spiræa. Order, Rosaceæ (Rosewort tribe).—A very handsome deciduous hardy shrub, having dark green sharply serrated lance-shaped leaves, and bearing branched cymes of brilliant rose-coloured flowers. It has the general appearance of *Spiræa bella*. It is from the north of China and Japan, and was re-introduced by Mr. Fortune in 1850, to the nursery of Messrs. Standish and Noble of Bagshot. It flowers in July and August, and appears to have been long since introduced for the Horticultural Society by Mr. Reeves, but lost ; see *Paxton's Flower Garden*, ii., 113.

CHRYSOBACTRON HOOKERI, *Colenso*. Dr. Hooker's Chrysobactron.—Order Liliaceæ (Lilywort tribe).—A showy summer-blooming half-hardy or greenhouse evergreen perennial herbaceous plant, having large fleshy fibrous roots and producing a tuft of radical leaves, which are linear strap-shaped and channelled, about eighteen inches long, and of a glaucous green colour. The flowers form an erect, rather open raceme at the top of a leafless scape, which grows from one and a-half to two and a-half feet in height. The perianth is of a rich golden yellow, composed of six oblong spreading sepals, which in size and arrangement have considerable resemblance to some of the large flowered Scillas. This plant is a native of New Zealand, where it grows in great clumps in boggy places, and, when in flower, clothes the plains in a sheet of yellow. It was introduced in 1848, by Mr. Bidwill, to the Royal Botanic Garden, Kew. See *Botanical Magazine*, t. 4602.

ANGRÆCUM ARCUATUM, *Lindley*. Arched-racemed Angræcum.—Order Orchidaceæ (Orchid tribe).—A greenhouse species, producing a stiff hard stem a few inches high, clothed with tough leathery distichous bluntly-two-lobed leaves, and bearing horizontal lateral racemes of white flowers, of which the sepals, petals, and lip, are almost alike in form, linear taper-pointed and reflexed, and the spur is a tapering blunt horn much longer than the lip. From the Albany district of the Cape of Good Hope. Introduced in 1850, by Messrs. Veitch of Exeter. Blossoms in July.—*Paxton's Flower Garden*, ii. 120.

ANGRÆCUM MONODON, *Lindley*. One-toothed Angræcum.—Order Orchidaceæ (Orchid tribe).—An inconspicuous stove epiphyte, having roundish oblong distichous leaves obliquely two-lobed; and bearing narrow many-flowered racemes of small reddish flowers, having somewhat the smell of horse chestnut seeds. The sepals and petals are ovate-acute, the lip roundish with a single small erect tooth in front of the opening into the spur. From Gabon in Africa, whence it was introduced to European gardens about 1849, by Mr. Pescatore of Paris.—*Paxton's Flower Garden*, ii. 102.

ZAMIA LINDLEYI, *Warczewits*. Dr. Lindley's Zamia.—Order Cycadaceæ (Cycad tribe).—A remarkable stove shrub, having a cylindrical trunk, six to seven feet high, which bears a tuft of narrow equally-pinnated leaves, consisting of many pairs of linear sharp pointed acuminate entire leaflets, and having hispid petioles. From the Cordillera of Veragua, at an elevation of from 5000 to 7000 feet, and introduced to continental gardens by M. Warczewits, about 1850.—*Allgemeine Gartenzeitung*.

ZAMIA SKINNERI, *Warczewits*. Mr. Skinner's Zamia.—Order Cycadaceæ (Cycad tribe).—This remarkable stove shrub has a trunk from four to six feet high, tapering upwards, and bearing a tuft of broad equally-pinnated leaves, consisting of many pairs of elliptic-lanceolate leaflets, which are acute at each end, serrated near the point, and have hispid petioles. From the Cordillera of Veragua, at from 5000 to 7000 feet elevation. Introduced to the continental gardens by M. Warczewits, about 1850.—*Allgemeine Gartenzeitung*.

DENDROBIUM CLAVATUM, *Wallich*. Club-stemmed Dendrobe.—Order Orchidaceæ (Orchid-tribe).—This beautiful summer-blooming stove epiphyte is one of the handsomest of the orange Dendrobes. It has terete pendulous stems a foot and a half to two feet long, bearing lateral racemes of about five flowers, the rachis when full grown being zig-zag. The flowers are rich orange colour, with a broad double brown blotch in the middle of the lip; the sepals are linear-oblong, the petals roundish obovate oblong and somewhat undulated, the lip slightly three-lobed, round, hairy all over the upper surface, and strongly ciliated though not fringed at the edges. It is near *D. fimbriatum* and *D. moschatum;* and has very recently been introduced from Assam by T. Denne, Esq. See *Paxton's Flower Garden*, ii. 104.

THE BEAUTY OF FLOWERS IN FIELD AND WOOD.*

SUCH is the title of a very enticing-looking little volume now before us, the aim of which, as explained by its author, is that of leading the rambler in field and wood to a higher order of pleasure than that which arises from mere general impressions of floral beauty; and this by acquiring a certain degree of knowledge of the plants which blossom around his path, and therefrom deriving certain edifying moral reflections.

The first object of the book is that of furnishing a reply to the enquirer, whose interest, excited by the beauty or singularity of some common flower, or the very inconspicuousness of some wayside weed, leads him to ask, first, What is it? and then, What is it like? These questions lead to a generalized explanation of all the more essential parts of a plant; next of the mode in which they are most naturally classified; and, finally, how this mode of classification may be practically applied, with the view of ascertaining the affinities and characteristics of any plant under examination. This part of the volume might consequently be called a popularized elementary sketch of structural and systematical botany. The remaining, and most bulky part, is occupied by a brief analytical survey of the more interesting British families of wild plants, treated in accordance with the "natural" method of classification, with which it is the author's especial endeavour to familiarize the reader. The distinctive features of the families, or natural orders as they are usually called, and of the most conspicuous and interesting wild plants, are given with sufficient exactness to render it a tolerably easy matter to recognize them by this aid alone; but we imagine that those who are thus far tempted within the domain of science—and this is the special object of the volume—will not rest satisfied without making further advances. We may briefly indicate some of the author's sentiments, as illustrative of the style of the volume :—

* The Beauty of Flowers in Field and Wood; comprising the Natural Orders, or Families of British Wild Plants, with their Moral Teachings Illustrated. By John Theodore Barker. Bath: Binns and Godwin. London: Whittaker & Co.

"There is not a plant but on minute investigation will reveal some peculiar beauty, or some exquisite adaptation, to reward the attention bestowed. What we despise as weeds, and condemn as inconspicuous, are only so in relation to our superficial view.

"For a garden, we select such plants as are suitable, on account of the size and brilliancy of their flowers, or of the unusual elegance of their foliage. But in a landscape, individual beauty is subservient to general effect. Even a mass of hemlocks or nettles is not without its relative beauty. The garden is cultivated for the sake of some favourite flowers, often unjustly, to the disadvantage of many that cannot be confined within artificial boundaries. For a landscape, *foliage* is the principal requisite, and thus every so-called weed has its appointed service. . . . . . Some flowers are common to both garden and country. Violets, Primroses, Snowdrops, Lilies of the Valley, &c., are as sweet in their wild haunts as in the protected enclosure. Many not found in the garden are splendid in their wild independence, such as the Mullein, Fox-glove, Viper's-bugloss, Speedwell, and the curious tribes of Orchis. Daisies, Buttercups, Anemones, Cowslips, Harebells, Vetches, &c., are more welcome in their wild habitats.

"Varied beauty is thus spread over the surface of the habitable globe, and cannot fail to delight every mind that is not blighted by the wretched conventionalities of the world, benumbed by cold utilitarianism, or besotted by selfishness.

> " ' Nature never did betray
> The heart that loved her; 'tis her privilege,
> Through all the years of this our life, to lead
> From joy to joy; for she can so inform
> The mind that is within us, so impress
> With quietness and beauty, and so feed
> With lofty thoughts, that neither evil tongues,
> Rash judgments, nor the sneers of selfish men
> Shall e'er prevail against us, or disturb
> Our cheerful faith, that all which we behold
> Is full of blessing.' "—WORDSWORTH.

The sketches of the families, and of the most noticeable plants in each, are, of course, very general and brief; but they are, as we have already remarked, in most cases, sufficiently clear for the end in view; and, with ordinary attention and tact, the commoner species of our wild plants might be recognized. The volume is not, however, intended to supersede the "Manuals" and "Floras" in which our wild flowers are described with more completeness and precision, but rather to excite a hungering for this branch of knowledge, and to supply the first cravings of the awakened appetite, as well as to give it a healthful tone and bearing. Hence we find moralizing reflections, in true harmony with the beauty of flowers, largely scattered among the more scientific details of the volume. Take, as an example, the remarks on the Honeysuckle :—

"The most interesting plant of this family [Caprifoliaceæ, or the Honeysuckle family] is certainly the Honeysuckle, associated with many others that cluster around the familiar and endeared scene of home and rural life. It often becomes associated with the Ivy, with which it has some natural affinity in structure. . . . . . The Honeysuckle, however, has more affinity with the living present, and its fragrance and beauty seem appropriate to the happy home it adorns. The Ivy is often a memorial of the past, and clings to the ruined habitation and neglected wall as if unwilling to part with the remembrance of ties and endearments that have long ceased, and solemnly reminds us of the transientness of earthly bliss, which even the tender herb may survive. Another lesson suggested by the Honeysuckle is thus beautifully expressed :—

> " 'Would'st thou soar, but strength hast none?
> Clings to earth thy grovelling heart!
> Seek, like yonder fragile flower,
> Fitting prop round which to twine:
> There 's an arm of love and power,
> Lean on it, and heaven is thine.' "

The volume is very elegantly printed, and is nicely illustrated by ten coloured plates, the execution of which, however, might be improved with advantage. It would form a very pretty and appropriate gift for youth.—M.

Gladiolus.
1 Wellington 2 Von Gagern 3 Prince Albert.

THE "WELLINGTON" GLADIOLUS.

HIS fine hybrid production is another valuable addition to a now universally-admired family of plants. It comes from the establishment of J. Willmore, Esq., of the Wellington Road, Birmingham (late of Oldford), whose name has been long known in the floricultural world as one of its most able and enterprizing supporters. Mr. Willmore's collection of seedling Gladioli is well known to be extensive, and of first-rate excellence; and we have to acknowledge his kindness in favouring us with the variety "Wellington" here represented, accompanied by the following account of its origin :—
"The parent plant was *Bidwilliana*, or, in other words, the orange variety of *gandavensis :* but what this was crossed with is not precisely known, as pollen was made use of indiscriminately. As, however, the flower is an orange scarlet, and as pollen from *vernalis spicatus, pyramidalis, albicans roseus,* and many varieties of *ramosus* was in requisition, it is probable that the pollen in question was obtained from one of these sources."

Along with some other varieties of equal, or even greater merit, the Wellington Gladiolus was exhibited, on the 4th of September last, before the National Floricultural Society, where it was awarded the certificate of merit. We understand that it, and others of Mr. Willmore's Gladioli, have been purchased by Messrs. Cole and Sharp of the Aston Lane Nursery, Birchfield, near Birmingham. Our plate contains, besides the Wellington, which is one of the natalensis section, two varieties of Dutch origin, belonging to the cardinalis section, named Van Gagern and Prince Albert, both of which possess considerable merit.—M.

THE GLADIOLUS AS A BEDDING PLANT.

The list of floral productions for the decoration of the garden, although very extensive, is constantly receiving numerous additions from various sources, not the least important of which is that opened up by skilful gardeners, who, by the care and judgment which they bestow upon particular plants, adapt them to a purpose for which they were not previously available.

New and approved varieties of established favourites which present any novel or distinctive feature, but more particularly such as possess any striking advantage as regards their hardiness or the season of their blooming, are hailed with no common satisfaction by all who can appreciate floral excellence. This is especially true of the class which is named at the head of these remarks, and to the most robust, as well as late-flowering members of which, my present object is to direct attention. A want of variety among them has hitherto presented an obstacle to their general cultivation; but skilful management, in combination with sound judgment, has done much to remedy the defect, and I have no doubt that every year will witness further changes, until we obtain every variety of shade, from white to scarlet, with great variety in marking, and an improvement in outline and truss. From their formal and soldier-like appearance in groups, they are not adapted to a low situation, and they ought not to be indiscriminately placed among common bedding-out plants. The most appropriate position for them would undoubtedly be the background of some geometrical arrangement, or upon a border facing a statue. In such situations they would present an extremely pleasing appearance during the autumnal months. As contrasts of colour are now attainable, no garden can be considered complete without them. I subjoin a list of those varieties which combine the qualifications of free and erect growth with the production of long spikes of bloom thickly set on the spike :—

Wellington (Willmore's).—Bright orange scarlet. This is a great acquisition; its height is from four to five feet, the flower-spikes being about eighteen inches in length.

Gandavensis superbus.—This is the best variety of *gan-*

davensis, as well as the strongest grower I have seen. It is from five to six feet in height; flower large; colour orange, deepening a few shades at the top of the upper petals.

Gandavensis aurantius.—This is a much weaker grower

than *superbus*, but desirable for the distinctness of its colour.

Gandavensis splendens.—This is also a strong-growing plant, and deep in colour, losing all the orange cast which distinguishes the *gandavensis* varieties.

Gandavensis coccineo-striatus is a new and strong variety, and a great acquisition, being a dwarf grower, from two to three feet high, producing a fine spike of bloom. The ground colour is orange, beautifully striated with brilliant orange scarlet.

These are the best of the dark varieties which I am acquainted with. I will now mention a few light ones :—

Floribundus superbus.—This variety of *floribundus* is a clear white, having the lower petals marked with a dense stripe of violet; it grows about four feet high.

Vernalis spicatus is an intermediate variety, of robust habit, and growing about four feet high. The flowers are French white, striated with rose colour.

Albicans roseus is the next in height. The colour of this branching variety is indicated by its name; height about three feet.

Ramosus superbus.—This erect-growing variety of *ramosus* is of dwarf habit, being much larger but more delicate in colour than the others. It attains the height of about two feet.

The above descriptions and explanations will assist those who are desirous of growing a selection of Gladioli suitable for flower-garden decoration.—J. COLE, *gardener to J. Willmore, Esq., Wellington Road, Birmingham.*

ON THE REPRODUCTION OF CRYPTOGAMOUS PLANTS.

MR. HENFREY in his recent report on the present state of our knowledge of the reproduction of the higher Cryptogams, laid before the British Association at Ipswich, after giving a summary of the facts now on record respecting the occurrence of the organs termed antheridia and pistillidia in all the higher cryptogamous families, as the Mosses, Liverworts, Ferns, Horsetails, Club-mosses, and the Rhizocarps, remarks, that "the phenomena in the Ferns and Equisetums, as well as in the Rhizocarps, Lycopods, and Quillworts less strikingly, seem to present a series of conditions analogous to those which have been described under the name of 'alternations of generations' in the animal kingdom; and seeing the resemblance which the pistillidia of Mosses bear to the 'ovules' of other families, we can hardly help extending the same views to them, in which case we should have the remarkable phenomenon of a compound organism, in which a new individual, forming a second generation, developed after a process of fertilization, remains attached organically to its parent, from which it differs totally in all anatomical and physiological characters." There is an "essential difference between such a case, and that of the occurrence of flower buds and leaf buds upon the same stem in the Phanerogams, as part of a single plant, yet possessing a certain amount of independent vitality, for these are produced from each other by simple extension, by a process of gemmation; while the Moss capsule, if the sexual theory be correct, is the result of a true reproductive process. Moreover, we have the analogy to the increase by germination in the innovations by which the leafy stems of the Mosses are multiplied." These anomalous conditions lose their remarkable characters to a great extent, if we refuse to accept the evidences of sexuality which have been brought forward. If the structures are all products of mere extension or gemmation, the analogies which have been supposed to exist between them and the organs of flowering plants, all fall to the ground. But in this view Mr. Henfrey does not acquiesce, believing the hypothesis of sexuality to be based on solid grounds.—*Botanical Gazette.*

ON THE HYBRIDATION OF PLANTS.

MY observations warrant me in laying down the following propositions as universal laws :—

1. Hybrid plants are produced readily only in particular genera. The artificial raising of hybrids involves great difficulties, and even when the greatest care is taken in the fertilization, the experiments are only occasionally successful.

Observation.—Gardeners talk commonly of hybrids produced by artificial fertilization where this is by no means the case. A hybrid is the intermediate form between two good species. The mass of the so-called garden hybrids which are annually produced are merely either "sports" of one and the same variable nature, or seedlings from hybrids. Of the latter I shall speak presently. As examples of the former, falsely called hybrid forms, I need only refer to the countless varieties of fruit trees and garden vegetables, to Dahlias, China Asters, &c., &c. In reference to artificial fertilization, I may add that it will only be successful when the plants operated upon are removed from all others of the same species blowing at the same time, and the flowers to be fertilized opened shortly before their natural expansion for the removal of their stamens; then, as soon as the stigma is seen to be ripe for fertilization, the pollen of another plant is applied to it. To make the fertilization "take" more readily, I usually cut the plants pretty closely, remove all the flowers, except a few which are to be fertilized, and break off all new shoots from the branch, or even from the whole plant, until the seed is ripe, so as to concentrate the vegetative force of the plant wholly upon the maturation of the seed.

2. The fertilization by strange pollen takes place the more readily in proportion to the proximity of the species which are crossed. The production of hybrids between even any closely allied genera is extremely rare.

Observation.—This fact is universally received. I have only succeeded once in raising a hybrid between two genera,* namely, between *Trevirania grandiflora* and *Diastema gracilis*. I called this hybrid *Diastema Rinzii*. It possessed the stamens, style, and the structure of the male parent; and in reference to the colour of the blossoms, the leaves, &c., it stood intermediately. Again, the degree of facility with which the cross-fertilization takes place, even between any nearly allied species of the same genus is widely different in different genera. In some genera these experiments never succeed, in others only when extreme precautions are taken (*Gesneraceæ*), in others, again, comparatively readily (*Begoniæ*, *Calceolariæ*, *Fuchsieæ*, &c.), and some even without any artificial aid (*Cupheæ*). Forms of one and the same species merely require to be placed side by side, and not artificially fertilized, for these take the pollen of each other as readily as they do their own.

3. Artificial hybrids are often infertile, but still they frequently bear seed.

Observation.—Botanists commonly assume that hybrids are barren. But this is only the case to a certain degree, inasmuch that the hybrid seldom bears seed in the first year, even when it is artificially fertilized. At least, so it happened with me in many cases, in the earlier years; but I was afterwards able to obtain a sufficient quantity of seed from the same hybrids. It seems as if the weather had also a good deal to do with this. I may mention, as an example, the hybrid between *Cytisus Laburnum* and *Cytisus purpureus*, which formerly blossomed every year in our garden, but never bore seed, while in recent years it has spontaneously "set" a quantity of fruits and matured them.†

4. It is a general rule with hybrids that they most resemble the male parent in the flowers, while the foliage and habit take after the mother plant. But exceptions to this general rule often occur, insomuch that sometimes one, sometimes the other, parent exhibits a preponderating influence; but the seedlings derived from one and the same fertilization, even when there are thousands of them, always present exactly the same characters.

Observation.—I formerly believed that various forms might arise from one and the same fertilization; but this was an error originating from the employment of different varieties for the fertilizations. Distinctions which sometimes show themselves at first in true hybrids, in regard to the colour of the flower, &c., disappear in the succeeding years.

5. Seedlings of hybrids mostly differ very much from each other.

Observation.—As soon as the path is opened, as it were, by obtaining a few true hybrids in a genus, and these hybrids can be brought to ripen seed, then commences an infinite series of forms, or in other words, in the eye of the botanist, an interminable confusion; for the seedlings of the hybrids mostly differ more or less from each other, since they return, in varying degrees, towards original species. I

---

* The "genera" mentioned are so closely allied as to have been formerly included under Achimenes.—M.

† Examples of this hybrid, which we have seen in this country, are barren while young, the flowers being of the true intermediate character. But as the trees grow older, the two species seem to separate from each other, and each to claim a portion of the buds, so that we see flowers of each parent, together with the hybrid's blossoms, all on the tree at once. In such cases only the "pure" blossoms ripen seed, that of the "cross" being always barren.—A. H.

will merely mention here, as an example, the genus *Calceolaria*, several clearly distinguishable species of which have become the parents of the countless varieties now cultivated with so much ardour. When these are sown with the most careful separation of the seeds, it is found that the most varied shades of affinity occur in the seeds of one and the same plant when this is a hybrid form. But if the seed has been obtained from a form recurring more to one of the primitive types, with yellow or red flowers, the seedlings will be found more uniform. When the characters of the species, or of the genus to which it belongs, have become uncertain through artificial fertilization, at least the cause of this can be satisfactorily demonstrated. This is more difficult when particular genera of plants produce such hybrid progeny in the wild state; as, for instance, the Willows, the Hawkweeds, the Thistles, the Gentians, and many others. If it amount merely to simple hybridation, the truth may always be discovered, since this always carries with it very definite characters. But, as we see in some Saxifrages, further hybridation and seeding of the hybrids give rise to new series of forms which are ordinarily much more difficult to reduce, and appear to connect two well distinguished species by gradual transitions.—*M. E. Regel, of Zurich: Botanische Zeitung.*

New Garden Plants.

IMPATIENS PULCHERRIMA, *Dalzell.* Handsome-flowered Balsam.—Order Balsaminaceæ (Balsam tribe).—A very handsome tender annual Balsam, with much the aspect of *I. platypetala*, with which, indeed, Dr. Lindley identifies it. It appears, however, from the published descriptions and figures to differ in being annual not perennial, in having the leaves alternate not whorled, and in having a fringe of glands at the base of the leaves, which *I. platypetala* has not; the flowers are also somewhat different in form. The stems are erect, smooth, simple, or branched, with alternate longish-petioled ovate-acuminate leaves. The flowers are large, a couple of inches across, flattish, and of a deep lilac rose colour. It was found near Warree, in Bombay, and was introduced by N. Dalzell, Esq., in 1850, to the Royal Botanic Garden, Kew. It flowers throughout the summer months. There is a figure in the *Botanical Magazine*, t., 4615.

DICTYANTHUS CAMPANULATUS, *Jordan.* Bell-flowered Dictyanth.—Order Asclepiadaceæ (Asclepiad tribe).—This fine and very singular-flowered climbing plant, has been introduced to the Belgian Gardens, and was exhibited by M. Joseph Baumann, of Ghent, at the exhibition of the Royal Horticultural Society of Anvers in 1851, where it was awarded the first prize. It has been said to grow in Mexico, at the foot of the Sierra Madre, near Durango, but Professor Morren, who figures it in *La Belgique Horticole*, states, on the authority of M. Baumann, that it is a native of Brazil. The base of the stem is woody, with white lines or fissures in the bark, which probably become corky with age. The stem is pubescent and twining; the leaves are opposite cordate-acuminate, with a red petiole three to four inches long. From their axils is produced a single flower, borne on a long peduncle. The calyx has five broad lanceolate lobes. The corolla is urceolate below, and green; its limb is turned back, and prolonged into five large horns, with recurved margins; this part is whitish, marked with innumerable small purple lines or striæ, which are horizontal on the limb, and vertical at the base of the tube. The staminal crown has five large rays in the form of a star. The flower remains open about a week. M. Baumann has grown it in the open air during summer, and in a warm orange-house during winter, and had bloomed it on a wire trellis, about two and a half feet high. It is the *Tympananthe suberosa* (Haskarl), and the *Stapelia campanulata* (Pavon).

SAXIFRAGA FLAGELLARIS, *Willdenow.* Spider-legged Saxifrage.—Order Saxifragaceæ (Saxifrage tribe).—This very curious plant, whose filiform stolons are cast out on all sides like the legs of an immense spider, was brought from Cornwallis Island, in the Arctic regions, by Captain Penny, to the Royal Botanic Garden, Kew, in October, 1851, the plants being in flower on their arrival. It has a compact rosulate tuft of spathulate glandular-ciliate leaves at the base of the short stem, which is surmounted by from one to five yellow five-petalled flowers. The stolons, bearing each a young plant at the extremity, have a very remarkable appearance. Arctic plants are difficult to cultivate, from the impossibility of giving them the absolute and extended winter rest to which they are naturally adapted; and this can only be imitated by placing them in a cold shady frame during the winter season. A sandy soil is desirable.

GRISSOIS RACEMOSA, *Labillardiere.* Racemose Geissois.—Order Cunoniaceæ (Cunoniad tribe).—This very fine stove shrub, sent last year by Mr. C. Moore, from New Caledonia, Dr. Lindley provisionally identifies with Labillardiere's plant. It bears crimson blossoms abundantly on the old wood. The leaves are opposite trifoliolate, with large obovate obtuse leaflets, woolly and serrated on young plants, entire and glaucous when they reach a blooming size. A roundish leathery sessile stipule is seated between each pair of leaves. The flowers grow in racemes from eight inches to a foot long; they are close packed, rich crimson, with globular buds, four leathery ovate sepals, hairy inside, and eight stamens with long crimson filaments. It has been introduced by the Horticultural Society, and is described in their *Journal* (vi., 273).

ACER VILLOSUM, *Wallich*. Villose Maple.—Order Aceraceæ (Maple tribe).—This is a very fine Acer, of the character of the common Sycamore, but a finer tree. It comes from the Himalayan mountains, and is described and figured in *Paxton's Flower Garden*. It is a large tree, with broad palmate leaves, downy on the under surface, and assuming in autumn a peculiar nankin tint. The flowers are fragrant. This tree has been introduced by Messrs. Osborn, of the Fulham Nursery.

BRASAVOLA ACAULIS, *Lindley*. Stemless Brasavola.—Order Orchidaceæ (Orchid tribe).—An interesting stove epiphyte from Central America, figured by a woodcut in *Paxton's Flower Garden*, ii. 152. It is almost stemless, and has short stiff quill-shaped leaves, and solitary cream-coloured flowers produced at midsummer; the sepals and petals are narrow, three inches long; the lip large roundish ovate, with a rolled-up claw. Presented to the Horticultural Society by G. U. Skinner, Esq.

PHILESIA BUXIFOLIA, *Lamarck*. Box-leaved Philesia.—Order Philesiaceæ (Philesiad tribe).—One of the handsomest plants of the Antarctic American Flora; a half-hardy shrub, from Chiloe and Patagonia, whence it has been recently introduced by Messrs. Veitch of Exeter. It is a slow-growing plant, forming large masses, throwing out long slender stems, which creep along beneath

DICTYANTHUS CAMPANULATUS.

the decaying bark of trees, and over rocks partly covered with soil, and root along the internodes. When it grows erect, it seldom exceeds a foot in height. It always grows about the base of dwarf stunted wood, similar to coppice. The flowers come near the extremity of the branches, and are produced in September; they are campanulate, rose-coloured, often as large as a tulip, with remarkably firm petals.

SPECULATIVE IDEAS ON WHAT IS TERMED FORCING.

THIS, the general term employed to express the means used to accelerate garden products, does not so aptly describe the practice of the present day as of that in bygone years. Then, it was in many cases *indeed forcing* ; now, perhaps, it ought to be called persuading. Good gardeners have taken a more rational basis for their proceedings.

In former days, the root action, as a concomitant of the procedure, was scarcely taken into account. Vines, &c., were " set to work," as it was practically termed, in November, with an outside root, and probably in a six-feet deep damp border, without hesitation. To be sure, they were pruned after some favourite recipe, and the houses made very smart; and the production of one crop of tolerable fruit was deemed conclusive of the triumph of branch over root—of fire heat over solar heat; or, at least, of the independent position the branch could assume when man chose. But, oh! in those times, what tales of Strawberries going "blind ;" Peach blossoms " dying unmarried ;" Vine branches furnishing a study for the curious by turning, in sudden metamorphosis, into tendrils, to amuse the puzzled phyto-logists of those days. Such things as these, although they might be pushed aside by practical men as things that *would happen* in the very best conducted establishments, have in their turn been the subject of keen investigation ; and it is now considered that a tree is endued with keen susceptibilities, and wondrous self-restoring powers.

My purpose in thus instituting a comparison between ancient and modern gardening is to draw attention to what is ordinarily termed "*bottom heat*" in forcing affairs. As for the Vine border *outside* the house, the Vines of which are to be forced tolerably early, there is not one practitioner in a score in these days who will leave his border unprotected ; whilst the majority employ heating material to create an artificial warmth. The question of bottom-heat does not, however, concern Vine-borders merely ; it is a principle of very wide application. In the fruit-forcing department, an important class equally demands an application of the same principles, in order that the root may be in a position to reciprocate with and meet the demands of the excited branches. I may name Peaches, Figs, Straw-berries, Raspberries, Cherries, &c. &c., whether in pots, tubs, or the open soil. And as for flower-forcing and retarding, the subjects are too numerous to be particularized.

Now, if the root-care exercised over the Vine border be right, these things are, and have been, sadly neglected or misunderstood.

Owing to the great vicissitudes in our clime, the accumulating ground warmth is liable to many controverting tendencies ; and, if our climate be really deficient in anything, as regards the vegetation on the earth's surface, it is probably in the ratio the ground heat bears to that of the atmosphere. It is not too much to suppose that our spring blossoms suffer very much from *this cause alone*—a fitfully excited branch, without any reciprocation of the root. It appears, then, to me, that a department in every garden of pretensions should be devoted to tender fruits and flowers ; and this should be termed, "*The Ground Heat Department.*" Such should be not far from the forcing processes ; and as nothing peculiarly interesting to the general observer would appear on the face of it, the whole might be enclosed, and form a very interesting little episode to those who wished to study principles. A few poles of ground would suffice for most establishments, and this might be readily heated by piping at a very moderate expense. One boiler might be well employed occasionally in working two five feet beds ; being placed so that a couple of pipes—flow and return—could traverse each plunging-bed at about a yard apart, parallel, and running longitudinally. What I suggest is, an autumn bottom-heat of an arti-ficial character, with but the ordinary atmospheric temperature of September, October, and, it may be, a portion of November ; or, in other words, a guaranteed ground or root warmth of some half dozen degrees in advance of the average atmospheric temperature. Such piping might be crossed by wide slates, and on these a foot deep of cinder-ashes might be levelled, or more if need be, to plunge in,—for plunging I would make a *sine qua non*. Under such circumstances, it is probable that a fire for a few hours, twice a-week, would suffice in ordinary seasons.

Such a plan properly established would, if I mistake not, be in very frequent request; and as to fuel, as a very moderate, but certain amount of bottom heat would be required, the cinders from the other fire-holes would in the main suffice. For the purposes to which it would be applied, a bottom warmth, capable of a range from 55 to 65 degrees, would probably answer: for it would be principally wanted in autumn, commencing as soon as the natural ground-heat began to decline.

Here, all the fruit trees, strawberries, &c., in tubs, boxes, pots, &c., might be plunged, as well as many things for the autumn and winter's decoration of the plant houses, such as bulbs, roses, violets, pinks, lilies, American shrubs, rhododendrons, &c.; and if (as we have to suggest) a canvas or other skreen could be drawn over at night, to arrest radiation and ward off cooling winds, slight frosts, &c., a climate would be secured within just enough to keep the fluids slightly in motion. It must not be understood that the heat of the whole *must be equal* at all times. Plants thus thrown into a state of preparation for a late autumn or winter display, or for what is termed forcing, might be removed progressively to their destination, whatever the structure or mode of heating, observing one thing, that for early fruits a continuation of bottom warmth would be most desirable. For retarded flowers, the ordinary shelves would answer; for these in general have only to waste in blossom the stored-up energies of the preceding summer. The roots never having acquired an actually quiescent state, to say nothing of having been frozen, would be prepared to reciprocate with any circulation of fluids induced in the foliage or branches; and it need hardly be suggested here that a thorough and harmonizing circulation of the fluids is of the utmost importance in all forcing, whether in the regions of Flora or Pomona.

One thing should be taken into consideration by those who feel disposed to give a thought to these —it may be—hypothetical suggestions, which is the fact that the roots of plants in a state of nature are seldom liable to the great extremes of temperature to which the branch is subject—neither does it by any means appear that such was the design in their formation, and as evinced by the well known functions assignable to each. We do know that with regard to most trees, to say nothing of the ordinary perennial tribes, the branches, by an extremely low temperature during the winter, are thrown into what may be considered a state of rest. But what is the condition of the fibres during that period?—the branches in perhaps an average temperature of some ten to twenty degrees of frost, whilst the soil at a foot deep or so indicating a temperature of about forty! Now, this is an enormous discrepancy, and it may continue for weeks. Theory, as well as practice, has repeatedly pointed to the fact, that the fibres are anything but inactive. No! much has to be done—many tubes to be refilled—before active vegetation can fairly commence, all this resulting from the perspiratory loss of the previous summer and autumn. Here, then, we seem to have a real principle; and it remains for art to control adverse matters and to see that the principle is duly carried out.

In considering this matter, the character of the autumnal atmosphere and autumnal light, as related to the heat of that period, should be taken into consideration. It may, I think, be taken for granted that the conditions which ripen corn well are those which will tend to a fructiferous condition, as well as a free subsequent development in fruits and flowers. And what are these conditions? Much remaining ground-heat, much light, and a very low temperature of air overhead—at least, in the night. Perhaps I have strained a parallelism in attempting to throw light on a subject hitherto rather obscure. The fact is, the question is, in a great degree, *untrodden ground*, and no wonder if the foot should slip in attempting to discover a track. My idea, however, of the use of an artificial bottom-heat is, that it should be more a guarantee against any *sudden depression* of ground-warmth, than a source of what is generally understood by bottom-heat.

I before suggested a covering of canvas, or some other material, simply on the ground of preventing a too free radiation. Not that the branches *would not endure* the low temperature to which they might be subjected; but that extremes are in most cases best avoided. And moreover, in the case of things for *forcing purposes*, the first stage of such forcing may be, if possible, commenced *out-doors*. Only observe the hyacinth! Who would not admire a fine stand of the finest of our imported kinds on New Year's Day? Yet we seldom see them fine so soon in the year. And why? Simply because they will not endure what practical men term "forcing," until they have produced plenty of fibres, which process (like the ripening of fruits) cannot be reduced simply to a matter of high excitement through temperature, but of time. However, plenty of fibres once produced, an affair of necessity occupying several weeks, the bulb may be introduced to a higher temperature—it may, in ordinary parlance, be "forced."—ROBERT ERRINGTON, *gardener to Sir P. M. Egerton, Bart., Oulton Park, Cheshire.*

ON THE COLLECTING AND IMPORTATION OF ORCHIDS.

THE following instructions, which have been prepared for a gentleman about to visit South America, with the intention of making a collection of the Orchids of those regions, are so clear and explicit on all the needful points, that they are submitted for the benefit of others interested in the importation of Orchids :—

The countries likely to be visited by the gentleman alluded to are Bolivia, and other portions of Central America, which abound in Orchids, many of the most gorgeous and showy kinds, more particularly the species of Cattleya, Peristeria, Oncidium, Chysis, and many other showy genera, which are mostly found growing on trees near the outsides of the thick jungle, and very frequently on decayed trunks that have fallen from age, but *rarely* in the dark or close part of the jungle. They are more abundant near rivers and water-courses than elsewhere. The best plan for their preservation is to cut them off whatever they may be growing upon, with as many of the roots whole as possible ; or, when growing on small pieces of wood, if that can be cut with them, the greater is the certainty of preserving them. Dry them a little in a *shaded* place, not allowing the sun to reach them. When dry, pack them in boxes, with a little dry moss, if to be had, between the layers of plants ; or, if moss is not procurable, the dried leaves of the Tillandsias, or wild Pine Apples, will answer the same purpose, and can be got in those regions without trouble. The sides of the boxes should be pierced by a half-inch centre-bit, with holes at about six inches apart, all over their surface. The cases are most convenient when about three feet in length, and eighteen inches in *depth and width*. They ought to be marked on the top as "perishable plants, to be kept as far from the boilers of the steam-ship as possible." In this way, nearly every plant may be imported alive and in good condition.

The same countries abound also in aquatics of the finest kinds. In the standing pools close to the Amazon and its tributaries, are hundreds of acres of *Victoria Regia*, and many other most beautiful water plants. The former is to be found in Bolivia, and from that country the first seeds of it were sent to Kew by Mr. T. Bridges of Valparaiso. Some vegetated ; but, having arrived late in autumn, died during the first winter. Soon after that Sir R. Schomburgh sent seeds from the Amazon. The best way of getting aquatics home is by collecting the seeds, and placing them in small balls of clay quite moist, putting the balls in bottles with *wide* mouths, like pickle bottles. Ram them tight, with a little water floating on the top, and then seal them so as to exclude air.* Roots of some of the kinds may be got home, but they require glass cases perfectly *air-tight*, so as to enable the soil to retain sufficient moisture.

All along the rivers of South America, and especially on the low banks of the tributary streams, bulbs of the very finest kinds are found in plenty, consisting mostly of Amaryllises, Crinums, and Pancratiums of the best sorts, many of which have never yet been introduced into this country. The above-named plants, and more especially the Amaryllises, are in every way deserving the attention of the collectors. There are also found by the rivers, and in the plains, many beautiful creeping plants, such as Echites, Allamanda, Passiflora, &c., seeds of which could easily be sent home.

On the Orinooko, about seven hundred miles up, there are to be found thousands of that splendid orchid, the *Cattleya superba*, in several varieties, with a vast assortment of other orchids.—H. L.

* The seeds of the Victoria have been transported much more successfully in phials of pure water.—M.

1. Ipomoea palmata. 2 Dillwynia scabra

IPOMŒA PALMATA.[*]

HE plant from which the accompanying drawing of this very handsome species of Ipomœa was taken, was raised from seeds gathered near the mouth of the Buffalo River, in British Kaffraria, by Captain E. Rooper, and sent by him in April 1849 to the Rev. T. Rooper, in whose garden at Wick Hill, Brighton, the flowers were produced for the first time in the autumn of 1850. It blossomed again in December last, when we had an opportunity of examining its flowers.

There seems no good reason to doubt its identity with the *I. palmata* of Forskahl, at least with that single or few-flowered plant to which the name of *I. cairica* has been applied, and which M. Choisy and others combine with it. Whether the few and many-flowered forms to which these names have been given, present any other permanent differences sufficient for their discrimination, we have no means of ascertaining, and we have accordingly concurred in the view taken in *De Candolle's Prodromus*, where Choisy also combines with it the *Ipomœa quinqueloba* of Rœmer and Schultes, and the *I. senegalensis* of Lamarck. Viewed in this collective form, the species is recorded to occur in Guinea, Senegal, Sennaar, Nubia, Egypt, Syria, and the Island of Santa Cruz.

The plant, a fleshy-rooted perennial of vigorous growth, produces smooth, slender evergreen stems. The leaves are quinate, the lobes lanceolate, the exterior pair usually bifid, the middle more oblong, and longer than the rest, all obtuse, mucronate, and very minutely serrulate. The longish petioles are slightly hairy at the base, where is situated a pair of palmately divided stipules. In our specimen the peduncles each bear one flower (1—3, rarely many-flowered, *Choisy*), and are somewhat shorter than the petioles, bracteate with a pair of small scales just above the middle. The sepals are smooth, equal, bluntly ovate, with membranous edges. The corolla is sub-campanulate, smooth, of a lightish rose-colour, suffused with purple; the stamens enclosed, unequal in length; the stigma slender, with a pair of roundish lobes. The ovary is two-celled, the cells two-seeded.

This very beautiful climber is no doubt suitable for a greenhouse, if not for the open air; but as yet, Mr. Rooper's gardener has not succeeded in blooming it freely, In the wild state, however, where it grows trailing over bushes, or climbing the trees, in sandy soil, by the river side, Captain Rooper found it so profuse that he could scarcely discern the leaves from the abundance of the flowers. We suspect that it requires considerable space to develope itself, and that its growth should be commenced early in the summer, in order that there may be time in autumn for the development of the flowers. Mr. Smyth informs us that in the summer of 1850, a small plant, placed at the foot of a south wall in July, had covered twelve square feet of the wall by September, when it was found to be covered with blossom buds, but the plant being lifted and removed to a conservatory, it sustained a check which prevented their development. When the little peculiarities of its cultivation are ascertained, we expect it will become a favourite plant. It was introduced many years since, but lost.—M.

DILLWYNIA SCABRA.[†]

FOR the opportunity of figuring this very pretty Australian shrub we are indebted to Messrs. Henderson, nurserymen, Pine Apple Place, Edgeware Road, by whom it had been raised about two years since from seeds sent by Mr. Drummond. It was exhibited by them at one of the Regent's Park Exhibitions last summer, when a medal was awarded to it.

It is a free-growing bushy shrub, with erectly-spreading branches, which when young are hairy, but afterwards clothed with a greyish bark. The leaves are scattered, linear, rolled inwards on each

* *Ipomœa palmata*, Forskahl, desc. p. 43.   † *Dillwynia scabra*, Schlechtendahl in Linnæa.

E

side so as to present a channel above, obtuse, clothed when young with short, stiff, spreading hairs, and having very minute deciduous stipules. The flowers grow in peduncles, axillary or terminal to the branches. The calyx is pubescent, somewhat bell-shaped, with the limb spreading, two-lipped, the upper lip larger and bifid, the lower with three more deeply divided narrow teeth. The standard of the corolla has a long claw, with a broad, short limb, emarginate, and laterally expanded so as to be almost two-lobed, folded slightly up the middle, reflexed, scarlet, with a yellow claw and central disk; the wings are narrow, oblong, half as long again as the claw of the standard, deep red; the keel is rather shorter, boat-shaped, and attenuated into a recurved point, purplish red above. The stamens are free, included in the keel, with short, subulate, glabrous, somewhat curved filaments. The ovary is shortly stalked, hairy, gradually attenuated into a short, slender, pyramidal style, half as long as the keel, and recurved suddenly at the summit; stigma slightly capitate.—A. H.

The Dillwynias are a tribe of free-flowering plants, of very neat growth, and generally great favourites among cultivators, and in consequence of blooming with great freedom and considerable certainty, they are found exceedingly useful for decorative as well as exhibition purposes. They are principally natives of New South Wales

Like most of the hard-wooded plants, they delight in a peaty soil, liberally intermixed with sand : a mixture in the following proportions is found very suitable for their growth :—Four parts rich turfy peat; two parts mellow turfy loam; one part sand; and one part charcoal, broken to the size of horse-beans. These ingredients should be passed through a sieve with half-inch meshes, and be intimately mixed together before using. In selecting plants, take care that they are strong and bushy, with plenty of healthy roots; but if the roots are not in a vigorous-growing state, do not pot the plants until they are so. If the plants are in good condition, the stronger-growing kinds will bear a comparatively large shift with advantage. It is, however, unsafe to shift any plants largely until you are quite sure that your soil is suitable; and therefore, in first receiving them from the nursery, it will be better to give them a slight shift, and if the soil is suitable, then, when the pots are full of roots, give a more liberal one, observing, however, as a general rule, that it is better for a plant to be short of pot-room than to have too much. In shifting, loosen a few of the matted roots round the sides of the ball, and take care to make the soil pretty firm at the time of potting. Now, if you procure nice bushy plants at this season (February), if they are nicely rooted in three-inch pots, they may be removed into pots one size larger, or even into six-inch pots, if they are of the more vigorous-growing kinds. In potting take care to use sufficient drainage, and with the very delicate rooting kinds a few crocks, broken small, may be intermixed throughout the soil in addition to the charcoal. Some cultivators recommend sand, freestone, or small pebbles for this purpose, but we prefer broken crocks, as being less likely to work their way to the bottom of the pots, or injure the roots. After potting place the plants in the warmest end of the greenhouse, or in a close pit or frame, and do not expose them to cold or arid draughts until they get into free growth. Almost all New Holland plants require more heat than plants from the Cape, and, indeed, those from low warm valleys are materially benefited in the growing season by a little extra heat, more than is usual for ordinary greenhouse plants. In the winter, all New Holland plants require more heat than Heaths, and similar hard-rooted plants. When the young plants give evidence of having their roots in action, it will be time to stop the shoots to induce a bushy growth, but do not attempt to stop the plants until they are properly established. In stopping you must be ruled by circumstances, such as the habit of the plant, and its disposition to produce side branches. Some of the kinds, as *D. clavata* and *rudis*, produce their flowers upon long shoots, while *D. juniperina*, *floribunda*, and several more, produce their flowers at the points of short shoots, and hence, while those first-named require but little stopping after they are once properly formed, except to cut them boldly in after they have done blooming, those of the habit of *D. juniperina* should have the points of the shoots pinched off in the growing season whenever they are three inches long, as it is upon the multiplication and maturing of a number of small branches that we must depend for a good head of bloom. Do not stop any of the kinds later than the end of July, or the young shoots will not get sufficiently ripened to produce flowers.

As the plants progress through the summer (they may be set in a warm corner out of doors after the middle of June) take care to attend them properly with water, and pot them as frequently as appears necessary, but not too late in the season. Syringe the plants frequently to keep them clear of red spider, and water them with weak liquid manure once or twice a-week if they are growing very freely. We have said nothing of staking and training, but that must be properly attended to, for unless a plant is properly formed in the young state, it will never make a fine and handsome specimen.—A.

ARTISTIC COMBINATIONS IN FLOWER GARDENING.

FOR some years past the planting of flower beds in masses of one colour has been the prevailing fashion, not only in this country but also upon the continent. That the practice is a very good one cannot be denied, as the violent contrasts of distinct or complementary colours has a very striking effect. The only drawback upon the system is a want of intricacy and variety, and hence some gardeners have adopted the mixed system, planting flowers of distinct and contrasting colours in concentric circles or distinct straight lines. In this new scheme it is questionable whether we are not exchanging the massive and decided for the "little prettinesses" of persons of small intelligence ; and it is quite certain that beds so arranged, though they may be individually striking and interesting, cannot produce the grand effect of bold masses of properly contrasted and distinct colours. If we wish to detract from the size of a garden, these mixed beds are well calculated to assist in such a work; but, if boldness and distinctness of expression is wished for, then masses of distinct colours must be employed. Originating in this system of planting, is what may be called "ribbon grouping," in which a long narrow border of distinct colours are blended in imitation of the gaudy ribbons which sometimes garnish the shop fronts of silk-mercers, and such borders, when of sufficient length, have a very remarkable and striking effect. Thus, for example, a row of dark blue Branching Larkspur for the back, with *Calceolaria viscosissima* next, and then Scarlet Pelargoniums in the front, is said to look very fine, and, no doubt, if the border has a margin of grass, a row of Mangles's Variegated or Silver Bedding Pelargonium, might be introduced in the front with advantage.

Again *Pentstemon gentianoides coccinea* with Orange Calceolaria, Purple Senecio—the dark variety, —Dwarf Scarlet Pelargonium and *Lobelia gracilis*, or any of the dark blue trailing varieties, would afford an excellent combination.

Among hardy plants, the following may be planted in lines together :—*Delphinium Barlowii* or *chinense*, blue ; *Lobelia splendens*, scarlet ; Yellow Lupine ; Crimson Antirrhinum ; *Campanula carpatica*, purple, with, if the edging is grass, Variegated Alyssum in front.

Of annuals of a permanent character the following are suitable :—Blue Branching Larkspur, *Eschscholtzia crocea*, Scarlet Intermediate Stock, *Phlox Drummondii alba*, *Eutoca viscida*, and dwarf dark French Marigold.

Mr. Beaton, a year or two back, recommended *Verbena venosa*, and the common Variegated Pelargonium to be intermixed, to form what some call a shot-silk bed ; and the dark red Calceolaria, intermixed with *Brachycome iberidifolia*, and edged with *Campanula rotundifolia alba*, is said to produce nearly the same effect. Intermixed with the pink Ivy-leaved Pelargonium—a low trailing plant,—the blue Lobelia, with its flowers resting upon the foliage of the Pelargonium, looks very pretty ; and a few plants of the old Verbena Favourite, with its pink flowers, look well mixed with the same Pelargonium. Indeed, we might multiply these combinations *ad infinitum :* but the rule of strong, and, as far as possible, complementary contrasts, once properly understood, the application of it to plants of all kinds is an easy matter—for Roses, Hollyhocks, Phloxes, Dahlias, Antirrhinums, and hundreds of our commoner plants are suitable for planting as indicated above. Of the formality of the system we say nothing : variety, change, and contrast must be had, and no doubt the new system will please for a year or two.—A.

GLAZED PROMENADES AND GLASS WALLS.

AMONG the wonders which the great 1851 has brought to light, glass walls for horticultural purposes are not the least remarkable for those interested in gardening pursuits. To Mr. Ewing, gardener to O. F. Meyrick, Esq., of Bodorgan, Anglesea, belongs the merit of directing attention to the subject at the present time, though a similar plan was proposed many years ago in the *Gardeners' Magazine* by Mr. Mallet, C. E. of Dublin. Cheap glass and the present building facilities, as exemplified in the erection of the Crystal Palace, enable us now to profit by the suggestion; though it is matter of doubt whether glazed promenades would not be very preferable to walls of glass. Walls, as proposed by Mr. Ewing, to make the best of them, being very narrow, will contain but a small volume of air, and hence must be liable to sudden variations of temperature, being in a few minutes, when the sun strikes upon them, exceedingly hot, and on frosty nights correspondingly cold. For the growth of Peaches and other stone fruits during the time of setting and stoning, they will require the utmost watchfulness as to ventilation, and, indeed, being all glass, in gleamy weather in March and April, it is doubtful whether it will be possible to keep anything like an equable temperature; and every Peach forcer

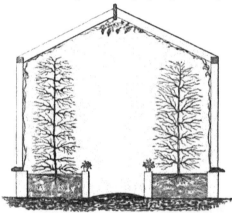

SECTION OF A GLAZED PROMENADE FOR FRUITS OR FLOWERS.

knows how difficult it is with the best management to set a regular crop of fruit. Apart, however, from their narrowness, and the small volume of air which they contain, we think with Mr. Rivers there is great waste of glass to no purpose, and that for the same, or a little more expense, narrow houses of great convenience might be constructed, which in addition to offering shelter as promenades, will also produce double the quantity of fruit.

The annexed engraving represents a house of this kind, in which either fruit trees or flowers may be planted, and the increase of glass for such a structure is only as thirty to twenty-one, and the additional expense at the same ratio. A house of this kind, fifty feet long by twelve feet wide, using the best materials and performing the work in first-rate style, would not cost more than £100, and if ordinary materials were used it might be constructed for much less. But we believe in all horticultural erections cheapness and durability are not synonymous terms, and though a house may be erected for £50, perhaps one of the same size at £100 would twenty years hence be the most economical. Besides, as fruit-forcing may be considered one of the luxuries of life, we should like to see the trees growing in respectable habitations. Mr. Ewing's glass walls, as shown by the drawings, would doubtless have a very elegant appearance; there is nothing make-shift about them, but they are worthy of a place in the best appointed gardens, being strong and substantial in every respect. In the house represented in the engraving, we suppose a neat iron or wood frame-work to be erected permanently, against which sashes (all made precisely the same size, viz., seven feet six inches long by three feet six inches wide) may be fixed by means of bolts and nuts, and the sashes to slide at the top in the usual fashion. If two houses of the same size were erected in the same garden, say one for fruit and the other for Perpetual Roses, one set of sashes would be sufficient, as the fruit would be ripe by the time the sashes were required for the Rose-house or winter promenade, and they might be removed from the Rose-house in time for the fruit in the spring. At the present time, the middle of January, we have buds of Géant des Batailles Rose, which have been exposed to a temperature of 16°, but still promise to open; and on Christmas-day last, we gathered a very nicely-expanded bud of the same kind from a plant quite unprotected. With the simple protection of glass, autumnal Roses might be had in abundance until Christmas, and a house so arranged with an admixture of Chrysanthemums, &c., would have a most charming effect. The frame-work of the Rose-house being in the dressed ground might through the summer be covered with summer climbers, and climbing Roses budded with the perpetual kinds, which might hang in festoons from the rafters. Standing upon the inner walls is shown a row of Strawberry pots in fruit; or a border one foot deep and nine inches wide, might be partitioned off by bricks on edge, in which strawberries might be planted, and Russian violets in the Rose-house.

In planting these houses, we propose to train the trees, whether fruits or roses, into pyramids, tall and short alternately, the tall growing to the top of the house, and the short ones about four feet high. These will be placed so that the sun will shine over the small trees on the larger ones on the opposite side of the pathway, and so all will be alike exposed to light. Trees trained into the pyramidal form will present a much larger surface than when trained flat; and we see no reason why peaches and apricots should not be covered with natural spurs the same as pears and plums.

Although we have heard it remarked by a learned authority, since the above was written, that it was not fair to draw comparisons between glass walls and such contrivances as this, until the former had been properly proved, we must take the liberty of stating, that if any reason can be shown why glass walls should not be adopted, the sooner it is done the better, for if they are what they are represented to be, no opposition that can be urged against them will be of any avail. We, however, advise all who read these pages to pause before they adopt them, for it is quite certain that glass can be turned to a much more profitable purpose than for the construction of walls. It is certainly not an economical application of glass to use it as Mr. Ewing does—viz., more than *twenty feet* to cover *two* superficial surface of ground, while it is quite certain that this might be made to cover sixteen feet. Making the best of glass walls, glass-houses must be very preferable to them; but we do not want them put up on the cheap plan. What is worth doing in gardening matters is worth doing well, and we are quite sure will be the most economical in the end.

Since the above was written we have seen a scheme similar to our own, from Mr. Spencer of Bowood, particulars of which we hope to give hereafter.—A.

MELLAGETTA PEPPER.

MELLAGETTA PEPPER is produced by the *Amomum Granum Paradisi*, synonymous, according to Sir W. J. Hooker, with the *A. grandiflorum* (Smith), the *A. exscapum* (Sims), and the *A. Afzelii* (Roscoe). The term Melegueta, or Mellegetta Pepper, has been applied to several zingiberaceous plants. It has usually, observes Dr. Periera, been considered synonymous with the terms Grains of Paradise, and Guinea Grains. Melegueta Pepper is said to have been known in Italy before the discovery of the Guinea coast by the Portuguese in the fifteenth century. It was brought by the Moors, who used to cross the region of Mandingha, and the deserts of Libya, and carry it to Mundi Barca (or Monte de Barca), a port in the Mediterranean. The Italians, not knowing the place of its origin, as it is so precious a spice, called it Grana Paradisi. Another kind of Amomum, known as Melegueta Pepper, is the *A. Melegueta* (Roscoe), figured in that author's work on scitamineous plants. The fruits of both kinds seem to be indifferently employed in lieu of pepper in Western Africa, and are esteemed the most wholesome of spices, and generally used by the natives to season their food.

The principal consumption of Grains of Paradise in Europe is in veterinary medicine, and to give an artificial strength to spirits, wine, beer, and vinegar. Although the seeds are by no means injurious, an act was passed (56 Geo. III., c. 58) that no brewer, or dealer in beer, shall have in his possession, or use, Grains of Paradise, under a penalty of £200 for each offence, and no druggist shall sell it to a brewer under a penalty of £500 for each offence. (*Bot. Mag.*)

The plant which produces this spice is of very curious structure. From a mass of tuberous knobs, covered by large red sheathing scales, the sterile stems grow up very much resembling those of the common ginger, and among these grow the flowers on very short scapes, also clothed with loose red scales, from among which the flowers issue. The conspicuous part of these flowers consists of two series of organs, the exterior tubular below, and cut into three erect oblong segments, white, tinged with yellow and rose; the inner series is reduced to one larger segment, whose tubular base is included in the tube of the outer series, and whose limb is rotundate, somewhat folded and undulate at the margin, pure white, with yellow at the base. Two or three such flowers are produced on each scape, and these are succeeded by the capsules containing hot acrid seeds, which form the Grains of Paradise.

THE SIKKIM RHODODENDRONS.*

DR. HOOKER'S account of the Himalayan Rhododendrons is one of the most beautiful of recent contributions to botanical literature, whether in regard to the character of the plants on which it treats, or to the execution of the plates, which are admirably drawn by Mr. Fitch, from Dr. Hooker's,

RHODODENDRON LEPIDOTUM, *var.* ELEAGNOIDES.

sketches made whilst travelling in the most elevated region of the globe. From this tract there are here enumerated no fewer than forty-three species of Rhododendron, most of them previously unknown to science; and of this number, thirty-one are depicted in inimitable folio figures. These species of the Himalayas, and those of Java recently brought into notice — of which latter group we lately observed some additional novelties in the Nursery of Messrs. Rollison of Tooting—must open up an entirely new field for planters and hybridizers, and give rise to a complete change in the aspect of this showy and favourite race of hardy shrubs. The cultivability and hardiness of the pure Sikkim species must, as yet, be considered an unsettled point; but they cannot fail to have a material influence on the future cross-breeding of our present hardy races.

Now that Dr. Hooker's work is completed, we purpose giving a brief and connected enumeration of the new kinds he has figured, embodying some corrections he has since published. We shall take another opportunity to offer a few observations on the climate of Sikkim, from another source. Dr. Hooker arranges the species as follows :—

I. Calyx obsolete. Corolla broadly campanulate, hemispherical at the base. Stamens 18—20 (rarely 10). Ovary 10—20 celled. Trees with ample leaves, and, capitate, often crowded flowers.

R. Falconeri (J. D. Hooker). Plate 10.—A large tree, thirty feet high, having very large broad blunt leaves, ferruginous and veiny beneath; and dense heads of small ten-lobed white flowers. Elevation 10 to 12,000 feet.

R. Hodgsoni (J. D. H.). Plate 15.—A bush twelve to twenty feet high, with large leaves, silvery beneath, and close heads of pale rosy-lilac eight to ten-lobed flowers. Elevation 10 to 12,000 feet, in moist alpine forests.

R. argenteum (J. D. H.) Plate 9.—A noble tree, thirty feet high, with very large obovate-oblong leaves, and large heads of pure white flowers. Elevation 8 to 10,000 feet.

* The Rhododendrons of Sikkim Himalaya. By Dr. J. D. Hooker. M.D., R.N. Edited by Sir W. J. Hooker. Complete in Three Parts. London: Reeve and Benham.

II. Calyx cupular, hemispherical or scutelliform, obsoletely lobed. Corolla campanulate, five-lobed. Stamens 10—16. Ovary 6—16 celled. Large flowering shrubs, with very glabrous leaves.

R. Aucklandii (J. D. H.). Plate 11.—A noble species, four to eight feet high, with large leaves, and heads of few large broad shallow flowers, white, tinged with pink, and veiny. Elevation 7 to 9,000 feet, in the drier valleys. This proves to be the *R. Griffithii* of Wight, which name must take precedence of *R. Aucklandii.*

R. Thomsoni (J. D. H.). Plate 12.—A magnificent bush, 8 to 10 or 15 feet high. The leaves are broad, flat, and rounded, and the campanulate flowers are of a deep blood-red colour, very brilliant. Elevation 11 to 13,000 feet. *R. candelabrum* (J. D. H.); plate 29; a very handsome bush, with the flowers sulphur-coloured, edged with rose, and growing at a similar elevation, is now found to be merely a variety.

III. Calyx subfoliaceous, five-partite, lobes submembranaceous. Corolla infundibuliform or campanulate, tube elongated. Stamens 10—18. Ovary 5—6 celled. Shrubs, frequently epiphytes, leaves lepidote beneath.

R. Dalhousiæ (J. D. H.). Plates 1 and 2.—This is the finest of the race. Its form an epiphytal shrub, six to eight feet high, with moderate-sized leaves, and very large lily-like fragrant white blossoms, which in age assume a delicate roseate tinge. Elevation 6 to 9,000 feet, in humid forests of the temperate zone.

R. Edgeworthii (J. D. H.). Plate 21. A beautiful shrub, of moderate size, often pendulous from trees or rocks, having large ferruginous leaves, downy beneath, and producing large white flowers two or three together. Elevation 7 to 9,000 feet, in damp temperate forests.

R. barbatum (Wallich.). Plate 3.—A tree forty to sixty feet high, bearing compact heads of rose-coloured flowers. Elevation 9 to 11,000 feet, in damp forests of the temperate zone. *R. lancifolium* (J. D. H.); plate 4; a shrub six to eight feet high, found at 8 to 10,000 feet elevation, is considered a variety of this superb species.

R. ciliatum (J. D. H.). Plate 24.—A small hairy shrub, two feet high, with largish leaves, and small clusters of purplish flowers. Elevation 9 to 10,000 feet, in temperate rocky valleys of the interior.

R. glaucum (J. D. H.). Plate 17.—A beautiful little shrub, averaging two feet high, the leaves small, oblong, very glaucous beneath, the flowers in comparatively large clusters, of a lively rose pink. Elevation 10 to 12,000 feet.

R. pumilum (J. D. H). Plate 14.—A very elegant little plant, the smallest of the Sikkim species, rooting amongst moss, growing three or four inches high, and bearing pretty pink flowers on long stalks. Elevation 12 to 14,000 feet.

IV. Calyx small or obsolete, rarely five-toothed, lobes equal. Corolla campanulate, or with the limb contracted below its base, and subinfundibuliform. Stamens 10. Ovary 5—10 celled. Shrubs sometimes lepidote.

R. Campbelliæ (J. D. H.). Plate 6.—A fine tree, the characteristic species of Darjeeling. The rose-scarlet flowers are in close round heads; the leaves are narrow and rusty beneath. Elevation 9 to 10, or 11,000 feet, in the temperate valleys. This is the *R. nilagiricum* of the *Botanical Magazine;* and is now considered only a variety of *R. arboreum.*

R. Wallichii (J. D. H.). Plate 5.—A shrub, eight to ten feet high, with broad elliptical leaves, and flowers of a lilac-rose colour. Elevation 11 to 13,000 feet. This and the following are now ranked by Dr. Hooker as varieties of *R. campanulatum.*

R. æruginosum (J. D. H.). Plate 22.—A handsome shrub, growing four feet high, with blunt leaves, rusty beneath, and large heads of lilac rosy flowers. Elevation 12 to 14,000 feet.

R. Wightii (J. D. H.). Plate 27.—A very handsome shrub, of ten feet high, with rather large flat leaves, rufous beneath, and large heads of pale yellow flowers, marked with red spots. Elevation 12 to 14,000 feet, in the alpine valleys, where it is the most prevalent species.

R. lanatum (J. D. H.). Plate 16.—A neat-looking large shrub; the young bark, stalks, and under part of the leaves covered with white cottony tomentum; the flowers are sulphur-coloured, spotted with red. Elevation 10 to 12,000 feet.

R. fulgens (J. D. H.). Plate 25.—A very showy shrub, growing four feet high, with broad foliage, woolly and purplish beneath, and dense round heads of the richest blood-red flowers. Elevation 12 to 14,000 feet, in the valleys of the interior.

R. campylocarpum (J. D. H.). Plate 30.—A handsome pale-flowered bush, of about six feet high, which, from its graceful and delicate inflorescence, Dr. Hooker regards as the most charming of the Sikkim species, claiming precedence over its more gaudy congeners. The leaves are short and broad, and the flowers are of a pure, spotless sulphur-colour, produced in large heads. Elevation 11 to 14,000 feet.

V. Calyx short coriaceous, five-lobed or toothed, the upper generally elongated, sometimes subulate. Corolla funnel-shaped, tube narrowed. Stamens 10—20. Ovary 5—10 celled. Shrubs with leaves lepidote beneath.

R. Maddeni (J. D. H.). Plate 18.—A fine shrub, six to eight feet high, with sharp-pointed leaves, bright ferruginous beneath, and heads of three or four large white long funnel-shaped blossoms. Elevation 6000 feet, in the drier temperate valleys.

R. cinnabarinum (J. D. H.). Plate 8.—A small, and, according to Dr. Hooker, very elegant shrub, with small pendulous cinnabar-coloured flowers. Elevation 10 to 12,000 feet. It is considered poisonous to cattle and goats, and the smoke of the wood when employed as fuel causes the eyes to inflame and the cheeks to swell. *R. Roylei* (J. D. H.); plate 7 ; a small shrub, with neat oval leaves, rusty beneath, and small heads of rosy coppery-tinged flowers, tipped with blue in the bud, and growing at an elevation of 10 to 11,000 feet, is a variety.

VI. Calyx subfoliaceous, five-partite. Tube of the corolla short, tinged at the base, the lobes patent concave.
     Stamens 5—10. Style subclavate. Ovary 5-celled. Shrubs often small, epiphytes or terrestrial, with
     leaves densely lepidote (except in R. pendulum).

     R. camelliæflorum (J. D. H.). Plate 28.—A small slender shrub, pendulous from trees or rocks, with elliptic leaves, brown and dotted beneath with rust-coloured scales, and producing from the ends of the shoots two or three abnormal white flowers, which in form resemble those of a single Camellia. Elevation 9 to 10,000 feet.

     R. pendulum (J. D. H.). Plate 13.—A small pendulous epiphytal species, with small white flowers growing two or three together from the top of the shoots. Elevation 9 to 11,000 feet.

     R. salignum (J. D. H.). Plate 23A.—A pretty diminutive shrub, two to four feet high, with small narrow leaves, the branches terminated by a few shallow spreading yellow flowers. Elevation 7,000 feet. Dr. Hooker now combines under the name of *R. lepidotum* (Wallich), this, *R. obovatum*, and the following :—*R. elæagnoides* (J. D. H.) ; plate 23B ; a charming diminutive plant, growing in clumps like heather, the small leaves arranged in semi-rosettes, and the broad shallow flowers more like a Cistus than an ordinary Rhododendron, varying in colour from yellow to purple. Elevation 12 to 16,000 feet.

VII. Calyx subfoliaceous five-parted or lobed, lobes short rounded. Tube of corolla, short funnel-shaped, lobes
      of limb elongated, narrow spreading entire. Stamens 8. Style slender. Ovary 5-celled. Lepidote
      shrubs, with Azalea-like flowers.

      R. virgatum (J. D. H.). Plate 26A.—A small glaucous shrub, growing four feet high, and producing small purplish red flowers. Elevation 8 to 9000 feet. A variety of this is the *R. triflorum* (J. D. H.); plate 19; which forms a small shrub, four to six feet high, bearing pale greenish-yellow flowers in threes at the end of the branches, and grows at an elevation of 7 to 9000 feet.

      R. nivale (J. D. H.). Plate 26B.—A small depressed shrub, spreading to a foot or two in diameter, with woody branches, bearing small leaves, and small rosy flowers. "The latest to bloom, and earliest to mature its seeds, by far the smallest in foliage, and proportionally largest in flower, most lepidote in vesture, humble in stature, rigid in texture, deformed in habit, yet the most odoriferous ; it may be recognised even in the herbarium as the production of the loftiest elevation on the surface of the globe—of the most excessive climate—of the joint influences of a scorching sun by day, and the keenest frosts at night—of the greatest drought, followed in a few hours by a saturated atmosphere—of the balmiest calm, alternating with the whirlwind of the Alps." Its odour resembles that of eau-de-cologne. This species grows at an elevation of 18,000 feet, far above the ordinary limit of phænogamic vegetation.

      R. setosum (Don). Plate 20.—A diminutive and elegant plant, from a span to a foot high, with small coriaceous leaves, and very numerous scattered lively rosy-purple flowers. Elevation 13 to 16,000 feet. It has a good deal the aspect of Rhodora, but the flowers are more copious and brighter, and the foliage is box-like and evergreen. "The Sikkim Bhoteas and Thibetians attribute the oppression and head-aches attending the crossing of the loftiest passes of Eastern Himalaya to the strong resinous odour of this and *R. anthopogon*. The species certainly abounds to within a few miles of the summit of all the passes, and after hot sunshine fills the atmosphere with its powerful aroma, too heavy by far to be agreeable." A useful volatile oil would probably be yielded by distillation of the foliage.

The most striking species among the foregoing are :—*R. Dalhousiæ, Maddeni, Edgeworthii,* and *Griffithii,* which are remarkable for their very large white flowers, the latter differing from the others in its shallow-cupped form ; *R, argenteum* on account of its fine foliage and compact heads of white flowers; *R. Falconeri* and *Hodgsoni* for their peculiarly dense globular inflorescence, and large broad blunt leaves ; *R. Thomsoni* and *fulgens* for their rich blood-coloured flowers; *R. glaucum* for its neat habit, glaucous leaves, and pretty pink blossoms; *R. campylocarpum, Wightii,* and *lanatum,* for their sulphur-coloured flowers; and *R. elæagnoides, salignum, virgatum, nivale,* and *pumilum* for their small size, and general dissimilarity from the ordinary aspect of Rhododendrons.

Setting aside the question of cultivability, which can only be settled by experience, and admitting all the larger growing species to be—if cultivable—fine conservatory ornaments, we should select as the most distinct and promising for general cultivation, the following species :—*R. Thomsoni, fulgens, Dalhousiæ, Maddeni, Wightii, glaucum, campylocarpum,* and *Griffithii.* It may be worth while to add, as an encouragement to cultivators, that two at least of the species—*R. barbatum* and *Campbelliæ,* have been successfully cultivated in this country, as also has been the epiphytal *R. javanicum.*

Some of the species naturally inhabit what may be called the temperate regions of the Himalaya, while others occur only within the alpine range, and some even rise above that to the arctic region and approach the perpetual snow. It will, therefore, be manifestly improper that they should all be treated alike, without reference to these peculiarities.—M.

Campanula Vidalii

CAMPANULA VIDALII.

THE accompanying figure of this very fine Bell-flower of the Azores, is made from a plant which bloomed last August, in the nursery of Messrs. Osborn and Son, of Fulham. The species was originally found by Captain Vidal, after whom it is named, on an insulated rock on the east coast of Flores one of the Azorean group of Islands, and specimens were presented by him to H. C. Watson, Esq. Subsequently it has been communicated by T. Hunt, Esq., Her Majesty's Consul at the Azores. Living plants appear to have been first obtained by Messrs. Osborn, from seeds sent to England by Mr. Wallace, and our figure is made from one of them. Last year, however, our coadjutor, Mr. Ayres, obtained seeds from the same source; and a further supply, recently received, will place the *Campanula Vidalii* (first described and named by Watson in Hooker's Icones Plantarum, vii., t., 684) within reach of cultivators generally.

The habit of the plant is sub-shrubby, with thickened branching stems. These grow up at first from four to six inches high, and retain foliage only at the top, in a semi-rosette fashion. Near the top is produced a series of branches (in our plants raised last spring, from four to seven in number), which also grow to the length of four or five inches, and then terminate in a tuft of leaves. From the centre of these shoot out the flower stems, which grow about two feet high, and bear, towards the end, their nodding, bell-shaped flowers, which are either disposed in a raceme, or in plants of greater vigour, in a somewhat paniculate manner below. The leaves are smooth, shining, spathulate-oblong, with crenated margins, very thick, between leathery and fleshy in texture; those scattered on the flowering stems being smaller, narrower, and less crenated. The flowers are white, and have the remarkable contracted form shown in the figure. The plant sketched in the background of the accompanying plate is one of the smaller examples selected from the seedlings of last spring. The largest plants from the same sowing are about a foot high, each with six or seven branches. The indication of paniculate inflorescence is taken from a native specimen. It is a very ornamental plant, and, unlike many maritime species, perfectly cultivable. It, however, requires protection from frost.—M.

Contrary to expectation, this Campanula proves to be of easy cultivation, and a very free-blooming and graceful plant; so much so that being quite shrubby in habit, it must become exceedingly useful for the flower-garden, and also for the greenhouse stage. In cultivation, the best time to sow it will be in February, using a light porous soil, and placing the pot in a temperature of from fifty to sixty degrees; water slightly, and the young plants will make their appearance in about a fortnight. When of sufficient size prick them off, either singly into small, or five or six into a larger pot, and place them in a frame with a little warmth, so that they can be properly nursed until they are thoroughly established. Through the summer they may be grown in a cold frame or in the open air, in a sheltered corner, supplying them plentifully with water, and shifting them into large pots as they require it. By vigorous growth, two or three sets of branches may be produced the first season, and each will produce a spike of flowers.

For growing specimen plants, a very suitable soil may be formed of turfy loam, leaf mould, and turfy peat in equal proportions, liberally intermixed with gritty stones and coarse sand. The pots must be thoroughly drained, and care must be taken that the plants are plentifully supplied with water whenever they require it.

For the use of the flower-garden, plants grown in three or four-inch pots will be sufficiently large; and, in planting out, one plant may be allowed to every square foot of border. Fresh plants will require to be raised every season, but whether from seed or by cuttings remains to be proved. The plant, however, is strictly a perennial, and hence will not, when raised from seed, flower until the second year. For bedding purposes we fancy this is likely to become an excellent plant. There can be no question but it will form an exceedingly interesting group.—A.

THE CULTURE OF ALPINE PLANTS.

LINNÆA BOREALIS.

OOKING through the range of ornamental gardening we find no class of plants that indicate better than Alpines the presence at least of pure taste and botanical knowledge. The possessor of a collection of these is always a person of superior intelligence, acquainted with at least some of the branches of botanical philosophy, and always possessed of a decided love of nature, and of a taste guided alone by her laws, unbiassed by the influences of art. The increasing desire for Alpine plants among horticulturists seems to indicate an increasing regard for the simple poetry, as well as the science of nature. In a public garden a collection of Alpines is of great importance in a scientific point of view, affording the student opportunities of studying in a living state those forms of vegetation that adorn inhospitable regions he may never have an opportunity of visiting, as well as those whose native homes on the summits of our highest mountains are often as effectually beyond his reach. But the gradual, and by no means slow, extension of a taste for Alpines throughout society generally, which has of late years been especially observable, does not arise alone from the extension of botany as a science, but from a desire for the reproduction of those traits of simple beauty in nature, which poets of the Wordsworth school love to contemplate, and which we all associate with our purest emotions, and with the first dawning of poetic fancy on our nature-loving hearts.

It is the purpose of the present papers to introduce, from time to time, to the attention of the readers of the *Garden Companion* some of the more interesting of the Alpine plants; and we have thought that we could not commence with a more appropriate subject than *Linnæa borealis*,—a plant whose intrinsic beauty and perfect applicability as an object of cultivation are only excelled by the interest and importance of its associations in the history of botany. Whether seen in its native fir woods, forming a carpet of leafy verdure, to the exclusion of every other plant, or as a garden specimen, enveloping with its dense foliage the pot in which it grows, it is alike an object of beauty and attraction to every one whose eye is open to the loveliness of the vegetable world. But to the naturalist the *Linnæa* is a plant of especial interest, commemorating as it does the memory of one whose name (whatever may be said of his *system*) will long be venerated above all others by the votaries of natural science.

We need scarcely mention that it is a beautiful little plant, with small trailing shrubby stems, and these entwining together and spreading in all directions amongst the thin grass of the wood, form bright green leafy patches, often of large extent, from which the graceful pendent flowers are produced somewhat sparingly, but sometimes in abundance. The flowers are said to be very fragrant at night with the scent of the Meadow-sweet; but this we have not observed. As Smith tells us, it was first found in "an old fir wood at Inglismaldie, on the borders of Mearnshire," in 1795, by Professor James Beattie, junior; but since Beattie's day many new stations have been discovered for the plant in different parts of Scotland, more particularly in the counties of Perth, Inverness, Edinburgh, Aberdeen, Kincardine, and Forfar. Only one locality is, however, recorded for it in England, viz., in a plantation of Scotch firs at Catcherside, in the parish of Hartburn, Northumberland, where it was discovered by Miss Emma Trevelyan. It generally grows in the open but shady parts of old fir woods.

In regard to the cultivation of this plant, it may be remarked that the nature of its native habitats would seem to indicate a plant of difficult culture, and such is indeed the prevalent opinion respecting it. This is however erroneous. Few plants so peculiar in the choice of native stations stand cultivation so well, and few that are so decidedly partial to the shade, stand exposure to sunshine with so happy results. It ought, of course, to be quartered in the frame of Alpines; but on being planted should receive a larger pot than almost any other species, in order that it may have room to extend its procumbent wiry shoots. In the preparation of the soil, decayed leaves and rotten wood ought to form the principal ingredients; and, indeed, if the plant is wished to be cultivated on a rockwork it cannot be better placed than in the hollow of an old trunk filled with soil, for under such circumstances it finds congenial conditions for growth, and soon covers the mass with better effect than perhaps any other plant that can be chosen. In this way it is peculiarly desirable for a *small* ornamental rockwork where neatness is requisite.

We have said that the *Linnæa* delights in shade; but it is only under certain circumstances that this delight ought to be indulged in by the cultivators. The more shade that is given the fewer flowers are produced, and *vice versa*. Where it is wished to have a good pot specimen or a small log one, it is therefore necessary, so soon as the plant is established to allow it pretty free exposure to the sun, of course sheltering it from the hot noonday sunshine of the summer months, as is essential for success with all "Alpines." When thus treated the plant assumes a much more compact habit, and flowers much more freely than when allowed to diffuse its long straggling flowerless shoots, under the influence of shade and moisture; indeed, a well established plant will be annually *covered* with blossoms. The cultivator will of course understand that moisture at the root is an essential requisite, although all flooding ought to be jealously guarded against.

Those plants that record in their names the memories of departed botanists are cherished with especial care by all who entertain feelings of gratitude towards those who have gone before them in the pleasant paths of our fair science. Every grower of Pines looks upon *Douglasii* as one of his most endeared treasures; who can grow Heaths without having *M'Nabiana* in some of its varieties? or what collection of Mosses is complete without the genus *Hookeria*, whose prototype may be justly regarded as their presiding genius in Britain? On the same principle we claim for *Linnæa* a place in every European collection of Alpines, as recording the memory of one dear to ever true botanist. The poet has well said—

"These *botanists* trust	This mutual confidence; if, from such source
The lingering gleam of their departed lives	The practice flow; if thence, or from a deep
To *floral* record, and the silent heart,—	And general humility in death!
Depositories faithful and more kind	Nor should I much condemn it, if it spring
Than fondest epitaph; for, if those fail,	From disregard of Time's destructive power,
What boots the sculptured tomb? And who can bla me—	And only capable to prey on things
Who rather would not envy—men that feel	Of earth, and human nature's mortal part."

While we warmly invite the extended cultivation of the *Linnæa*, we would caution every reader to abstain from being instrumental in aiding the extermination of this rare plant from even *one* of the stations where it is found in wild luxuriance. Long may the *Linnæa* flourish in the woods of northern Europe, a lasting monument to the unparalled zeal, perseverance, and love of nature, that characterized the "Father of Naturalists!"—G.

THE CANNA TRIBE AS BEDDING PLANTS.

THE culture of this tribe of plants for bedding purposes is at once so simple, and attended with so little trouble, as to deserve the attention of every one who has space to spare for them. Their appearance, in suitable situations, is magnificent in the extreme, and planted in beds on a lawn, they impart an exotic character which no other plant that I know of can be employed to produce. Last season I succeeded in producing a very fine effect by planting six plants of *Canna gigantea*, at two yards apart, through a large bed of scarlet Geraniums, which, from being situated on level ground, and in a conspicuous situation from several points, required something to break the monotony of the bed in that particular place. This arrangement was much admired, and not without reason—for the splendid foliage and bright flowers, waving gracefully about with every gust of wind, imparted an effect at once lively and unique.

Our plan is to take up the plants when the frost has cut them down in the autumn, and to pot them in eight-inch pots, and place them under the stage of a greenhouse, or the back part of a conservatory, keeping them nearly dry until the first week in February, when they are placed in an early vinery, and watered freely until they have made a tolerable growth. We then begin to inure them gradually to a lower temperature by transferring them to the greenhouse, then to cold pits, and finally to the open air; and in the last week in May, or the first in June, we plant them in beds previously trenched and enriched with good strong decomposed manure. We give them abundance of water when they are planted, and afterwards treat them occasionally to a copious soaking of liquid manure. For the outsides of the beds we use *Canna coccinea*, which grows two feet; the next range is *C. patens*, from three to four feet; and in the centre *C. gigantea*, four to six feet.—JOHN COX, *gardener to W. Wells, Esq. Redleaf.*

New Garden Plants.

CAMPTOSEMA RUBICUNDUM, *Hooker and Arnott*. Ruby-flowered Camptosema.—Order Fabaceæ (Leguminous plants).—The *Kennedya splendens* of some. A luxuriant climbing stove shrub, with trifoliolate leaves, consisting of smooth petiolate oblong or oblong-elliptical retuse leaflets. The flowers produced in summer are in long drooping racemes, and are deep ruby-red, and about as large as those of *Kennedya rubicunda*. It is from Southern Brazil, and was introduced from the German gardens about 1848. It is a very showy plant for a warm house, where there is abundant space for its growth, but does not flower when restricted. See *Botanical Magazine*, t. 4608.

CEDRONELLA CANA, *Hooker*. Hoary-leaved Cedronella.—Order Lamiaceæ (Labiate tribe).—A showy border flower, apparently quite hardy and free-growing. It is a branched hoary herb, two and a-half to three feet high. The leaves are cordate-ovate, or approaching to hastate in the lower parts of the plant, smaller and narrower above. The false whorls of flowers form a long and crowded spike at the ends of the numerous compactly branched stems; the corollas have a long narrow tube, and a toothed middle-lobe to the lower lip, and are of a lively rose-colour. It is a native of Texas, and has been introduced in 1850 to Kew. It flowers through the summer months. See *Botanical Magazine*, t. 4618.

POTENTILLA AMBIGUA, *Cambessedes*. Three-toothed Himalayan Potentilla. Order Rosaceæ (Rosewort tribe).—A very handsome hardy perennial plant, well figured in the *Botanical Magazine*, t. 4613. It is of suffruticose habit, with ascending purplish stems from a woody root; they grow six inches to a foot high, and bear ternate leaves on longish petioles, the leaflets are cuneate-obovate, trifid at the apex, and of a deep green colour, paler beneath. The large showy flowers consist of five obcordate spreading petals, and grow singly on terminal peduncles. It comes from Sikkim and other parts of the Himalayas, where it is found at 12,000 to 13,000 feet elevation. It was introduced by Dr. Hooker in 1850, to the Royal Botanic Garden, Kew. It is a summer-flowering plant.

ACER CIRCINATUM, *Pursh*. Circinate Maple.—Order Aceraceæ (Maple tribe).—A handsome moderate-sized hardy deciduous tree, with pendulous-crooked branches, and palmate leaves, which are of a delicate green when young, and change in autumn to a lovely rose-crimson. The leaves burst in spring from a case of crimson leaf-scales. The flowers are purple, with white petals. The wood is fine-grained, white, and very tough. This tree, or rather large bush, has been introduced by the Horticultural Society from Oregon, and its foliage is represented in *Paxton's Flower Garden*, ii., 147.

PHILADELPHUS SATSUMI, *Siebold*. Japanese Mock Orange.—Order Philadelphaceæ (Syringa tribe).—An ornamental hardy deciduous summer-blooming shrub, nearly allied to *P. laxus*. It is a slender bush, with the lower leaves oval-lanceolate acuminate with a few sharp serratures, and the upper leaves lanceolate very much acuminated and entire; the under surface is slightly hairy, the upper deep green. The flowers are large, white, four-petalled, growing either singly or in pairs at the end of slender lateral shoots, or, as Dr. Lindley suspects (*Paxt. Fl. Gard.*, ii. 102), from a dried specimen supposed to be of the same species, coming, in mature plants, in interrupted racemes with linear, almost filiform, bracts. It was introduced from Japan in 1850.

PERNETTYA CILIARIS, *Don*. Ciliated Pernettya.—Order Ericaceæ (Heathwort tribe).—A hardy evergreen low-growing bush, with hard dark green ovate serrated leaves, covered slightly with stiff brown hairs on the under side. The flowers grow in numerous erect dense racemes, and are succeeded by deep reddish brown depressed berries, which render the plant very ornamental for an American border. It is figured in the *Horticultural Society's Journal*. vi. 268. From the mountains of South Brazil. Introduced in 1849, by Messrs. Veitch of Exeter.

EUCRYPHIA CORDIFOLIA, *Cavanilles*. Heart-leaved Eucryphia.—Order Hypericaceæ (Tutsan tribe).—A fine evergreen shrub, supposed to be hardy or nearly so. It has a stiff hard-wooded habit. The leaves are sessile, leathery, two to three inches long, oblong heart-shaped, dark green, and downy beneath. The flowers appear to be white, about as large as a small Camellia, and grow singly in the axils of the upper leaves. Messrs. Veitch of Exeter having imported it from Chiloe and Patagonia, whence it was sent in 1850 by Mr. Lobb. Its flowering season is not known.

LILIUM SINICUM, *Lindley*. Chinese Lily.—Order Liliaceæ (Lilywort tribe).—This is a small greenhouse summer-flowering bulbous plant, very closely related to *L. concolor*. The stems are about a foot high, covered with short down, and furnished with scattered oblong linear leaves; they bear two or three flowers at the top; these are small, deep scarlet, with revolute segments destitute of warts, but having the nectariferous channel at the base bordered by short hairs. It is a native of China, and was introduced originally in 1824; Mr. Fortune re-introduced it in 1850 to the nursery of Messrs. Standish and Noble of Bagshot.

BROMELIA LONGIFOLIA, *Rudge*. Long-leaved Bromelia.—Order Bromeliaceæ (Bromeliad tribe).—A fine pine-apple-like stove perennial, with narrow, channelled, coarsely-spine-toothed leaves, nearly two feet long, and pro-ducing a large central compact head of showy rose-coloured flowers, with a few narrow crimson spiny bracts at the base. It is a very showy plant, and was produced in August last before the Horticultural Society, by Mr. Hender-son, of the Wellington Nursery. A native of Guiana. It is figured in *Paxton's Flower Garden*, ii., t. 65.

VIOLA PYROLÆFOLIA, *Poiret*. Pyrola-leaved Violet.—Order Violaceæ (Violetwort tribe).—This is a very beautiful dwarf hardy herbaceous plant, in-troduced from Patagonia a year or two since, by Messrs. Veitch of Exeter, and grown by them and distributed under the erroneous name of *V. lutea*. It produces a tuft of small cordate-ovate radical leaves, with ovate or linear-lanceolate fimbriate stipules, and produces very large bright yellow blossoms each elevated considerably above the foliage on a slender stalk. The flowers have a short blunt spur, and the petals are bearded inside with club-shaped hairs; the lower petal is obcordate, streaked with red lines. It is found in Chili, as well as in the straits of Magellan; and is the *V. ma-culata* (Cavanilles), *V. glandu-losa* (Dombey herb.), and the *V. lutea megaphyllos* (Com-merson herb.). It has been figured by M. Van Houtte in the *Flore des Serres*.

KLUGIA NOTONIANA, *De Candolle*. East Indian Klugia. —Order Gesneraceæ § Cyrtan-dreæ (Cyrtandreous Gesner-wort tribe).—This soft-stem-med stove annual is remark-able for having its large cordate leaves remarkably diminished on one side at the base. The flowers are very rich deep blue, and come in secund racemes, opposite the leaves; the corolla being very unequally two-lipped, the lower lip large, blue, and

VIOLA PYROLÆFOLIA.

yellow at the base, the upper small and yellowish. It is abundant in some parts of the East Indies, and pro-bably inhabits Ceylon, having been sent to Kew by Mr. Thwaites, from the Botanic Garden at Peradenia. It flowers in September. There is a figure at t. 4620 of the *Botanical Magazine*. It bears the names of *Wulfenia Notoniana*, *Glossanthus Notoniana*, and *G. malabarica*.

ON PREPARING SOILS AND COMPOSTS.

SINCE the use of manure in a liquid state has become so very fashionable among both professional and amateur cultivators, it is doubtful whether too little attention has not been paid to the use of proper soils and composts, for though manure, in the liquid state is a convenient and excellent aid, it is quite certain that a properly prepared compost, as containing all the ingredients which a plant can require from the soil, is the best to be used. According to old rules, or, indeed, to practices of the present time, composts consist of various ingredients mixed together in the prepared or decomposed state, as mellow loam, leaf-mould, rotten dung, &c. These, though good and healthy, except in special cases, are not calculated to induce luxuriant growth, for the manure of old hot-beds, the kind generally used, is not rich, neither is the soil from old commons, which is generally preferred. Now, in the growth of plants, more especially for purposes of exhibition, it is customary to limit the size of the pots for certain kinds of plants, and hence those who aim at high cultivation, have to seek in rich compost what the plants under other circumstances would find in a quantity of soil; in fact, they endeavour to concentrate, in a given space, the fertility of a larger volume of material. Without entering into the rationale of the subject, it is well-known that annual and soft-wooded plants require more manure than shrubs and trees, and hence, to get the greatest quantity of nourishment into the smallest space, without, at the same time, making the soil or compost unhealthy, is a secret worth knowing.

Although much has been written in favour of guano, superphosphate of lime, and other manures, we never use them. In the stable, the cow-shed and the sheep-walk, all that is required for horticultural purposes may be found, and hence no risk need be run of this being too strong, or that too weak. If it were given as a problem, "What is the best compost to prepare for the general cultivation of soft-wooded plants?" the following would be our answer:—Procure from a suitable place two cart loads of rich loam with the turf on, and as free from oxide of iron as possible; then get from the nearest stable, where the horses are highly fed, a large cart load of dung, selecting that which has been thoroughly soaked with urine—for it must be recollected the urine carries off the soluble salts of the food of the animal, and the excretia the mineral, and hence it is very important that both should be had. When you have got the loam and manure home, place each in a separate heap, three or four yards apart, shaking the manure out, and mixing it together just the same as you would to prepare it for a hotbed, only do not allow it to heat too violently; to prevent which it will be necessary to shake it out every three or four days. In a fortnight it will be fit for use; then commence, as you would to form a hotbed, by marking out the ground, say six feet long and four feet wide, and upon this place a layer of the hot dung nine inches deep, and then a layer of loam, and so proceed, reserving a good layer of loam for the top, until all is used. In forming the bed, beat the manure firmly as you proceed, but leave the loam loose, and square the work up properly at the last. Then place over the heap loose litter to the thickness of twelve or eighteen inches, and cover the whole with mats closely pegged down; the object being to excite fermentation, and to prevent the escape of the ammonia and other essential gases. The heap may remain in this state for a fortnight or three weeks, or until the heat begins to decline, then turn it over, taking care to throw the sides into the middle, and to mix the loam and dung thoroughly throughout. The covering must be again put on as before, and remain on until fermentation has almost ceased. Here then we have a compost as rich as the manure it is formed of; but it is so strong that great caution must be exercised in its use, or injury will be the result. To prepare it, however, lay it out in thin ridges, fork it over once a-week to expose it to the ameliorating influence of the weather, but protect it from drenching rains, which would soon wash all the nutriment away. After being exposed for a few weeks to the full air, the outsides of the ridges will be fit for use; but if it could be exposed for twelve months before using it would be all the better. Except for very strong-growing plants, this soil is too strong for general purposes, and hence—more especially when used in a fresh state—a portion, say one third, of fresh loam should be mixed with it.

The above is a compost which we can recommend for soft-wooded plants of all kinds, and in it, when properly prepared, plants may be grown stronger, and more healthy, in three-inch pots than they are generally seen in pots of double the size. Nurserymen would do well to pay more attention to this subject, as they frequently put their patrons to the expense of carriage of large pots when smaller ones would do. This, or soil similarly constituted, forms the staple in which the magnificent Pelargoniums, Fuchsias, Calceolarias, Cinerarias, Roses, &c., seen at the London exhibitions are grown, and its strength accounts for the wondrous growth attained in such small pots. The spring is the best time to prepare such compost, keeping it turned weekly throughout the summer; but a good stock should always be kept, so that it may be properly sweetened before using.—A.

"THE QUEEN OF FLOWERS"—VICTORIA REGIA.

"A fair imperial flower;
She seem'd design'd for Flora's hand,
The sceptre of her power."—COWPER.

IT is little more than two years since the Royal Water-Lily was successfully introduced to cultivation. No other merely ornamental plant has, in so short a period, given rise to so profuse a literature as now exists peculiar to itself, and which details almost every phase of its history. Not to speak of the magnificent works of Lindley and Hooker, which have been published to illustrate this most magnificent of all plants, our periodical literature has, during the last two years, devoted more attention to it than to any other single topic connected with the science of Botany. Magazines of Science, of Literature and of Art, Newspapers, Journals of Botany, Natural History, Horticulture, of Light Reading for the Million, and of Philosophy for the Learned, have all and each done homage to the Queen of Flowers.

The *novelty* of the Royal Water Lily has now passed over, at least in England; and with it some prophetic botanists portended that the interest and admiration accorded to the plant would likewise become a mere matter of history. That this is not likely to happen, any one may be readily satisfied who will contemplate for a moment the position in Horticulture which the Lily holds, and the fact of its having given birth to a branch of cultural art scarcely recognized before in Britain, but with the development of which our ideas of Landscape and Artistic Gardening are likely to widely expand, and which, as it gains favour and gradually wins over horticultural taste, will insure the continued and extended cultivation of the Victoria. The materials, as well as the element necessary for their cultivation, which aquatic plants place at the artistic gardener's disposal, are calculated to lead to a much more perfect representation of vegetable physiognomy, and of the botanical traits of different regions, than has hitherto been realized, or even attempted by art.

The history and early cultivation of the Royal Water-Lily being recorded in the *Gardeners' Magazine of Botany*, I purpose to confine myself at present to some tracings of the Victoria's *subsequent* history, accompanied by an interesting letter just received from M. Eduard Otto, Curator of the Botanic Garden at Hamburg, a zealous and successful cultivator of this as well as of aquatic plants in general.

One of the most important instances of the Victoria's cultivation in England during the past summer, is that at the establishment of Messrs. Weeks and Co., of Chelsea, where, as many readers are aware, it has been grown in an open air pond, with only occasional protection. As I have elsewhere remarked, few cultivators (especially in Scotland) save those who have "been there to see," incline to give credit to the reported success of the experiment, surmising that the plant *must be* almost constantly protected with canvas and glass-frames. This is by no means the case. The pond is of very simple construction, heated usually to 76°, by means of hot water pipes from an adjoining house, and protected during the night and early morning by means of canvas. I have no doubt but this experiment will lead to many trials of the Victoria in the open air during 1852.

The Victoria Lily has also been introduced from Kew to the United States of America; it began to flower in August last, in the garden of Caleb Cope, Esq., Philadelphia, where it has been grown with much success. The salver-edge of the leaf appeared on the twenty-fourth and succeeding leaves. During September the plant continued to produce two flowers a-week, the twenty-seventh leaf measured six feet six inches, and others six feet two inches.[*]

[*] *Hooker's Journal of Botany*, iii., 346.5 (Nov. 1851.)

The Victoria is also thriving in the Calcutta Botanic Garden, from seeds received last March from Chatsworth. On the 26th of May the seedling was planted out on a hillock of prepared earth in the tank. On the 5th of September the first flower-bud opened. The flowers have averaged ten inches across, and at first are of a purer white, and subsequently of a brighter pink or rose than those produced in England. The leaves develope with great rapidity. On July 25, 4 P.M., the entire foliaceous surface was 45 square feet, four-fifths of which had attained full growth; on July 26, 4 P.M., it was 54 square feet; showing an increase of 9 square feet, produced by the united efforts of three leaves during a period of 24 hours, in an average temperature—air 89°, water 94°, Fah.; the youngest leaf trebled its foliaceous surface by adding 4 square feet, nearly one-half of the whole increase. At that time (July 26) none of the leaves, when fully grown, exceeded 3 feet in diameter, and all leaves produced since have been under 4 feet across.

Perhaps the flowering of the Royal Water-Lily on the Continent of Europe has created more excitement than anywhere else. It bloomed at Hamburgh for the first time on 28th August, when immense crowds flocked to see it; and on the two days during which the first blossom was expanded, nearly 3000 tickets of admission (issued at about two shillings of our money) were disposed of. In a letter just received from M. Otto, he gives an account of the cultivation and progress of the plant at Hamburgh; of this the following is an abridged translation :—

"The treatment of my Victoria has been an imitation of what has been previously practised in Britain. Last spring, I had a span-roofed house, of 31 feet each way, and containing a circular basin of 25 feet diameter, and four feet deep, built for the purpose. In this basin I introduced a mound of earth, consisting of equal parts vegetable mould, loam, and sand, upon which I planted, on the 31st May, a small plant of the Victoria, having only four leaves. The plant flowered on the 28th of August, having up to that time produced seventeen leaves, of which the largest had reached a size of five feet, eight inches. Although the water in the tank had no continual and gradual flowing in and off, twenty-five to thirty buckets of water were daily added to it, while a like quantity was either run off, or used for watering other plants. The young plant, nevertheless, succeeded well from the commencement, despite the frequent reduction in the temperature of the water in the tank to 14° Reaumur (63½ Fah.), that of the house being often no more, especially at the end of June and in the beginning of July. From the middle of July, the temperature of the house was seldom below 18° R. (72½ Fah.), and that of the water never less than 21° R. (79¼ Fah.), the temperature of the house being generally at from 28° to 30° R. (95° to 99½ Fah.), and that of the water from 22° to 24° R. (81½° to 86° Fah.) At first, a new leaf was produced by the plant every eighth day, afterwards every fifth, till at last two leaves came to maturity in a week. The length of the leaf stalks, which only extend after the leaves are nearly full grown, is from 12 to 13 feet. The nineteenth leaf was the first on which the brimmed margin was developed, and it appeared on all the following ones. The first flower made its appearance on the 11th August, expanding on the 28th. The second bloomed on the 7th September; the third on the 14th September; and up to the 17th of October eight flowers had been produced. The rest did not come to perfection, the house being then purposely very slightly heated, as I intended to reduce the plant to a dormant state, in which I have now nearly succeeded. The flowers had a diameter of from 12 to 14½ inches.

"The flowering of the Royal Water-Lily has created great sensation here; for, with the exception of the one in Hanover, which commenced flowering some weeks sooner, none had blossomed elsewhere in Germany. M. Van Houtte flowered the Victoria last year. M. Borsig of Berlin has also erected a beautiful house, but his plant has not yet flowered. I have got seeds from which I purpose to raise plants for blooming next year.

"Along with the Victoria, I had *Nelumbium luteum, Nymphæa rubra, N. pygmæa. N. micrantha, N. cærulea, N. cyanea, N. dentata, N. odorata. N. thermalis;* also *Pistia Stratiotes, Limnocharis Plumieri and Humboldtii, Pontederia crassipes, Cyperus Papyrus,* and *alternifolius, Saccharum officinarum, Caladium,* various species, &c., mostly all of which have flowered."—GEORGE LAWSON, F.R.P.S., *Curator to the Botanical Society of Edinburgh.*

1 Gastrolobium-ovalifolium 2 Epiphyllum Rollissoni 3 E. Buckleyi.

GASTROLOBIUM OVALIFOLIUM*.

THIS very pretty New Holland shrub was bloomed, for the first time, last spring, by Messrs. Henderson, of the Pine Apple Nursery, and we are indebted to them for the opportunity of publishing it. It is one of Drummond's collection, and will become a very useful ornamental plant.

It forms a dwarf branching shrub, very downy on all the young parts, glabrate when old. The leaves are elliptical opposite, stalked, the petioles half embracing the stem, and having erect, triangularly subulate, brown stipules: the summit of the leaves is bluntish, and with a soft mucro produced from the midrib, most evident in the young leaves. The inflorescence forms short racemes, terminal on lateral branches, the base of the peduncle clothed with many brown bracts resembling the stipules. The calyx has a bell-shaped tube, and almost equal teeth, which are rolled back in the flowering period. The corolla is showy, deep maroon or reddish brown-purple outside, brilliant yellow and veined within.—A. H.

The culture of the genus *Gastrolobium* is so similar to that of *Dillwynia*, which is sketched at page 26, that it is unnecessary here to repeat it.—M.

HYBRID TRUNCATE CACTUSES.†

THE very distinct and pretty forms of truncate Epiphyllum, or Leaf-Cactus, figured on the accompanying plate, were raised at the nursery of Messrs. Rollisson of Tooting, along with another distinct, but less striking variety, which differs from *E. Rollissonii* chiefly in its smaller size and more acute petals, and in having a decided coppery tinge in its colouring; this may be called *E. cupreum*. The latter has been sold under the name of E. Russellianum elegans; *E. Rollissonii* under that of E. Russellianum rubrum; and *E. Buckleyi* as E. Russellianum superbum. Mr. Buckley, by whom these hybrids were raised, has communicated the subjoined account of their origin.—M.

" I had often admired the extreme beauty of the flowers of *E. Russellianum*, in respect to their colours and form, and also their graceful disposition on the plant; and it occurred to me, that if the *E. truncatum* could be made to produce flowers of the same *form* as these, still retaining its superior size, a desirable object would be attained. The hybrids you have figured are the result of an attempt to realize this object. They were obtained by impregnating *E. Russellianum* with the variety of *truncatum* called *Ruckerianum*.

"No 1 [*E. cupreum*] has the peculiar coppery tinge of its male parent, slightly suffused with purple from the female; it has also the reflexed petals of the latter, which it resembles in form and size, whilst in growth and in freedom of blooming it resembles *truncatum*; this is the smallest of the three.

"No 2 [*E. Rollissonii*] is double the size of *Russellianum*, and in colour differs from both parents, being of a bright rose-red; the growth is similar to that of *truncatum*, but the flowers have the regular (not gaping) form of the female parent, as well as its straight stamens and short angular seed-vessel; it is a very free bloomer.

"No. 3 [*E. Buckleyi*] has the colours of both parents beautifully blended; the 'petals' are gracefully reflexed, especially the lower series; thus presenting the appearance of two corollas. In common with No. 1 and No. 2, it has the short angular seed-vessel and straight stamens proper to its female parent; in habit this is more slender than the others, but is still nearer the male than the female parent; in size it is intermediate.

" These hybrids were all raised from one plant by the same cross, and at the same time; thus showing, that in order to procure a numerous and *varied* offspring from one plant, the best way is to *put the variety on the species*. I maintain I have in this instance gained the following advantages :—

---

* *G. ovalifolium*, n. sp.: leaves opposite shortly petiolate elliptic with a setaceous mucro, the younger ones on both sides as well as the branches villose, becoming glabrate on the upper surface, stipules large triangular-subulate scariose villose, racemes terminating the lateral branches, densely clothed with numerous stipule-like bracts, calyx villose, its teeth sub-equal revolute when in flower, ovary stipitate villose.—A. H.

† *Epiphyllum Rollissonii* (hyb.: ♂ truncatum ♀ Russellianum).—Stems as in truncatum; flowers large, the divisions of the perianth in two remote series, sub-regular, crimson-red; petals broadly oblong, abruptly acute; filaments and style straight; ovary angular.—M.

Epiphyllum Buckleyi (hyb.: ♂ truncatum ♀ Russellianum).—Stems as in truncatum; divisions of the perianth in two remote series, regular, rose-purple; petals narrow oblong, tapering to an elongated acute point; filaments and style straight; ovary angular.—M.

A free-flowering progeny from a shy-flowering parent, securing at the same time its superior form, for they are entirely free from that peculiar ringent appearance which is characteristic of the flowers of *truncatum*; and a distinct period of flowering, for they are fully two months later than *truncatum* in opening, and at that time—January—flowers are very scarce; in this respect, namely, their time of flowering, they are intermediate between their parents.

"I need scarcely add that their culture is as easy as that of *E. truncatum*. I find they do well in a mixture of peat, loam, and brick-rubbish, in equal parts, with good drainage, and using rather small pots."—W. BUCKLEY, *Tooting*.

THE BEAUTIES OF NATURE.*

THE beauties of Nature! What a theme for poetry! One might almost expect to see the paper kindle beneath the poetic fire inspired by such a subject! But alas! in the "poem" before us, we cannot promise our readers that they will find any such like result, and we regard the adoption of the poetic form as particularly unfortunate on the part of the author, because he has scattered through his pages many good hints and suggestions of the plain common-sense complexion, such as might really benefit those persons who, as is quaintly observed, having "got rich in a hurry," and desiring to create for themselves some enjoyable rural retreat, oftentimes, in carrying out that desire, exhibit "curious fancies." We are afraid, however, that the unlucky attempt at poetry will inspire but little confidence in the writer's ideas, on the part of those who would be most likely to derive benefit from advice of the kind he has offered. Neither does the appearance of the book convey a very favourable impression, for the proper names both of places and plants, of which latter, especially, a good many occur, are sadly disfigured by incorrect orthography. Perhaps one of the best passages is the following episodal sonnet on the daisy:—

"There is a little simple flower
That cheers the wanderer aye;
On hill and dale and lonely bower,
In many a distant sky.
It seeks the towering mountain's brow,
Where does the tempest reign,
And, too, the valley deep below,
And, too, the spreading plain.

It does delight the eye of youth,
And, too, the day of age;
In east and west, in north and south,
It gilds fair Nature's page.
No velvet mantle it adorns,
Yet lovely is its glow;
It smiles wherever mankind turns,—
The mountain daisy low."

The object of the poem is stated to be no less than "to introduce a new era in the art of landscape gardening, and to lay down fixed principles for the production of real beauty in that art." For the purpose of gaining this object, "parallel lines," either in the shape of roads, flower borders, grass or gravel walks, or in any other way, are totally disused;" and this being so, we are told that "hereby this method of laying out ground is strictly original, and totally different from any other ever used in this or any other country." Beyond this, which the author says for himself, we can only add, we much fear that his efforts—well meant, no doubt—will fail to accomplish the revolution in taste to which he appears to look forward.—M.

SCIENTIFIC GLEANINGS.

THE *Hieraceum plumbeum* of Fries has been ascertained to be a native of Britain, by Mr. J. Backhouse, junr., of York. It grows on Falcon Clints, in Teesdale. Mr. Backhouse, who has had an opportunity, during the past summer, of examining specimens of the Norwegian Hieracia, describes it as nearly allied to *H. cæsium*, but differing strongly in having more truncate involucres, with *broad based acuminate* apiculate scales, of a dark colour, margined with green; also, in the

* "The Beauties of Nature, and how far they transcend those of Art in Landscape Gardening." By James Sinclair. London: Houlston and Stoneman.

involucres and peduncles being almost or entirely *destitute of stellate pubescence*. *H. cæsium* from the same place, and from Cronkley Scar, has narrow, *acute*, involucral scales, and usually a *large* amount of stellate down on the peduncles and involucres. *H. plumbeum* flowers *very early* (about July), while *H. cæsium* is in perfection, or nearly so, in September. In cultivation the plants become still more dissimilar.—*Report of Edinburgh Botanical Society.*

Professor Simpson recently communicated to the Botanical Society of Edinburgh the results of some experiments relative to the growth of Alpine plants, after having been kept artificially covered with snow in an ice-house for many months. Seed and plants, when kept in this way during winter, and then brought into the warm air of summer, were found to germinate and grow with great rapidity. In Arctic regions the rapid growth of plants during the short summer is well known; and the importance of similar experiments being made on the different kinds of grain was suggested. The rapidity of the harvest in Canada and other countries, where the cold lasts for many months, seems to indicate that if grain was kept in an ice-house during winter, and sown in spring, there might be an acceleration of the harvest. The subject is certainly deserving the attention of cultivators.—*Ibid.* [A writer in the *Scottish Gardener* recommends to try this plan with the *Rhododendron nivale* of the snowy summits of the Sikkim Himalaya: see ante p. 32.]

The *Pe-la*, or *Insect-wax of China* has been largely used in China since the thirteenth century, and has been occasionally imported into France and Britain for many years past, but its natural history is still very imperfectly known. Its chemical properties were investigated in 1848, by Mr. B. C. Brodie, of London, who showed that, even as it is met with in commerce, it is nearly in a state of chemical purity, and that it most closely resembles *cerin*, the base of bees-wax. The Pe-la is perfectly white, translucent, shining, not unctuous to the touch, inodorous, and insipid. It melts at 100° Fahrenheit. It is found adhering to the branches of certain shrubs, whence it is collected yearly in June. It seems to be produced by myriads of minute insects, which either excrete, or are changed into, the wax. Dr. Macgowan, Medical Missionary at Ningpo, is inclined to believe that the insect undergoes what may be called aceraceous degeneration, its whole body being permeated by the peculiar product, in the same manner as the *Coccus cacti* is by carmine.—*Report of Royal Physical Society.*

In the village of Gries, four leagues from Strasburg, stands a tree of *Æsculus Hippocastanum*, one of the oldest in the country, certainly dating further back than the year 1680. At a foot above the ground it measures twelve feet in circumference. The peculiarity of this tree is that from an unknown period it has annually blossomed on *one side alone*, one year on the west side, the next only on the east. The bare half does, indeed, present a bunch of flowers here and there, though seven-eighths of the branches are without blossom; but the leaves exhibit a more vivid green hue, while those on the flowering half of the tree are of a dull, unpleasant colour.—*Flora.*

Those who have paid little attention to the Mosses, can hardly imagine the great variety of beautiful forms they present to the enquiring eye; and indeed, excepting the Ferns, there is, perhaps, no tribe of plants which look prettier than a collection of these in a dried state, and neatly fastened to small sheets of paper. We mention this just now, because a very nice series of specimens of the British Mosses are in course of publication, by Mr. F. Y. Brocas, of Basingstoke; and these would form an excellent ground-work for those who might wish to begin to collect and study these interesting lowly forms of vegetation, and would also furnish materials for those who could only find leisure to study—not to gather for themselves, The two fasciculi published, containing each fifty species, consist of excellently preserved specimens, and, as far as we have observed, very correctly named.—M.

It appears that the flowers of the *Victoria regia* evolve a considerable amount of latent heat during the period of their development, similar to what has been observed to occur in *Caladium* and other Araceous plants. M. Otto, of Hamburgh, has observed that a thermometer plunged into the *Victoria* flower, at the moment of its expanding its anthers (7h. 11m. p.m.), rose to 21¾° R., the temperature of the house being 17¾° R., and that of the tank 16¾° R. Upon being sunk below the anthers, a gradual decrease took place. On another occasion, the temperature of the air being 18° R., that of the water 16¾. and the thermometer at 16¾° R., in the course of fifteen minutes the latter rose, in the flower, to

32$\frac{1}{2}$° R.   These experiments were made at the suggestion of Professor Lehmann, who thought he had formerly noticed an increase of temperature to occur in the flowers of *Nymphæa alba* during their development.—*Hooker's Journal of Botany*.

The Chinese Rice-paper plant, of which so much has been conjectured, and so little hitherto known by Europeans, proves to be a tree of the Araliaceous family, and has been named *Aralia* (?) *papyrifera* by Sir W. J. Hooker, in the *Journal of Botany*.   It is a "good sized" tree, occurring apparently only in swampy ground, in the northern parts of the Island of Formosa.   The pith, which occupies a very large space, and is beautifully white, is the part from which the rice-paper is cut in thin sheets.   The leaves of the plant are very large, palmate, not unlike those of a Sycamore, and clothed beneath with brownish stellate tomentum.   It would appear that a living plant, sent many years ago by J. Reeves, Esq., of Clapham, to the Horticultural Society, arrived alive, but soon died.   An attempt recently made by Mrs. Layton, to introduce a living plant for Sir. W. Hooker, has also failed, but the remains have sufficed for the determination of the real nature and affinities of the species, which before were entirely problematical to European naturalists.

THE PELARGONIUM GARDEN.

FOR the preparation of the annexed plan I am indebted to my tasteful friend, M. H. Seitz, of Chatsworth.   There is apparent in this garden a judicious blending of gravel and grass, productive of a light and airy elegance that garden artists of greater celebrity would not do amiss to profit by.   Unfortunately for good taste, gardens of this kind in general exhibit such a crowding clumsiness and incongruity of disposition in the several figures, as to render the *tout ensemble*, in good

perspective, the very reverse of elegant, comprehensive, and dignified.   Too many figures in a plan, or the separate parts of the latter too widely spread asunder, when the entirety should rather be expressive of nicety in design, can but result in deformity and dissatisfaction when displayed in practice on the ground, however well suited the same arrangement might previously have appeared, on paper, to the uninitiated in such matters.

The vignette exhibits in perspective the accompanying ground plan circumscribed with trelliage arches about nine or ten feet high, formed of stout rod-iron, inserted into blocks of stone beneath the surface of the ground; and a marble figure of "Flora" is presumed, not inappropriately, to occupy the centre of the parterre. The Pelargonium garden at Oakley, the Duke of Bedford's, is thus circumscribed with iron arches; and the airy elegance thus imparted, when entwined and festooned with

hardy and summer greenhouse climbers in great variety, is not the least attractive feature of the scene. A seldom used, but most classic plant for this kind of decoration, is the Grape Vine. And when in early autumn the foliage of various hardy species of *Vitis* assume a variety of tints, and ripe and unripe bunches of Grapes in "bacchanal profusion reel to earth," or rather depend from these arches, partly concealed by green, and red and green, and purplish foliage, the effect is extremely pleasing, reminding one of Byron's lines on Italy—

> "Who love to see the sunshine every day,
> And Vines (not nailed to walls) from tree to tree
> Festooned, much like the back scene of a play."

The only difference being, that the sun, perhaps, does not shine so brightly as it does in Italy, and that *our* Vines, instead of being "festooned from tree to tree," are merely trained from arch to arch. In addition to the Grape Vine, Clematis, Jasmine, Roses, Virginian-creepers, Honeysuckles, and other hardy climbers, are rendered decidedly more elegant and graceful in summer time by having such half-hardy greenhouse creepers as *Maurandia*, *Lophospermum*, *Rhodochiton*, *Loasa*, *Tropæolum*, *Cobæa*, &c., planted at their base annually, and induced to loosely enwreath themselves, and ramble over their more sturdy compeers.

The flower-basket shown below is also an interesting feature in connection with the Pelargonium garden at Oakley; and, since this particular kind of ornament is not in

very general use, the following particulars relative to it may not be considered out of place :—The basket portion is composed of robust, closely-interwoven wickerwork, annually painted green, both for effect and for the preservation of the comparatively frail material of which it is composed. In form it is circular, and made to rest upon a substantial wooden frame or support, constructed with a view to strength as well as ornament. This ornamental stand is about eighteen inches or two feet high, square in shape, with a circular top corresponding to the diameter of the basket bottom, and, like the latter, is painted green to preserve the wood, as also to harmonize in colour with the superstructure which it upholds. The flower-basket itself is about five feet diameter at top, two-and-a-half feet across at bottom, and about three feet in depth. The interior is necessarily furnished with a portable lining of sheet-iron next the wickerwork, perforated at bottom with numerous apertures for the escape of moisture descending through the soil, and, since the basket itself is bottomless, the circular false bottom of perforated sheet-iron (though, of course, placed inside the basket) is necessarily made to rest chiefly upon the ornamental latticed frame which supports it. It is, of course, a portable contrivance *in toto*, being disposed in winter in some dry airy place for the sake of preservation from damp, and consequent decay, until again required for use as a summer ornament. Drainage and soil are, of course, renewed annually when re-introduced to the flower-garden; and, albeit the species of ornament I have described is composed, in part at least, of frail materials, if painted over yearly, and taken care of in the dead season, it will last for many years.

At Oakley these flower-baskets are exclusively decorated with a miscellaneous assortment of choice hybrid and fancy Pelargoniums, fringed with the trailing ivy-leaved and variegated kinds, which depend over the sides in rich profusion, producing a luxuriant and yet most elegantly unique appearance. Scarlet Pelargoniums are omitted from these baskets, as being too conspicuous and glaring in colour, when thus elevated so nearly to a level with the eye of the observer; and the *coup d'œil* presented is more reposing and softer in consequence of their omission. In planting them the plants are so thickly disposed as to confer upon these beautiful flower-stands, when in full bloom, an appearance of what in truth they are—magnificent, tastefully-formed bouquets of Pelargoniums.

Reference.—The accompanying plan being uniform and pretty well balanced throughout, it will be indispensable, in order to obviate any violation of the effect as a whole, that the corresponding parts be arranged so similarly in respect of the habit, height, colour, &c., of the different varieties of Pelargoniums employed in its decoration, as to confer an expressive air of unity and harmony upon the entire disposition,—the respective parts of the design being thus made to reflect, as it were, the corresponding ones. This is easy of accomplishment, provided the plan be carefully studied on paper previous to planting it; and which is assuredly well worth the pains, when it is known that any material mistake in the arrangement must inevitably prove destructive to the equipoise and harmony of the picture.

The fastigiate tree and dwarf bush profiles indicated on the plan are intended to represent specimens of some strict-growing and spreading plants, as Irish Yew or evergreen Cypress for the former, and Phillyrea or Laurustinus for the latter. Doubtless, however, well-managed examples of standard or pyramidal Pelargoniums would be equally as appropriate in these positions; and the small angular beds on grass, *g*, near which they are planted, might most appropriately be furnished alike with masses of the "Frogmore improved" scarlet, zoned with some variegated Pelargoniums, for effecting a suitable contrast with the grass.

The small square, *c*, within the circular figure, *i*, in the centre of the gravel parterre, *a*, and grass-plats, *b*, are consecutively the sites of the statue of Flora and flower-baskets shown in the vignette. The circles, *i*, surrounding the basket-stands, being furnished with fragrant Pelargoniums, intermingled with Heliotropes and Mignonette; the base of Flora being planted with Pelargonium Lucia roseum, margined with the gold-leaf variegated variety: *a* represents gravel walks, respectively, eight, six, and two and a-half feet in width; and *b* indicates the grass portion of the plan.

The dotted line extending round the circumferential border, *f*, shows the direction of the iron trelliage arches exhibited in the vignette,—the border itself being filled with the most brilliant kinds of scarlet, margined on both sides with the variegated Pelargonium called "Mangles' silver bedding."

The small circles, *e*, are devoted to handsome full-grown specimens of pyramidal Pelargoniums, zoned with the old dwarf Frogmore scarlet. The best and most select bedding varieties of the "choice," and "fancy" hybrids, with a goodly intermixture of fragrant-leaved Pelargoniums, are apportioned to the beds, *d*, composing the large interior circle of the garden.—GEORGE TAYLOR, *Chatsworth.*

GARDEN NOTES OF THE MONTH.

THERE is an old truism that a man whose taste does not direct him to the admiration of either music, poetry, or flowers, "has no soul," and though we concur in the intended inference, it is questionable whether so far as flowers are concerned, there is not vulgarity as well as taste; or rather, to put the matter more plainly, may not that taste which is satisfied only with a glare of flowers be considered vulgarity! Those who can only admire a flower for its gaudy flowers have no very elevated idea of beauty; and hence we think the introduction of plants, remarkable for the splendour of their foliage, into flower gardens, as practised in Germany and other parts of the continent, is a sign of progress which we may copy with advantage, for we can imagine nothing more appropriate in a highly artistic, and more especially an 'architecturesque' garden, than single plants, or groups of plants remarkable for the beauty of their foliage. Such things are quite in accordance with high finish, or if we may be allowed the term, are nature's finishing stroke to high art. *Phormium tenax*, the New Zealand

Flax, is said to be an admirable plant for filling vases, and no doubt it would look much more graceful when properly grown than stiff and formal Aloes. Mr. Beaton has lately recommended the old Senecio cinerarias, or *Cineraria maritima*, the Sea Ragwort, a plant frequently seen in cottage windows, as admirably adapted for decorative purposes, having under strong artificial light the appearance of frosted silver, and, when mixed with scarlet Pelargoniums, either in zones or planted alternately, it forms an exceedingly rich group. Grown also as a single specimen for the drawing-room, more especially in the winter season, it is found exceedingly useful. We have often been surprised that variegated plants are not more used for decorative purposes, more especially for balls, routs, &c. Such things as variegated Pelargoniums, *Croton pictum*, and *variegatum*, *Dracæna terminalis*, and many other plants are likely to be found very interesting. A group now standing before us, consisting of variegated plants, Primulas, Cinerarias, Hyacinths, Tulips, and Ferns, has a splendid effect, more especially by candle light.

Among winter-blooming plants nothing is more useful than the *Tropæolum Lobbianum*, which with a temperature of fifty to sixty degrees, blooms magnificently through the whole winter, and for *bouquets* is almost equal to Scarlet Pelargoniums. It is, however, impatient of a moist atmosphere, but succeeds admirably in the plant stove. *Echeveria secunda*, a greenhouse plant, which merely requires protection from frost, and is of a succulent nature, blooms beautifully at this season, and five or six plants in a shallow pan forms a splendid group, and will continue to bloom for several months. *Selago distans*, which simulates white Mignonette, though not sweet, forms a beautiful specimen plant, and is also useful for winter cutting; and *Jasminum nudiflorum*, one of Mr. Fortune's acquisitions from China, blooms throughout the winter in the open air. For growing in small pots for the greenhouse this will be found a very useful plant, and for a wall, though not sweet, it will take rank with the *Chimonanthus fragrans*.

As forcing plants, *Weigela rosea* and *Forsythia viridissima* have long been favourably known; and now we suspect that *Escallonia macrantha*, when properly prepared, and *Mitraria coccinea*, will be found equally useful at this season. Of more modern introductions, we find *Deutzia gracilis* blooming when only an inch or two in height, and Messrs. Veitch's *Berberis Darwinii* is now showing bloom in our propagating house in beautiful style, and no doubt will form an admirable plant. Though more humble, *Cheiranthus Marshallii*, for its delicious scent of violets, will be found worthy of a place in every greenhouse, and will force in gentle heat.

The fumigating of plant-houses and frames is a troublesome matter, especially to amateurs, and hence the following plan, which we have practised lately, may prove interesting to some. Provide a strong solution of nitre in water, in which soak some sheets of strong brown paper, and afterwards dry it slowly, and cut into lengths of convenient size, the largest eighteen inches by twelve inches, then get some strong tobacco, and strew it thinly over the paper, and, with a coarse pepper-box, dredge in a good coat of common cayenne pepper; wrap the whole up rather loosely, like a "cigarette;" paste the end over, and when dry it is fit for use. Two or three of these suspended by a wire under a greenhouse stage, and lighted at each end, will quickly settle the accounts of the green fly and thrip, and that with comparatively little trouble. Indeed, if a quantity of these "cigarettes" are kept ready made, a few plants may be put into a pit or small room, and be cleaned, at least have their insect pests destroyed in a very short time. By using cayenne, much less tobacco is required, and the effect of the two combined is most deadly, for as the cigarettes will burn for a considerable time, say an hour or more, it is impossible for insects to live in an atmosphere so thoroughly impregnated with the elements of suffocation. Since writing the preceding, we have tried an experiment with "cigarettes" against tobacco paper, and three houses, each about thirty feet long, have been effectually fumigated with eight ounces of tobacco, two ounces of cayenne, and about four sheets of brown paper, with a handful of damp hay to make a smoke. The expense was three shillings. The same houses hitherto have required seven pounds of tobacco paper, at an expense of ten shillings and sixpence!

OSPHRESIOLOGY OF FLOWERS.

CLOQUET has given the name of *Osphresiology* (from Οσφρασία, an odour, or Οσφρησις, smelling) to the theory of the knowledge of odours. He has written a large treatise on this subject, which naturally has found its application to horticulture; and has well observed that we cultivate the *Reseda* not for its beauty, but for its perfume. It is agreed, that a flower, though not brilliant, if fragrant, is always modest and full of virtue.

We are accustomed to admire flowers, when they are fresh and in the full exercise of their functions. Our love for them is allied to their fragrance. Physiologists even believe that odour is given in particular to flowers that these fragrant emanations might attract insects, and even birds, for the purpose of placing in contact by their predations, the pollen and the stigma. They add, that since camphor, if cast on a plate of wet glass, dries up the moisture on the part where it falls, the perfume emitted from corollas dries the air, by depriving it of watery vapours which are ungenial to the pollen. We are very willing to admit these facts and arguments as being in accordance with truth.

There are, however, with flowers, posthumous odours, that is to say, odours that survive the flowers; and there are instances also of the odours not being emitted till the flowers have arrived at a certain state of decay. The latter emissions take place after the process of fecundation; they must have functions, the mystery of which physiology has not yet penetrated. In the consideration of this subject, I read, in a collection of papers which I edited in 1836, as follows:—

" The fresh spike of flowers of the *Orchis mascula*, newly opened, has no appreciable odour; but when the flowers decay, and especially when they have dried on the stalk, they emit an offensive feline smell. Two plants that I gave to a lady, produced, in drying, a smell of this kind so strong, that during several days, no one suspecting the supposed innocent flowers, a vigorous search was kept up for the feline pest, which, it was believed, had contrived to secrete itself in the room. At last, however, the real culprit was discovered. On another occasion, a child, having returned from the woods with a bouquet of the flowers of this species, left it to wither in a room which was found uninhabitable so long as the flowers remained."—*Professor Morren : La Belgique Horticole.*

PENTSTEMON COBŒA.

WE were favoured last summer by Messrs. Downie and Laird, of Edinburgh, with a fine specimen of the rare *Pentstemon Cobœa*, of which we regret the limited space afforded by the plates in this work will not allow us to republish a figure, which this fine species well merits. Mr. Downie, however, who has had much success in its cultivation, has kindly sent a brief account of his mode of treatment, which we subjoin :—

" I have hitherto been very successful in cultivating this beautiful plant by following the plan I will now describe :—I strike the cuttings in small sixty-sized pots, in light sandy soil, putting them into a dung hot-bed frame until they are struck, when I remove them to the stove, and place them under a hand-glass, until they are well taken with the pot, always taking care, however, to exclude *air* and *sunshine*. I afterwards gradually inure them to the ordinary atmosphere of the stove, in which they remain until such time as I consider them strong, and able to bear a colder atmosphere, to which they are gradually inured, and finally removed to the open air. It is of the greatest importance in the early stage of their culture, to keep them from a current of cold air.

" The plants I wish for stock I plant in the open ground, in deep rich loam, where they stand till September, or the beginning of October. They are then lifted and put in a cool greenhouse for the winter. As, however, this is a plant very subject to mildew, and prevention being better than cure, I generally dust them well over with sulphur when housing them, even although there be no appearance of mildew present."—J. DOWNIE.

1 Castradenium cuneatum 2 Linaria reticulata

GASTROLOBIUM CUNEATUM.*

WE are glad of the opportunity of presenting a figure of this fine greenhouse shrub, which was exhibited by the Messrs. Henderson of Pine Apple Place, at one of the Royal Botanic Society's exhibitions last summer, and is worthy to rank among the best of this class of plants, being a compact grower and an abundant bloomer. It was raised from seeds sent by Mr. Drummond, collected in Australia. It forms a dwarf-branching shrub, with the leaves growing in whorls of four; the shoots and lower surfaces of the leaves covered with minute silky hairs. The leaves are narrowly wedge-shaped, very obtuse at the summit, sometimes slightly emarginate, mucronate. The inflorescence consists of racemes terminal to the branches, with the flowers arranged in leafless whorls of about four. The calyx is distinctly two-lipped; the upper being very obtuse, and the division into two sepals only indicated by a shallow notch. The flowers are bright yellow; the standard with a deep purple marking on the disk, the wings and keel tinged with brownish red.—A. H.

For CULTURE, see *Dillwynia*, p. 26.

LINARIA RETICULATA.

THE Reticulated Toad-flax is, in cultivation, a pretty perennial herbaceous plant, with the stems erect and glabrous, except about the flowers. The leaves are flat, linear or subulate, in whorls of four below, somewhat glaucous. The racemes are pubescent, with flower-stalks shorter than, or nearly equalling, the calyx; segments of the calyx unequal, broadly linear, with the margins usually somewhat membranous. The flowers are very handsome, large, and variable in colour, from rose, blue, and purple-veined, to rather deep purple; the inside of the throat is whitish, perhaps sometimes yellow; the spur is straight, or slightly incurved and conical, about equalling the tube of the corolla.

It is the *Linaria reticulata* of Desfontaines; the *Antirrhinum reticulatum* of Smith; the *Antirrhinum pinifolium* of Poiret; and the *Linaria arabida* of gardens. Our specimen was raised by Mr. R. M. Stark, nurseryman of Edinburgh, from seeds brought from Portugal by Dr. Welwitsch, and was sent us under the name of " *Linaria arabida.*" This name appears to have been given to it through a misconception. Probably Dr. Welwitsch's label ran "Linaria ?——. Arrabida," the latter word referring to the Sierra d'Arrabida, the locality in which the Linaria, then undetermined, was found.

We have identified our specimen with the *Antirrhinum reticulatum* of Smith, which is well figured in his "Illustrations of Rare Plants," from a specimen which flowered in the Botanic Garden, at Chelsea. We presume that it has been lost for many years, since it is represented as an annual; and hence the plant now figured was considered a new species. *Linaria reticulata* is a native of both Portugal and Algeria.—A. H.

To this, we can only add, that it is certainly a very pretty plant, suitable for warm rock-work, flowering freely in the summer, and propagating by cuttings. It will probably require the protection of a frame in winter. At present it is only in the hands of Mr. Stark, who favoured us with the specimen from which our drawing was made. We believe, however, it is to be let out this spring.—M.

SCHLEIDEN'S VIEWS ON THE DISEASES OF CULTIVATED PLANTS.

IN an appendix to his newly published work on " Vegetable Physiology and Agriculture," Professor Schleiden puts forth some views respecting the diseases of plants, which are deserving of great attention, since, though they may not be regarded as conclusive, they are calculated to direct inquiry into a profitable field. It may, therefore, prove of interest to English readers, if we give a brief summary of that celebrated botanist's opinions.

In the first place, we must separate really wild plants from the cultivated and the weeds (which

* *G. cuneatum*, n. sp.—Leaves in whorls of four, shortly stalked, and furnished with setiform stipules, minutely silky below, narrow wedge-shaped, obtuse, sometimes sub-emarginate, mucronate; racemes terminal, many-flowered, the flowers disposed in distant leafless whorls of four; calyx minutely silky, its teeth subequal, the two upper coherent, and forming a blunt upper lip.—A. H.

being placed in the same condition as the cultivated plants, are exposed to like influences). The question then arises, whether the truly wild plants are subject to diseases properly so-called; whether the blights, &c., which we see them suffer from occasionally are not altogether a result of external causes, such as peculiar seasons, &c., and, arising from transitory influences, have but a transitory duration? This question the author leaves open, his immediate business being with the cultivated plants.

Here the conditions are totally different. Scarcely any one of our cultivated plants is in a natural condition; almost all deviate, more or less, from their typical specific form, as defined by the naturalist. The unnatural and excessive development of particular structures or particular substances, destroys the equilibrium and lays the plant more open to suffer from injurious external influences, some of which are direct results of the methods of cultivation. Moreover, the greater part of our seed or fruit crops grow in a foreign or unfavourable climate, and are thus exposed to a number of unavoidable causes of disease.*

The condition of a plant in cultivation may be regarded as identical with that of a plant in which disease has commenced. Almost all our cultivated plants have, by modification of the chemical processes of their vegetation, been caused to deviate from the normal type, and though we consider them improvements, because they are profitable to us, it is an improvement of the same sort as that where the enlarged liver is produced in geese for the Strasburg pies. This *general morbid condition* is heightened into *specific predisposition to disease*, when the conditions of cultivation are opposed too strongly or too suddenly to those of nature, as when natives of light or sandy soil, such as the Oat or Potato, are planted in heavy land; or when Wheat, Rye, or Barley are sown in land in the first year of its being manured; or when the climate is very unlike the original one of the plant, as in the case of Maize in most parts of Europe.

The outward forms of disease in plants are sufficiently known. The internal appearances are less understood, and, for their proper apprehension, require some knowledge of vegetable anatomy. The characters are essentially similar in all living vegetable cells; we have a *wall* or *membrane* composed of *cellulose*, devoid of nitrogen; this wall is lined by a semifluid layer of viscid mucilage (the *primordial utricle*) composed of a proteine-compound abounding in nitrogen; the cavity of the cell is filled up with watery juice containing little nitrogenous matter, but having all the other compounds, such as gum, sugar, vegetable acids, inorganic salts, &c., dissolved in it. The chemical force of the plant would appear to reside in the nitrogenous mucilaginous layer; all growth depends on this and it does not disappear, until the cell-wall (really the skeleton of the plant, like the horny or stony substance of the coral polypes) has become perfectly developed.

Now, when diseased plants are examined in an early stage, whether it be smut in Wheat, rotting of succulent parts or of stems, or the Potato disease, the first morbid appearance is found in this nitrogenous mucilaginous layer, which becomes discoloured, coagulated, and granular; then it seems to penetrate into and affect the cellular wall of the cell. These appearances are so general that it may fairly be asserted that all *internal diseases* of plants commence in this way, in the nitrogenous internal coating of the individual cells, in which their chemical force seems to be concentrated.

Professor Schleiden adopts the view of Liebig, that all the variety of the vegetable world, so far as it depends upon chemical processes, arises exclusively from the varying qualitative and quantitative composition of the inorganic part of the soil; and that poor or luxuriant development, healthy or diseased condition, must be attributed to this. The experiments of Boussingault and Liebig show that the formation of the organic substances of the *dextrine* and the *proteine series* depends exclusively on the presence of certain inorganic substances. It is not yet decided whether the formation of the *proteine* (nitrogenous) substances depends on the presence of phosphoric acid, and that of the dextrine series on the presence of alkaline salts without phosphoric acid, but the following facts render it probable :—

* The unsatisfactory deduction from this, that we must not hope to exterminate disease in our cultivated plants, even by improved knowledge, points to the natural mode of proceeding in such matters—to the principle of *assurance*—finding averages of the good and bad times, and making the former pay for the latter.

Phosphoric acid is rare in most geological formations; soils solely or chiefly composed of these, therefore, rarely contain it; but in soils composed of accumulated remains of vegetables, still more of animal substances, phosphoric acid salts abound; above all, in well-manured garden grounds, where they usually exist in higher proportion than the plants normally contain. Plants do not select their food, but absorb all the soluble matters in contact with their roots: therefore, when the salts which they require for their nutrition are present in wrong proportions, they are forced to take up more than they should of certain kinds,—in this case, of phosphates,—and hence inevitably follow morbid deviations from the natural modes of growth.

From this we derive the following general law:—The more the proportion of phosphoric salts is increased in a soil, either through the mode of origin of the soil, or by its culture, the more will the plants growing upon it be inclined to deviate from their original type, to form *sports, varieties*, &c., and finally to be attacked and destroyed by internal diseases.—A. H.

THOUGHTS ON PLANTING ROCK-WORK.

THERE is as much exercise of mind required in disposing plants on rock-work as there is in building the masses of stones together. In fact, the placing of the plants in positions not only to exhibit their own beauties and peculiarities, but to bring more visibly into view the forms and colours of the rocks, in all their natural irregularity, is a work demanding even more taste and skill than building up the stones.

Plants give animation to rock-work, and are suggestive of many a thought which the bare rocks could never impart. The depths of darkest shade should embrace within their stony folds plants of light coloured flowers or foliage, to relieve their gloom, and assist the eye in tracing out their intricate windings. *Cerastium Biebersteinii*, with its white leaves and whiter flowers, and procumbent habit of growth, is admirably adapted for such a purpose, either planted in a recess or suspended gracefully over the front of some stone. *Arabis procumbens* is also a beautiful plant for a like purpose, though less effective than the former, from its flowers being small and white, and its leaves green; still its close symmetrical character renders it very suitable for setting off some rough irregularly-formed stone. *Aubrietia purpurea grandiflora*, as its name implies, is a charming purple-flowering spring plant, differing from its congeners in its larger flowers, and will be seen to best advantage planted on some external or prominent part of the rock-work, where its colder-coloured flowers will bring forward the rocks; while the white-coloured flowers will add depth and extension to the view, and therefore heighten the irregularity of the whole. True to its nature, the eye demands the sunshine as well as the shade; and with our many-sided stones and differently-formed plants, as well as great variety of colour amongst flowers, it is in our power to meet the eye's requirements.—JOHN CAIE, *Gardener to the Dowager Duchess of Bedford, Camden-hill, Kensington.*

THE TALLOW TREE OF CHINA.

THE *Stillingia sebifera* is prized for the fatty matter which it yields; its leaves are employed as a black dye; its wood, being hard and durable, is used for printing blocks and various other articles; and finally, the refuse of the nut is employed as fuel and manure.

It is chiefly cultivated in the provinces of Kiangsi, Kongnain, and Chehkiang. In some districts near Hangchan, the inhabitants defray all their taxes with its produce. It grows alike on low alluvial plains and on granite hills, on the rich mould at the margin of canals, and on the sandy sea-beach. The sandy estuary of Hangchan yields little else. Some of the trees at this place are known to be several hundred years old, and though prostrated, still send forth branches and bear fruit.

In mid-winter when the seed-vessels are ripe, they are cut off with their twigs by a sharp crescentric knife, attached to the extremity of a long pole, which is held in the hand and pushed upwards against the twigs, removing at the same time such as are fruitless. The capsules are gently pounded in a mortar to loosen the seeds from their shells, from which they are separated by sifting. To facilitate the separation of the white sebaceous matter enveloping the seeds, they are steamed in tubs, having convex open wicker bottoms, placed over cauldrons of boiling water. When thoroughly heated, they are reduced to a mash in the mortar, and thence transferred to bamboo sieves, kept at an uniform temperature over hot ashes. A single operation does not suffice to deprive them of all their tallow, the steaming and sifting is therefore repeated. The article thus procured becomes a solid mass on falling through the sieve, and to purify it, it is melted and formed into cakes for the press; these receive their form from bamboo hoops, a foot in diameter and three inches deep, which are laid on the ground, over a little straw. On being filled with the hot liquid, the ends of the straw beneath are drawn up and spread over the top, and when of sufficient consistence, are placed with their rings in the press. This latter apparatus, of the rudest description, is constructed of two large beams placed horizontally, so as to form a trough capable of containing about fifty of the rings with their sebaceous cakes; at one end it is closed, and at the other adapted for receiving wedges, which are successively driven into it by ponderous sledge-hammers wielded by athletic men. The tallow oozes in a melted state into a receptacle below, where it cools. It is again melted and poured into tubs, smeared with mud to prevent its adhering. It is now marketable, in masses of about eighty pounds each, hard, brittle, white, opaque, tasteless, and without the odour of animal tallow : under high pressure it scarcely stains bibulous paper ; melts at 140 deg. Fah. It may be regarded as nearly pure stearine, the slight difference is doubtless owing to the admixture of oil expressed from the seed in the process just described. The seeds yield about eight per cent. of tallow, which sells for about five cents per pound.

The process for pressing the oil, which is carried on at the same time, remains to be noticed; it is contained in the kernel of the nut. The sebaceous matter, which lies between the shell and the husk having been removed in the manner described, the kernel and the husk covering it are ground between two stones, which are heated to prevent clogging from the sebaceous matter still adhering. The mass is then placed in a winnowing machine, precisely like those in use in Western countries. The chaff being separated, exposes the white oleaginous kernels, which, after being steamed, are placed in a mill to be mashed. This machine is formed of a circular stone-groove, twelve feet in diameter, three inches deep, and about as many wide, into which a thick solid stone wheel, eight feet in diameter, tapering at the edge, is made to revolve perpendicularly by an ox harnessed to the outer end of its axle, the inner turning on a pivot in the centre of the machine. Under this ponderous weight, the seeds are reduced to a mealy state, steamed in the tubs, formed into cakes, and pressed by wedges in the manner above described: the process of mashing, steaming, and pressing, being repeated with the kernels likewise. The kernels yield above thirty per cent. of oil. It is called *Tsing-yu*, sells for about three cents per pound, answers well for lamps, though inferior for this purpose to some other vegetable oils in use. It is also employed for various purposes in the arts, and has a place in the Chinese Pharmacopœia, because of its quality of changing grey hair black, and other imaginary virtues.

Artificial illumination in China is generally procured by vegetable oils; but candles are also employed by those who can afford it. In religious ceremonies no other material is used. As no one ventures out after dark without a lantern, and as the gods cannot be acceptably worshipped without candles, the quantity consumed is very great. With an unimportant exception, the candles are always made of what I would designate as vegetable stearine. When the candles, which are made by dipping, are of the required diameter, they receive a final dip into a mixture of the same material and insect-wax, by which their consistency is preserved in the hottest weather. They are generally coloured red, which is done by throwing a minute quantity of Alkanet root (*Anchusa tinctoria*), brought from Shantung, into the mixture. Verdigris is sometimes employed to dye them green.—DR. MAC-GOWAN : *communicated to the Agricultural and Horticultural Society of India.*

STROBILANTHES AURICULATUS.

THE order of Acanthads contains many pretty stove plants of the "soft-wooded" class, which, from their affording considerable variety, and from many of them being winter-bloomers, are desirable in gardens where conveniences exist for the cultivation of plants of this peculiar stamp. There are the Aphelandras, the Porphyrocomas, the Schauerias, the Eranthemums, the Goldfussias, the Beloperones, the Ruellias, the Cyrtantheras, and many other family groups, all yielding species of a more or less ornamental character; and though not quite so striking as some of these, there are some Strobilanths, such as *S. Sabinianus*, and the subject of the present notice, which possess sufficient merit to claim admission, if only for variety's sake.

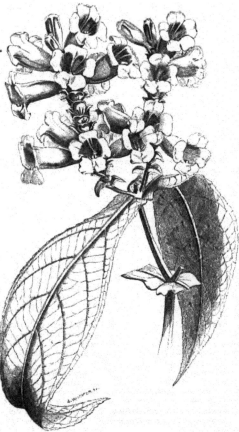

STROBILANTHES AURICULATUS.

Strobilanthes auriculatus is a vigorous-growing branching plant, of from two to three feet high, bearing stem-clasping elliptic-oblong leaves, which are narrowed to the base, and strongly auriculate; they are hairy on both surfaces. The flowers come on short axillary branches, and issue, as is usual in this genus, from a spike of imbricated leafy bracts, which, having the character of a strobilus or cone, seem to have suggested the generic name. They are very pale blue, prettily veined, and when a considerable number are expanded at one time, are rather attractive. Their defect is, that they individually fall too soon.

The plant is a native of the East Indies. We have no exact information as to its introduction to this country. The plant was presented about twelve months since to the Chelsea Botanic Garden, by Messrs Henderson, Pine-apple Nursery, Edgeware Road. With us it has blossomed in February.

Nothing can be easier to cultivate or increase. It grows vigorously in a stove, if potted liberally into a free compost, which should not be too rich. To develope its ornamental qualities, a good plant should be grown on through summer and autumn, and then allowed a short rest. The excitement of additional heat will then cause it to throw out the flowering branches. To produce smaller blooming plants, cuttings taken from a nearly matured growth, will usually branch into flower, as happened with that from which the accompanying sketch was taken.—M.

New Garden Plants.

BEGONIA STRIGILLOSA, *Dietrich.* Bristly Begonia.—Ord. Begoniaceæ (Begoniad tribe).—Introduced into Germany from Central America. A very singular-looking stove plant, with a creeping stem. The leaves are fleshy, oblique, cordate acuminate, dark green on both sides, glossy above. The surface is studded with reddish glandular hairs, accompanied with the fringing usual in *B. manicata.* The petioles are thick, long, round, green, spotted with red, from which spots arise single scales, terminating in long white hairs, which gives the plant a bristly appearance. The flowers are bright-red, and supported in large corymbs on stalks about a foot long, the stalks covered with scales. This species is of easy culture, and is considered a valuable acquisition for a stove or warm conservatory.

PITCAIRNIA FUNCKIANA, *Dietrich.* Funck's Pitcairnia.—Ord. Bromeliads (Bromeliad tribe).—This flowered in the establishment of M. Nauen, at Berlin, last October, and is inserted in the catalogues as *Puya Funckiana.* It was introduced from Merida by Messrs. Funck and Schlim. Dr. Dietrich considers it a Pitcairnia, and not a Puya.´ The flowers are white, and surrounded with yellow cups and bracts, which are arranged on a flower stalk about three and a half feet long. It is cultivated as other species of this genus. A temperature of 60°—65° is sufficient to flower it, and it has a very showy appearance when in bloom.

IMPATIENS CORNIGERA, *Hooker.* Horn-bearing Balsam.—Order Balsaminaceæ (Balsam tribe).—A coarse stove annual, growing four feet high, with large ovate acuminate leaves, and rather pretty flowers, growing several together in the axils of the leaves; the lower sepal is yellowish and downy, the upper bears a green horn, and is with the rest of the flower of a pinkish lilac. It flowers the whole summer and autumn. Sent from Ceylon to Kew, by Mr. Thwaites, in 1851.—*Bot. Mag.,* t. 4623.

MACHÆRANTHERA TANACETIFOLIA, *Nees.* Tansy-leaved Dagger-flower.—Order Asteraceæ § Asteroideæ (Composite plants).—A branching half shrubby biennial, growing a foot high, with sessile oblong pinnatifid leaves, and terminal flower heads, consisting of numerous dagger-shaped purple ray florets, and a yellowish disk. It was sent by Dr. Wright from New Mexico to Kew, where it flowered during summer. It is the *Aster tanacetifolia* of Humboldt, and the *A. chrysanthemoides* of Willdenow.—*Bot. Mag.,* t. 4624.

EUGENIA UGNI, *Hooker and Arnott.* The Myrtilla.—Order Myrtaceæ (Myrtle tribe).—A charming free-flowering evergreen shrub, hardy at Exeter, and therefore well adapted for conservative walls, and cold conservatories. It grows two to four feet high, with numerous opposite ovate myrtle-like leaves, and axillary four or five petalled globose flowers, white, tinged with rose. It is the *Myrtus Ugni* of Molina. Messrs. Veitch bloomed it in July, 1851. It is a native of South Chili and the islands, and was introduced by Mr. W. Lobb. The flowers, as well as the leaves, when bruised, are fragrant.—*Bot. Mag.,* t. 4626.

PENTSTEMON BACCHARIFOLIUS, *Hooker.* Baccharis-leaved Pentstemon.—Order Scrophulariaceæ (Linariad tribe).—A handsome erect growing plant, flowering during summer and autumn. It grows about a foot and a half high, with opposite distant spinescent-toothed leaves, the lower ones spathulate, the upper oblong and rotundate. The flowers are rich scarlet, in a terminal elongated panicle. Sir W. J. Hooker, in *Botanical Magazine,* t. 4627, conjectures it may be annual, but it is stated to increase by cuttings. Native of Texas, and recently introduced to Kew.

GRINDELIA GRANDIFLORA, *Hooker.* Large-flowered Grindelia.—Order Asteraceæ § Asteroideæ (Composite plants).—A showy orange-flowered biennial, four feet high, branched corymbosely at top, with alternate sessile lanceolate leaves, having a broad cordate semi-amplexicaul base, and the terminal flower-heads measuring fully three inches across. It is from Texas, and flowers in autumn. Introduced to Kew, where it is found to increase readily from cuttings.—*Bot. Mag.,* t. 4628.

CENTRANTHUS MACROSIPHON, *Boissier.* Long-tubed Centranth.—Order Valerianaceæ (Valerianwort tribe).—A showy autumn-flowering annual, with a stout dwarf erect branched fistular stem, ovate leaves, the lower ones almost toothless, the upper deeply cut at their base, and compact dichotomously corymbose panicles, of deep rose-coloured flowers. It is allied to *C. Calcitrapa,* but is larger, and has longer flowers. Native of Grenada, and introduced from the French Gardens. It is well figured in *Paxton's Flower Garden,* ii., t. 67.

GRAMMATOPHYLLUM SPECIOSUM, *Blume.* Showy Grammatophyl.—Order Orchidaceæ (Orchid tribe).—A very fine caulescent stove epiphyte, with distichous sword-shaped leaves, and racemes of large yellow flowers, thickly spotted with red; the sepals and petals are alike obovate-oblong and leathery, and the lip is rolled round the column. It is from the Malay Archipelago, and was flowered last summer by Messrs. Loddiges, "after years of patience." Figured in *Paxton's Flower Garden,* ii., t. 69.

SALVIA CANDELABRUM, *Boissier.* Chandelier Sage.—Order Lamiaceæ (Labiate tribe).—This fine hardy herbaceous plant was introduced from Malaga by E. Delins, Esq., and is figured by a woodcut in *Paxton's Flower Garden* (ii. 161). Its leaves resemble those of common Sage; but it throws up a branching naked panicle of flowers, which have a greenish yellow upper lip and a rich violet lower one. The flowers, though handsome, drop too soon, which render its appearance shabby.

PODOCARPUS NUBIGENA, *Lindley.* Cloud-born Podocarp.—Order Pinaceæ (Conifer tribe).—A yew-like hardy evergreen bush or tree, with stiff linear deep-green leaves, having a double glaucous band beneath. It is a native of Southern Chili, and has been imported by Messrs. Veitch. See *Journal of Horticultural Society,* vi. 264.

ONCIDIUM SCHLIMII, *Linden*. Schlim's Oncid.—Order Orchidaceæ (Orchid tribe).—A pretty stove epiphyte, collected by Funck and Schlim, in the province of Merida, in Central America, at the height of 7000 feet above the sea. The pseudo-bulbs are narrow, each bearing a pair of long thin sword-shaped leaves, and producing a long, weak, scrambling, branched panicle of small yellow flowers, slightly and irregularly barred with brown. It has been bloomed in the garden of T. Brocklehurst, Esq., of the Fence, Macclesfield. Introduced by Mr. Linden.

FAGUS OBLIQUA, *Mirbel*. Oblique Beech.—Order Corylaceæ (Mastwort tribe).—A fine evergreen tree, probably hardy, inhabiting the slopes of the Andes, from the sea level to the line of perpetual snow, attaining the height of forty to fifty feet, with a stem as straight and smooth as a Pine-tree. The foliage is more like a Hornbeam than a Beech; between lozenge-shaped and lance-shaped, serrated, with strong straight veins, and of a beautiful pale green. It grows freely in Messrs. Veitch's nursery, at Exeter, in the open air.

LUXURIAGA RADICANS, *Ruiz and Pavon*. Rooting Luxuriaga.—Order Liliaceæ (Lilywort tribe).—A climbing plant from South Chili, where it inhabits cool shady woods, and covers the trunks of trees. It throws out branches much resembling the fronds of Ferns, producing small, flat-ribbed, somewhat succulent leaves, arranged in two rows, and bearing on the under side white pendulous whole-coloured flowers, something like snowdrops, and delightfully fragrant. Introduced by Messrs. Veitch, and closely related to the following, which grows with it.

CALLIXENE POLYPHYLLA, *Hooker*. Many-leaved Callixene. — Order Liliaceæ (Lilywort tribe). — The *Luzuriaga erecta* of Kunth. It is similar to *L. radicans*, but the fragrant flowers are speckled with brown. If these plants would prove hardy, it would be a great gain to our gardens; but experience is unfavourable to the supposition. Mr. Lobb, however, thinks they will be hardy on elevated parts of the mainland. He describes the climate of Chiloe as much like that of Cornwall—raining almost incessantly in winter, but not so cold as in England, the frosts being of short duration. The summer is also wet and cold; the thermometer seldom exceeding 65°. The south winds are very cold and cutting. See *Journal of Horticultural Society*, vi. 267.

DAMMARA OBTUSA, *Lindley*. Blunt-leaved Dammar.—Order Pinaceæ (Conifer tribe).—From the representation given of this fine tree in *Paxton's Flower Garden* (ii. 146), it seems a remarkably distinct species. It was found by Mr. C. Moore in the New Hebrides, and a living plant has been received during the past year by the Horticultural Society. In its native localities it grows to a large size, having the appearance of the New Zealand Kauri, *Dammara australis*, and producing a valuable timber. The leaves are exactly oblong, with the ends rounded, four inches long, and rather more than an inch wide. The cones are cylindrical, with the ends rounded, three inches long, the ends of the scales convex, about four times as broad as long. It will form a greenhouse evergreen tree.

ABELIA UNIFLORA, *R. Brown*. One-flowered Abelia.—Order Caprifoliaceæ (Caprifoil tribe).—A small erect evergreen shrub, nearly, or quite, hardy. It has ovate leaves growing opposite or ternately, and from the axils of the upper leaves the flowers grow singly, each subtended by three bracts; the funnel-shaped corolla is white, with a slight violet tinge on the upper side. It comes from the North of China, whence it was sent about 1849, by Mr. Fortune, to the nursery of Messrs. Standish and Noble, of Bagshot.

The following novelties are of less general interest as garden plants :—

CENTROSOLENIA PICTA, *Hooker*. Painted-leaved Centrosolenia.—Order Gesneraceæ (Gesnerwort tribe).—A rather coarse procumbent stove herb, with fleshy stems, and large opposite hairy oval or ovate leaves, the pairs unequal in size. The flowers, clustered in the axils, are white, funnel-shaped, and parted above into five spreading rounded lobes. The younger leaves are said to be beautifully painted or mottled with pale green and brown. It has been figured in the *Botanical Magazine* (t. 4611) from plants sent in 1850 to Kew, from the Amazon River, by Mr. Spruce.

SPHÆROSTEMMA PROPINQUA, *Blume*. Dr. Wallich's Sphærostemma.—Order Schizandraceæ (Kadsurad tribe).— A neat-foliaged, somewhat climbing warm greenhouse shrub, having ovate acuminate leaves and axillary flowers; those in the male plant are pale yellow, and either solitary or in fascicles. The fruit is said to consist of many berries attached to a receptacle, and the latter elongating as the fruit advances to maturity, gives them the appearance of a long bunch of red currants. From Nepal and Sikkim. Introduced by Dr. Wallich some years since to Kew. Flowers in June.—*Bot. Mag.*, t. 4614.

PEDICULARIS MOLLIS, *Wallich*. Soft-leaved Indian Lousewort.—Order, Scrophulariaceæ (Linariad tribe.)— A small herb, probably perennial, but uncultivable. It has an erect, simple stem, a foot high, bearing pinnate leaves, with pinnatifid pinnæ, the leaves passing into bracts upwards. In the axils of these, forming whorls, grow the small, deep purple, two-lipped flowers. From the mountains of Northern India; introduced about 1849 to Kew.—*Bot. Mag.*, t. 4599.

EPIDENDRUM VOLUTUM, *Lindley*. Volute-flowered Epidendrum.—Order Orchidaceæ (Orchid tribe).—A greenish-white-flowered terete-stemmed stove epiphyte, of no beauty. It is from Central America, and was introduced in 1849 by G. U. Skinner, Esq., to the garden of the Horticultural Society.

CAPSICUM CEREOLUM, *Bertoloni*. Waxy-fruited Capsicum.—Order, Solanaceæ (Nightshade tribe.)—A curious, half shrubby plant, with oval tapering leaves, downy all over. The flowers are succeeded by curved-down conical fruit, of a bright lemon colour, and having a waxy appearance. It is from the west coast of South America, and was introduced by Messrs. Veitch of Exeter in 1850.

HOYA CUMINGIANA, *Decaisne*. Cuming's Hoya.—Order, Asclepiadaceæ (Asclepiad tribe.)—A curious scandent, summer-blooming, stove shrub, of erect growth, with dense sessile cordate leaves, somewhat downy beneath, arranged in a decussate manner. The axillary clusters of flowers are not showy, they being of a yellowish green colour, the coronet purplish brown. It is from the Philippine Islands, and was introduced in 1850 by Messrs. Veitch of Exeter.

SWAMMERDAMIA GLOMERATA, *Raoul.* Cluster-flowered Swammerdamia.—Order, Asteraceæ (Composite plants.) —A worthless half-hardy evergreen bush, with small roundish leaves, dull green above, and white with down beneath, the straggling branches bearing small clusters of white flowers. From New Zealand ; introduced about 1850. Flowers in spring.

MIMOSA URAGUENSIS, *Hooker* and *Arnott.* Uraguay Mimosa.—Order, Fabaceæ (Leguminous plants.)—A curious spiny half-hardy shrub, with bipinnate finely-divided shining foliage, and bearing in the summer months balls of thread-like flowers of a reddish or brick-dust colour. From the Banda Oriental. Introduced in 1841 by the Hon. W. F. Strangways, to the Horticultural Society of London.

ARBUTUS VARIANS, *Bentham.* Variable Strawberry tree.—Order, Ericaceæ (Heathwort tribe.)—Syn. *A. mollis*, Hooker ; *A. xalapensis*, Lindley.—An evergreen, spring-blooming, greenhouse shrub, with dull green leaves, hoary beneath, and having terminal panicles of white and pink urceolate blossoms. From Mexico. Introduced by Mr. Hartweg in 1846.

GAULTHERIA NUMMULARIÆ, *De Candolle.* Moneywort-leaved Gaultheria.—Order Ericaceæ (Heathwort tribe). —A neat trailing evergreen greenhouse plant. It has roundish, hairy, alternate leaves, and axillary small white flowers, hidden by the foliage, and succeeded by reddish purple berries. It is a native of the Himalaya, and was introduced to the gardens of her Majesty at Frogmore.

CATASETUM SANGUINEUM, *Lindley.* Red-spotted Catasetum.—Order Orchidaceæ (Orchid tribe).—A strong-growing, but not handsome stove perennial, with long pseudo-bulbs, light glaucous green leaves, and close racemes of greenish flowers, speckled with brown and dull red. It is from Central America, and was introduced by Mr. Linden. It is in cultivation as *Myanthus sanguineus.*

CLEISOSTOMA BICOLOR, *Lindley.* Two-coloured Cleisostoma.—Order Orchidaceæ (Orchid tribe.)—A stove epiphyte of little beauty, the stems and leaves of which are not described. The flowers are small, pink, stained at the base with dingy purple. From Manilla. Introduced in 1848 by Messrs. Veitch of Exeter. The latter have been described in *Paxton's Flower Garden.*

AMARYLLIDEAN PLANTS.

WE cultivate these plants at Redleaf very successfully, on a simple and inexpensive plan ; and as we find them to attract general admiration as an ornament to the conservatory when in flower, a succinct detail of our mode may not be unacceptable.

We preserve them during the greater part of the year in a two-light forcing pit, which is constructed on the M'Phail system, that is, the size of the pit being fixed upon, say eight feet by six feet, four feet of nine-inch brick-work is built up in the pigeon-hole fashion ; on this is built two feet of single brick-work, on which rests the frame and lights. An arched entrance is left at one end of the pigeon-hole work, and the interior, in the autumn, is jammed full of oak leaves. Linings of leaves are also provided at the same time, and these are confined by nine-inch brick-work, eighteen inches from the pit at bottom, two feet six inches at top, and four feet six inches in perpendicular depth. It is best to sink at least three feet below the ground-line. For the support of the plants, slate slabs are laid on the ledge formed by the junction of the nine-inch and single brick-work.

The culture is very simple and easy. We procure the bulbs in September or October, when quite dormant, and pot them in a soil composed of two parts rich friable loam and one part leaf mould, with a little silver sand, leaving nearly half the bulb exposed. They are placed in the pit, and no water is given. About February, they will begin to throw up the flower stems, when watering may begin, and they should be removed to a light part of an early vinery or forcing-house. Just before the flowers expand, remove them to the conservatory, and water freely. After the flowering is over, remove them back to the pit, and as . .on as the leaves begin to turn yellow, gradually withhold water until they are again dry and dormant. Top dress in the autumn, and shake out and re-pot every second year.

The linings require to be topped up now and then ; and every autumn both the linings and interior bed are renewed with fresh leaves. They are covered up securely in severe weather, the same as with other plants in cold pits.—JOHN COX, *Gardener to W. Wells, Esq., Redleaf.*

1 Stylidium Armeria 2 Acacia undulaefolia

STYLIDIUM ARMERIA.

LABILLARDIERE gave this name to a species of Stylewort found in Van Diemen's Land; and the present plant, collected, we believe, by Mr. Drummond, in New Holland, does not appear to differ in any material feature. Our drawing was made in the Chelsea Botanic Garden last summer, from a plant which had been presented by Messrs. Henderson of the Pine Apple Nursery. It is a very pretty plant, well deserving of cultivation, having the aspect of *S. graminifolium*, but possessing broader leaves, and larger, as well as deeper-coloured flowers. It comes near the plant which Dr. R. Brown has named *S. melastachys*, and perhaps that is not distinct from the *S. Armeria*. In cultivation, it proves to be a herbaceous perennial, with tall leafless flower-stalks issuing from tufts of linear sword-shaped leaves. The scape is smooth below, but clothed with small glandular hairs on the upper part among the flowers. The flowers are arranged in a long and tolerably close raceme, arising from short stalks in the axils of acute lanceolate bracts of about equal length; they are large and showy, of a purplish crimson colour. The flowering stem becomes much longer than the leaves as the flowering period passes over, and at seed-time greatly exceeds them.—A. H.

This pretty species of Stylewort, though a native of New Holland, like many plants from the same country, enjoys a little extra heat in the growing season, and the warmth of an intermediate house is a suitable excitement for it from February until it begins to show its flowers, when full air and light are necessary to give colour. Indeed, a great number of New Holland plants, to grow them to perfection, like a gentle moist heat in the growing season, which is, in fact, only in imitation of their native habitats, where the heat is much greater than in our ordinary greenhouses. This plant is best propagated by seeds, which are produced freely, and require to be sown in sandy peat soil, and to be kept in a close frame afterwards, until the young plants get well established, after which they may be kept in the greenhouse. The plants may also be increased, but not so readily, by division. The established plants require a light rich soil, consisting of sandy loam, peat, and leaf-mould, to which plenty of gritty sand and charcoal must be added. After they are potted, place them in a gentle heat, as indicated above, and encourage them to robust and healthy growth. To form a fine specimen an established plant is necessary, and therefore a succession of young plants must always be grown on. Indeed, to produce a fine mass, several seedling plants might, at the final shifting, be placed together in a large pot. When the plants are thoroughly established, manure-water may be used once or twice a-week, and the plants must be syringed to keep them clear of insects, especially of the red spider. Should this, or the thrip, another insect pest, at any time infest them, give a good dusting of sulphur after syringing, allowing it to remain on for a few days, and then washing it off again.—A.

ACACIA UNDULÆFOLIA.

THIS fine species of Acacia is cultivated in Messrs. Henderson's Nursery at Pine Apple Place, under the name of *A. oleæfolia*, but it is undoubtedly the *A. undulæfolia* of Allan Cunningham, a species many years since introduced to our gardens, but apparently lost; for we do not remember to have recently seen it in cultivation. It is, of course, an Australian plant, and is one of the finest species we possess for the conservatory. Our drawing was made at Messrs. Henderson's, where it flowers in the early spring months.

It forms a graceful shrub, seldom exceeding four feet in height, and is of variable, irregular habit, much branched, the branchlets being of dark colour, crowded with axillary flowers to their very extremity, and densely clothed with short, cinereous hair. In the cultivated state the branchlets are brown, sub-angular, pilose, and of spreading, dependent habit. The phyllodes are copious, alternate, often an inch long, sometimes but little longer than broad, elliptical or ovate, as frequently equilateral as oblique, especially in wild specimens. They are of very flexuose surface, with undulated thickened margins, or are almost entirely plane, acuminate, with an attenuated, curved mucro; the upper margin more wavy than the lower, and, near the base, furnished with a rather prominent oval gland; smooth,

ı

having several faintly marked primary veins, diverging from the midrib at an angle of 45 degrees, and running parallel to each other. The flowers are bright yellow in solitary heads, and pairs of heads, projecting beyond the phyllodes, upon stalks arising from the axils of the latter.—A. H.

In a genus of plants remarkable for the sameness of their flowers, the present subject is certainly one of the most distinct and desirable, not only on account of its profuse habit of blooming, but likewise for the distinct character of the plant. The Acacias are not difficult to cultivate. Most of them strike root with facility; and they may also be raised from seed, which some of them produce with great freedom. The best cuttings are the little, short, sturdy pieces, produced from the sides of the main branches; and when they can be taken off with a heel or piece of the mature wood adhering, they are less liable to damp. When the cuttings are procured, smooth the bottom of each with a sharp knife, and insert them about half an inch deep, making the sand tolerably firm. The cutting-pot should be prepared by first thoroughly draining, and then filling it to within an inch of the rim with turfy loam, peat, and sand, filling the remaining portion with silver sand. If you have a close pit, frame or hand-glass, bell-glasses will not be necessary, but if not, they must be used. The cuttings, at the time they are taken off, must be about half ripe, and the cutting-pots should be placed in about the same temperature as that from which the cuttings were taken. Acacias may also be increased by cuttings of the roots, and a well-established plant will furnish a considerable supply. The strong roots must be cut into pieces about two inches long, and be inserted like cuttings, leaving about a quarter of an inch exposed to the light, from which young shoots will be produced.

If you are desirous of growing large specimens, select well started young plants, and pot them, any time during spring, in equal portions of peat and rich turfy loam, to which some charcoal and gritty sand may be added. The soil should be broken tolerably fine, and, if the plants are well rooted, a tolerable shift may be given. As the plants will grow with great freedom, supply them liberally with water, and syringe them daily in the growing season, not more to promote free growth than to secure their being kept quite clear from insects. Manure water may be used occasionally when the pots are full of roots, and care must be taken to stop the plants regularly, and to train them into proper form. Towards the end of the season, when the growth is nearly completed, place the plants in the full sun, to secure the ripening of the wood, as, unless the wood is properly matured, they will not flower profusely, especially if the plants are in free and luxuriant growth. The Acacias are very liable to be attacked by white scale, the best remedy for which is hot water, applied with a syringe until the insects are washed off.—A.

<hr />

THE VINEGAR PLANT.

VERY interesting series of observations respecting the Vinegar plant, were recently laid before the Botanical Society of Edinburgh, by Dr. Balfour. Of these, which we have not hitherto been enabled to notice, we now present a summary :—

Much interest has been recently excited by the statements relative to the Vinegar Plant. This plant, which has a tough gelatinous consistence, when put into a mixture of treacle, sugar, and water, gives rise to a sort of fermentation by which vinegar is produced. After six or eight weeks the original plant can be divided into two layers, each of which acts as an independent plant, and when placed in syrup continues to produce vinegar, and to divide at certain periods of growth. The vinegar thus produced is always more or less of a syrupy nature. Various conjectures have been hazarded as to the origin of the so-called Vinegar plant, some stating that it came from South America, or other distant regions, and others that it is a spontaneous production. Lindley states that it is a peculiar form of *Penicillium glaucum*, or common blue mould. There seems to be no doubt that it is an anomalous state of mould, or of some fungus allied to it, and the peculiarity of form and consistence appears to be owing to the material in which it grows. In place of producing the usual cellular sporiferous stalks, the mycelium increases to an extraordinary extent, its cellular threads interlacing together in a remarkable manner, and producing one expanded cellular mass, with occasionally rounded bodies like spores in its substance. The cellular filaments are seen under the microscope. The tendency to divide in a merismatic manner is common in many of the lower classes of plants, and this seems to be what occurs at a certain period of growth, when the plant divides into two laminæ in a horizontal manner. If the plant is allowed to continue growing, it forms numerous laminæ, one above the other, somewhat like the mode in which some monocotyledonous stems or corms increase. The anomalous forms of fungi, in certain circumstances, have lately excited much interest, and Mr. Berkeley has called attention to some of the remarkable transformations which they undergo. These transformations are such, that many forms considered as separate genera are now looked upon as mere varieties of one species.

That mould of various kinds, when placed in syrup, shows the same tendency to form a flat gelatinous, or somewhat leathery expansion, is shown by the following experiments:—Some mould that had grown on an apple was put into syrup on the 5th March, 1851, and in the course of two months, there was a cellular flat expanded mass formed, while the syrup was converted into vinegar. Some of the original mould was seen on the surface in its usual form. Some mould from a pear was treated in a similar way at the same time, and the results were similar. So also with various moulds growing on bread, tea, and other vegetable substances. The effect of these moulds was in most cases to cause a fermentation, which resulted in the production of vinegar. In another experiment on the 8th November, 1850, a quantity of raw sugar, treacle, and water, were put into a jar without any plant being introduced, and they were left untouched till March 5, 1851. When examined, a growth like that of the Vinegar plant was visible, and vinegar was formed. The plant was removed and put into fresh syrup, and again the production of vinegar took place.

It would appear from experiment that when purified white sugar alone is used to form syrup, the plant when placed in it does not produce vinegar so readily, the length of time required for the change varying from four to six months. There may possibly be something in the raw sugar and treacle which tends to promote the acetous change.

Dr. Greville, than whom few are better acquainted with the lower orders of vegetation, has stated his belief, that the Vinegar plant is an abnormal state of some fungus. It is well known that many fungi, in peculiar circumstances, present most remarkable forms; for instance, the so-called genus *Myconema* of Fries, as well as the genus *Ozonium*. Even some of the Agarics present anomalous appearances, such as the absence of the pileus, &c., in certain instances. The remarkable appearances of Dry-rot, in different circumstances, are well known.

GARDEN NOTES OF THE MONTH.

MR. VAN BUREN, in the American Horticulturist (vi., 575), notices, in respect to blue flowers:—1. That a large majority of our native plants, bearing blue flowers, bloom either early in spring or late in autumn, and he enquires,—Do blue flowers require and consume more oxygen than those of other colours? The bruised petals or expressed juice of red flowers exposed to the atmosphere change to a blue colour: Is this caused by absorption of oxygen? If so, may not plants consume a greater quantity at these seasons than when the air is in a more rarified state? Or does the intensity of the solar rays alone cause a redundancy of brighter coloured flowers in summer? 2. Wild blue-flowering plants are more frequently found in moist, shaded situations, than in more exposed, sunny spots. The colour of many plants may be changed from pale red to blue, by employing "swamp mould," and keeping them in the shade. Pursuing these hints, he suggests that blue flowers might, by perseverance through several generations, be produced on many plants now producing flowers of other colours.

Heartsease in pots are likely to form quite a feature at the Metropolitan exhibitions. We hear that our indefatigable friend, Mr. Turner, of the Royal Nursery, Slough, will have plants, fine compact specimens (covered with scores of flowers), eighteen inches to two feet in diameter. Such plants will do more to draw attention to the growth of pansies than as many cut flowers as would cover a rod of ground.

As an example that pine growing is progressing in other countries as well as Britain, a friend writes us from the Azores that he cut, in 1851, "a Cayenne Pine, weighing twelve pounds; five Trinidads, averaging eight pounds each; and twelve Moscow Queens, six pounds each (one over seven pounds). The only accommodation I have for growing them is a dung-pit, twelve lights long. As soon as the fruit is cut, which is about the end of August, the plants are taken up, the bed refreshed, or renewed, and the strongest suckers are planted out, and by growing them late into the winter, which this climate admits of, and keeping them a little later at rest in the spring, I expect to start even a better lot than I had last year." This is gratifying intelligence; and considering that St. Michael is only fourteen days, if the wind is favourable, from England, would not pines pay there as a commercial speculation? for if cut just as they began to ripen, they would be in prime condition for the table when they got to this country.

Chrysanthemums promise to become very general favourites, and blooming, as they do, in the very depth of winter, deservedly so. We have recently received a little *brochure*, "The Cultivation of the Chrysanthemum for the production of specimen blooms," by G. Taylor,* and a very useful little work it is. Mr. Taylor is certainly one of the most successful of the metropolitan growers, and though the plan he recommends for specimen blooms is not calculated to produce "specimen" or handsome plants, still there can be no question but that his practice is a good one. We saw his productions at the Stoke Newington Show, in November 1851, and we must confess the flowers surpassed our notions of perfect growth, some of the blooms being more than six inches in diameter. We therefore can confidently recommend the work as being a good shilling's worth, and a book from which the amateur may glean much information, not only upon treatment, but also upon the most suitable kinds to grow for cut flowers, for specimen plants, and also of the pompons.

In buying plants, amateurs cannot commit a greater mistake than that of purchasing plants, deficient in quality, for the sake of their cheapness; for though they may accord with the free-trader's notion of "cheap, cheap," yet, in the majority of cases they will, as compared with good plants, be found dear. An illustration occurs to us :—Six months back we purchased a quantity of plants, for which we paid from half a guinea to two guineas each. Among them was one plant of which the nurseryman said, " ——, you will see, is not my growth, but it is the best I can procure;" and true enough it bore good evidence of not being his growth, and even to the present time, though it has been subjected to precisely the same treatment as the others, it is not worth so much as kinds purchased at the same price by seventy-five per cent. It is, therefore, quite certain, that a properly started, well-grown plant, may be "cheap" at ten shillings, while a badly grown one, though quite as large, would be dear at half-a-crown. Prices in nurserymen's catalogues must be regarded as representing a certain article, and that which upon paper may be regarded as "dear," will, when quality is taken into consideration, be found very cheap. We have never bought plants at a "cheap shop" but once, and we paid so dearly for our experience, that we shall never deal at such a shop again. The "labourer is worthy of his hire;" and good plants are worthy of their price. In this as in all other garden requisites, the best will be found the cheapest.—P.

The *Anomatheca cruenta* is an excellent little plant for small beds, or for planting near the edges of large ones or borders, and answers exceedingly well under the following treatment :—Early in March pot the bulbs in equal parts of loam, dung, and leaf-mould, with a good admixture of sand, putting four bulbs in a pot; place them in a pit, or cold frame, until the season arrives for turning out, when they should be planted in a bed of similar compost, without disturbing the roots. With ordinary attention they will then grow vigorously, and flower profusely, from June to November. If bloom is all that is required, the seed-pods should be cut away as the blossoms fail; but if increase of stock be required, seed may be easily saved, and bulbs raised; they are also readily increased by offsets. The bulbs should be taken up before frost sets in, potted in silver-sand, and stored in a dry place secure against frost for the winter.

* London : Published by the Author, 7, Park Street, Stoke Newington.

THE WARINGTON PLANT CASE.

WE have already (p 5) given a view of the parlour aquarium, contrived by Mr. Warington, and which may well bear his name; and have also explained in his own words the principles on which success depends. These principles, it must be obvious, admit of various modes of application so that our former illustration is to be regarded rather as an exemplification of the principle than as a model.

We now subjoin another design for an aquarium, or Warington case, with the view to indicate, to some extent, the variety which may be attained, by combining this with the Wardian case. It will be obvious that this combination will afford scope for a much greater variety of form than would have been brought out by confining them chiefly to the growth of aquatic plants, and this amount of variety will afford opportunity for the display of a greater amount of ornamentation.

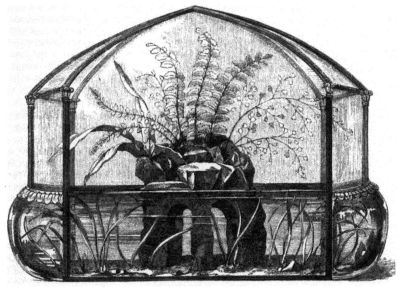

THE WARINGTON PLANT CASE.

The design now submitted, from the pencil of A. Aglio, Esq., jun., is intended to consist of an ornamental zinc frame-work, a slate bottom, and the whole of the sides to consist of glass, used in plates, as large as the fittings will allow. The front and back will thus each consist of a single plate, and the absence of frame-work of every kind will admit of the whole interior being viewed without obstruction. The convex ends of the basin portion are also intended to be of glass formed into the exact shape and size required.

The mass of imitation rock in the centre must be formed expressly for the reception of the plants, good drainage being an essential feature, so that the soil may not become soddened. The whole is supposed to be supported by an appropriate and elegant stand.

It is interesting to mention that the Zoological Society intend to fit up a case on Mr. Warington's principle in their garden in the Regent's Park.

THE CAMELLIA.

OF all the greenhouse plants this has been generally esteemed as the best, because of the fine appearance of the plant at all times, and its extreme beauty when in flower. The plant is always grand, the foliage being broad, deep green, and shining; but there is nothing so rich as its bursting blossoms.

When the cultivation of Camellias is commenced with plants sent in small pots from a nursery, and they are intended to be grown of a good form,—if they are at all lanky in their growth, it is best to cut off their heads at once, or to cut them in pretty severely, taking care, however, not to cut below the point where they were "worked. The plants will branch out freely and become much handsomer for this operation; and it is as well to lose the first season as to grow a plant that is ugly, and will require to be cut down ultimately, for the older it gets the less tractable it is.

It is often complained that Camellias will not set well for bloom: this arises from bad management. As soon as they begin to grow they require greater warmth and no check. In the summer months they often get put out in the open air to experience the changes of wetness and dryness, hot sun, cold winds, &c., whereas they should be in some well sheltered place, where neither the mid-day sun nor the north or east wind can reach them. A greenhouse without fire heat, and with shade against the mid-day sun, will be found perhaps the best place for them, unless they are placed in a canvas house such as Tulips are grown under; they continue growing there till the bloom-buds are developed, which is almost a matter of certainty. The fault in the management of these is much the same as that which attends American plants. Directly we have had the bloom we are careless of the plant; instead of which, it is the time, of all others that we should be most careful; for stinting them of water, giving them the hot sun, exposing them to north-east winds or high winds of any kind, or allowing them too much wet—which, if exposed in a rainy season is inevitable, will assuredly spoil the next year's bloom.

When, therefore, we commence growing the Camellia from a small plant, the greenhouse—and a part of it out of the draught,—or the coolest part of an airy stove, would be the best place, and they should not be exposed to the open air until they have completed their growth and set their bloom buds. If we grow the plant in the stove, it must be brought by degrees into the greenhouse, and then into a cold pit. It is rapid change from heat to cold, or from cold to heat, excess of water, or too little of it, that makes them cast their buds. The Camellia is by no means a tender plant, but it does not thrive well in rapid changes.

As often as a pot gets filled with roots, so often should they be shifted to larger pots; but this should be as the bloom declines and before they make their growth, or not till they have begun to swell their buds in the early months previous to opening, in both which states the plant wants extra nourishment; but the shifting must be managed without the least disturbance to the fibres, or the plants would throw their buds. The soil for the Camellia should be loam from rotted turves, one-half; cow or horse dung fully rotted to mould, one-fourth; peat, one-fourth. These ingredients should be well mixed.—X. Z.

SCIENTIFIC GLEANINGS.

CYCADEÆ, which, from the number of their fossil species, must have occupied a far more important place in the ancient, than in the present vegetable world, accompany their allies, the Coniferæ, from the coal formation upwards, but are almost entirely wanting in the variegated sandstone, which contains the remains of a luxuriant growth of certain conifers of peculiar form, Voltzia, Haidingera, and Albertia. The Cycadeæ attain a maximum in the keuper and the lias, which contain twelve different species; in the cretaceous rocks marine plants and naiades predominate. Thus, the forest of Cycadeæ of the oolitic period has long disappeared, and in the oldest groups of the tertiary formation this family is very subordinate to the coniferæ and the palms. The lignites, or beds of brown coal, which are found in each division of the tertiary period, contain, among the earliest land cryptogamia, some palms, a great number of coniferæ with well-marked annual rings, and arborescent forms (not coniferous) of a more or less tropical character. The middle tertiary period is marked by the re-establishment, in full numbers, of the families of palms and cycadeæ; and finally, the most recent shows great similarity to our present vegetation, exhibiting suddenly and abundantly various pines and firs, cupuliferæ, maples, and poplars. The dicotyledonous stems in lignite are occasionally characterized by colossal size and great age. In a trunk found near Bonn, Nöggerath counted 792 annual rings. In the turf bogs of the Somme, at Yseux, near Abbeville, a trunk of an oak tree has been found above fourteen feet in diameter, which is an extraordinary thickness for the extra-tropical parts of the old continent.—*Humboldt's Cosmos.*

The Spanish Dagger Plant, *Yucca aloifolia*, a plant very commonly used in Jamaica for making fences, yields a fine paper-looking substance, which is got by breaking the lower part of the leaf along the midrib, then pulling each half gently from the cuticle which covers the upper surface. It is most easily got from the young leaves, as in them only it separates freely. It can also be got equally well from the young leaves of the *Yucca gloriosa*. It is an excellent article for making artificial flowers, as it takes on colours freely.

In Junghuhn's " Travels in Java," we find an account of the remarkable forests completely covering an ancient volcanic mountain (Manella-wansie), over 9000 feet high. The woods near the summit have a very peculiar character. One of the most frequent and conspicuous trees is *Thibaudia vulgaris*, the trunks of which here attain enormous thickness, some as much as ten, others eight, most above six feet in circumference. Affected by the exposure of the elevation, they are gnarled, curved, and abundantly branched at a height of three to six feet from the ground, their branches being very much contorted, and spreading widely. *Thibaudia rosea* and *Gaultheria leucocarpa* (fifteen feet high), *Photinia integrifolia* (twenty-five to thirty feet high), *Gnaphalium javanicum*, and *Vireya retusa*, are other characteristic plants; but *Leptospermum javanicum*, with its white-spotted dome of leaves spreading over the *Vireya*, or a *Gnaphalium*, and *Hedera squarrosa*, creeping far and wide among the trunks and branches of the other trees, are particularly striking. Scarcely a tree is found of which the trunk is not short and divided low down into numerous gnarled, curling, and most irregular branches. The tree-fern *Cyathea oligocarpa*, which rises fifteen or twenty feet high, straight as a dart, and bearing its radiating crown of fronds at the summit, becomes thereby the more conspicuous. Herbaceous ferns are abundant, as also other Cryptogams, such as fungi. But the most curious of this tribe are the mosses (*Hypna, Leskeæ*, &c.), which clothe the trunks and main branches of the trees with cushions a foot and more in thickness, exaggerating the monstrous appearance already given by the irregular, twisted mode of growth. They also cover the damp ground to such an extent, that the flowers of the rhizanth, *Balanophora elongata*, parasitical in the roots here, can scarcely cut their way through. While the mosses clothe the trunks and main branches with their deep green cushions, heightening the gloom of the forest, the smaller branches and twigs are overgrown with whitish grey lichens (*Usneæ*), fluttering in the wind, and completing the character of such an ancient forest, hoary with time.—A. H.

CALCEOLARIA TETRAGONA.

POSSESSING considerable beauty in itself, this shrubby species of Slipperwort promises to afford materials which may effect that improvement in the worn-out garden Calceolarias which the Cape species of Pelargonium are beginning to bring about in the case of the enfeebled florists' breed of this latter popular flower. If its properties can at all be brought to bear upon the domesticated Slipperwort, we may yet hope to see some of their acquired beauty of flower, united with a vigorous constitution and good habit of growth.

The species has been lately introduced from Peru by Messrs. Veitch of Exeter, and was produced by them at the London exhibitions during the past summer. It forms a true shrub with a compact and dwarf branching habit of growth, and bears oblong-ovate blunt entire leaves. The flowers, which form loose corymbs at the ends of the stems, are large, with a pale-green calyx, and the lower lip of the corolla forms a broad squarish pouch of a pale yellow colour.

The habit of this new Slipperwort being all that can be desired in an ornamental plant, and being accompanied by clean-looking, ample, shining foliage, and numerous showy flowers, the form of which,

CALCEOLARIA TETRAGONA.

though not exactly agreeing with the artificial " cherry-bob " standard, is not at all inelegant, it is to be hoped that some persevering hybridizers will at once endeavour, by its aid, to rescue the Calceolaria as a garden flower from the neglect into which the execrable habit it has now acquired has almost everywhere consigned it.

Like the other shrubby species of Slipperwort, the present may be increased readily by means of cuttings of the young shoots; and the plants will grow freely in a mixture of equal parts of turfy loam, peat, and leaf mould. It, of course, requires greenhouse protection.—M.

1 Swainsona Osborni   2 Hypoxis Rooperii

HYPOXIS ROOPERII.*

WE are indebted for our drawing of this fine greenhouse perennial to the Rev. T. Rooper, of Wick Hill, Brighton. It is a most elegant plant, even when not in flower, but it has also the recommendation of being a very free bloomer, Mr. Rooper's plant having continued in blossom from March until August. Under the influence of sunshine, the golden stars of these Hypoxids are very attractive, and especially so in this *H. Rooperii*, from their size as well as their number. The species is allied to *H. stellipilis*, but is a larger and much more showy plant.

On a short stout erect rhizome, the elongate leaves are disposed in three ranks, about four being produced at one time in each series; they measure from nine to eighteen inches in length, and are about an inch and a half in breadth; the base is narrowed, and there they embrace the stem; the apex is drawn out into a long tapering point. Both surfaces bear stellate hairs, but those on the upper surface are scattered, whilst those below are more dense, and produce a hoary appearance. The flower-scape is about a foot long, and bears from four to six flowers, disposed in a kind of two-tier umbel. At the base of each pedicel is a subulate bract shorter than the pedicel itself, and having a membranous border; the pedicels are about as long as the perianth, and, as well as the bracts and outer surface of the perianth, are covered by long shaggy white hairs. The flowers are bright clear yellow inside, green without, and, when expanded, are nearly an inch and a half in diameter, forming a brilliant golden six-pointed star. The three outer divisions of the perianth are ovate-lanceolate, shaggy on the outside, the three inner broader, very obtuse, and hairy only at the very base. There are six yellow erecto-patent stamens, having an arrow-shaped base, and attached to short flat conical filaments.

We have not found any described species which agrees with the present, and have therefore much pleasure in appending to it the name of its discoverer, Captain E. Rooper, by whom also it has been introduced to our gardens. It was found by Captain Rooper growing near the mouth of the Buffalo river in Kaffraria, and was introduced in October 1848.

This is an easily managed greenhouse or frame plant. It requires complete rest and drought in winter, with immunity from frost, and a sunny situation through the summer. The soil should be sandy, and the pots thoroughly drained. The only means of increase is by seed, which Mr. Rooper's plant has already essayed to perfect, but we believe no progeny has as yet been obtained.—M.

SWAINSONA OSBORNII.†

THIS novel and very distinct species of Swainsona has been raised by Messrs. Osborn & Sons of the Fulham Nursery, and flowered with them in October 1851, when our drawing was made. It had been sent them by a correspondent from the Darling Downs, in Australia, where it was found growing by the side of water. Messrs. Osborn expect it to prove nearly hardy, it having been kept by them during winter plunged under shelter along with hardy herbaceous plants. The plants potted early in spring, and kept in a cold frame, bloomed in the course of the summer and autumn. It is a very ornamental half-hardy sub-herbaceous perennial.

The habit of the plant is dwarf, and it is a very free bloomer. The stems are suffruticose, erect, branched, and faintly streaked. The unequally-pinnate leaves consist of many (nine to fifteen, usually twelve) pairs of small linear-oblong retuse leaflets, narrowed towards the base, channelled by a sunken midrib, and having a smooth surface to the naked eye, but under a lens seen to be sprinkled over, especially when young and on the lower surface, with minute transparent warts or glands. They have small bluntly triangular stipules at their base. The flowers are large, few in number on the racemes, but the latter are numerous, and grow about as long as the leaves, sometimes longer; the

* *H. Rooperii*, n. sp.—Pilose; leaves trifarious, recurved, elongate, acutely keeled, narrowed below and imbricate at the base, tapering into a long point, clothed above with scattered stellate hairs, lanate beneath; scape four to six flowered, much shorter than the leaves, and as well as the bracts pedicels and exterior of perianth shaggy with long hairs; pedicels as long as the perianth, exceeding the subulate membranous-edged bracts.—M.

† *Swainsona Osbornii*, n. sp.—Suffruticose, smooth; leaves of nine to fifteen pairs of linear-oblong retuse leaflets; racemes few flowered, about equalling the leaves; pedicels without bracteoles, twice as long as the ciliate-toothed calyx.—M.

K

pedicels are twice as long as the calyx, and come from the axil of a small bract, but are, in our speci-men, entirely without bracteoles ; the calyx teeth are fringed with minute transparent hairs, which are probably glandular when fresh. The colour of the corolla is a deep rose, darker on the keel, and fading purplish. In the dried state we find but imperfect traces of calli on the standard. The stigma is bearded on one side along the back, which character, conjointly with its habit and the propor-tions of the corolla, has led us to refer it to Swainsona. The fruit we have not seen, but the ovary is shorter than the stamens, smooth, and attached by a footstalk about as long as the calyx.

To cultivate this plant well, it should, when growing freely, be liberally shifted into a good com-post of peat and loam, and early in spring the tops of the shoots should be removed, in order to pro-duce a greater number of stems, and these should be suffered to grow on till they flower. Cuttings of the young shoots will afford means of propagation. Until its hardiness has been ascertained, it should be treated as a frame plant.—M.

TREATMENT OF THE JAVANESE RHODODENDRON.

ADMIRERS of the Rhododendron must look upon the recent additions to this group of flowering shrubs with high anticipations, and, no doubt, a new era is about to commence in the history of these favourite shrubs. · *Rhododendron javanicum* stands conspicuous among the novelties, being new in colour, the flowers bold, of much substance, and freely produced; and the foliage broad and glossy. In Java, this plant is found growing on volcanic mountains, at an elevation of 9000 feet and upwards. In the same locality are found the *Gaultheria leucocorpa*, a dwarf shrub, with red hairy stems, alternate cordate-acuminate serrated leaves, and small lily-of-the-valley-like flowers, but chiefly remarkable for the numerous white berries with which it is studded in the winter season, even when the plant is not more than one foot in height. On the same mountains grows the crimson-flowered *Vaccinium Rollissonii*.

Rhododendron javanicum is partly epiphytal in habit, being found occasionally on the decaying trunks of trees ; at other times on the sides of the mountains, in a rich vegetable deposit, intermixed with spent lava, and which is also overgrown with Mosses, and a *Hymenophyllum* very much like our native *H. tunbridgense*. Various Lichens, of delicate thread-like texture, cling to the stems and branches. It has also been detected, in some instances, on the crumbling walls of old buildings, said to be the Idol Temples of the Javanese. In these native wilds it rarely attains a greater height than six feet, and forming a spreading bush. The stems of imported plants of *R. javanicum* are strangely contorted in their growth, which appears to be produced by the efforts of the plant to disentangle itself from the surrounding vegetation ; but seedlings raised in this country are free from curvature, either of stem or branch. It is a difficult plant to import in a living state ; the long sea voyage—generally five months—the pent-up atmosphere, and the extremes of temperature to which it is sub-jected, being anything but congenial to the well-being of a mountain plant.

The majority of the plants at present in this country were raised from seeds ripened and collected in Java in 1847, and received early in the spring of 1848. They were immediately sown in the usual manner, and had germinated in about three weeks; and, although they require the greatest attention during the first twelve months of their existence, after that time they are as easily managed as an ordinary Rhododendron or Azalea. If the plants require re-potting, let it be done as soon as the young leaves begin to unfold themselves. The pots should be rather small in proportion to the size of the plants : the drainage should occupy fully one-third of their depth, and the remaining space covered with a layer of rough fibrous peat. The amount of drainage may appear excessive, but it must be borne in mind that the natural locality of the plant offers the most effective drainage, and altogether prevents the retention of water at the roots; the fibres, also, are exceedingly fine, and are soon injured by any excess of moisture.

The most suitable soil for it is Wimbledon and Shirley peat, in equal proportions, well chopped-up together, and passed through a coarse sieve, with a liberal addition of sharp silver sand; if the peat abounds in pebbles, so much the better; if not, a few may be added with advantage to the plant. Where such a compost cannot be obtained, use the same as for Cape Heaths, adding rather more sand.

The plant is rather impatient of the knife, and frequently does not break for a long time after pruning, where the ordinary method is adopted. To remedy this habit, examine the plant carefully when first placed in the heat, and if it has no appearance of becoming bushy, take a small knife and scoop out the central bud or buds, and allow it to break again before it is re-potted.

When the young shoots are fully developed, and the leaves have arrived at their full size, and are beginning to harden, remove the plants to an airy greenhouse or cold pit, where they may remain through the winter; if placed in the latter, give air daily, according to the weather. Keep the foliage dry, and supply water very sparingly to the roots. In the spring, as soon as the plants show symptoms of growth, place them in a house where the atmosphere is kept moist, with a temperature of 55° to 60°, or 5° higher in the sun; sprinkling them daily with tepid water,—three times a-day, in bright sunny weather, will not be too often. They may remain in this situation till the end of May or beginning of June; and they should then be plunged up to the rim of the pot in an open border, where the sun can shine fully upon them; the spaces between the shrubs of an American border will be found suitable, provided they do not crowd too near. The attention now required will be to keep them well-watered in dry weather. The leaves will soon acquire a fine glossy surface, dark colour, and a leathery consistency; and if the season is mild and showery, they will not unfrequently make a second growth out of doors, and set flowers on the shoots so produced. The plants may remain in the open border until the month of September, or later if there is no appearance of frost, when they should be placed in a cold greenhouse for the winter as before.

When the flower-buds are beginning to throw off their numerous scales, preparatory to opening, place the plant at the warmest part of the house; they will expand all the better for it, especially if it be early in the season. By this method as many as twenty flowers have been produced in one head, all perfect, the individual flowers measuring exactly two and three-quarter inches across, of a rich orange-yellow, and of remarkably firm texture: the entire head formed a globular cluster, upwards of two feet in circumference, which continued in perfection more than a fortnight. The probability is that much larger heads may be obtained, as this was from a seedling of only three years age.

There is a variety of *R. javanicum*, with long lanceolate leaves, which vary in size exceedingly on the same plant, being from two to five inches in length, and from half an inch to two inches in width at the widest part; it is from the same locality as the broad-leaved sort, and of much slower growth, but has not yet flowered.

Although among the recently-introduced Sikkim Rhododendrons there are many splendid kinds, it is remarkable that yellow is a scarce colour among them. *R. lanatum R. Wightii*, and two or three others, are of a straw colour, and *R. lepidotum* is described as having flowers of a dark yellow, but here the heads are small, and the habit is weak. Hybridists must therefore look to *R. javanicum* for a new race of hardy yellow hybrids. That these will be obtained, no one who is at all conversant with the history of our hardy scarlet sorts, can for a moment doubt; directly, or indirectly, these have all been obtained from *R. arboreum*, some partaking of the character of trees, and others flowering freely when less than a foot in height. The hardy scarlets at the present time amount to upwards of thirty sorts. For the purposes of the ornamental planter, the importance of having a new and distinct colour, for grouping in clumps, or planting in the American border with the sorts already in cultivation, can scarcely be overrated.

Whether *R. javanicum* will eventually prove hardy, it is difficult to say; but, if not, its progeny most assuredly will be. It has already been made to produce seeds in this country, hybridised with several leading hardy sorts, and the young plants have passed through the first six months of their existence. *R. zeylanicum, R. Rollissonii*, and *R. cinnamomeum* were treated as greenhouse plants for very many years, but it is now satisfactorily proved that they are as hardy as the common kinds, at least in the neighbourhood of London; the foliage is also much finer than when kept in-doors. *R. cinnamomeum* sets its flower buds abundantly when planted in the open border, and if taken up, and potted late in the autumn, or early in the spring, makes a showy conservatory ornament, to be returned to the border after flowering. *R. Dalhousiæ*, as a parent, appears to promise flowers of extraordinary magnitude, and, what is better, sweet-scented; and *R. ciliatum* will probably be the parent of a new race, admirably adapted for pot culture, being of a dwarf habit with the foliage of a lively green. In fact, there are now sufficient materials for producing almost any given form or colour, and to render this charming family suitable for any required purpose.—W. BUCKLEY, *Tooting.*

ALCOVE-AVIARIES AND BOWERS.

THE grand general principle of propriety in garden decorations is, that they should never be object-less; and this, with the selection of sites, which should be so felicitously chosen as to give to each structure the appearance of being in a position, as it were, predestined for it, forms the fundamental law of the code of landscape gardening.

The accompanying design for an alcove-aviary is intended to occupy a position not distant from the

AN ALCOVE-AVIARY.

residence, and yet concealed from it. It should form a point of attraction capable of inducing frequent visits, by its convenient proximity, and yet convey to the spectator an impression of agreeable surprise every time it is approached. These conditions are not difficult of fulfilment. The readiest mode would be the following :—Let us suppose a side garden-door of a country house (not the principal entrance) opening upon a small lawn enriched by geometrical flower-beds, or a rosary, through the midst of which a dry, broad path leads towards the shrubbery, which is entered by a winding walk, at a given point of which, about half way through, the visitor is introduced, by a sudden turn, to an open space of long, oval form, running longwise in the direction of south-east to north-west. This space should be bordered with a neat, but somewhat bold and massive, cement coping, which would form a support of congenial character to the pedestals and vases which are intended to stand on each side of the entrance, and, at distances, all round. The entrance should be at the south-eastern end of the oval, opposite to the alcove-aviary, which would thus have a favourable aspect, securing the early morning sun, so essential to birds, especially in a state of comparative confinement. Both the entrance and the way out should be concealed by well-designed windings.

I propose that the front and exterior sides of those portions of the structure devoted to the aviary should be of one piece of strong glass, which would enable birds to be seen without the disagreeable intervention of wire-work, and at the same time form a protection from cold winds and beating rain, highly important to the healthy keeping of the birds. On the interior side of each compartment of the aviary, I would have wire-work only, as open as the size of the birds might render advisable. This, with the addition of proper ventilation planned under the thatch, would admit a sufficient quantity of air, and would place the birds in more open and immediate intercourse with the visitors, snugly seated within the shade of the alcove, and watching the varying play of sunshine upon the plumage of the moving birds, or renewing the food and water of the inhabitants of the aviary, which, it is scarcely necessary to state, should be done every day at least once, but if twice, so much the better. For these purposes, it is of course necessary that a wire-work door, large enough for a person to enter, should be framed into the interior wire-work.

It will be seen by the design that a more decorative style of rustic-work is suggested than that usually employed, a branch of garden decoration on which I intend to offer some advice, accompanied by designs, on another occasion.

Rustic-work of this character, if found impracticable by the usual mode—that of unbarked branches judiciously interlaced—should be roughly carved in wood, and varnished with transparent, but deep brown, varnish; or might be modelled, and then cast in cement, or even in iron; and I wonder much that low fences, &c., have not been cast in iron in that style, of which, however, I shall treat in a paper on that subject. The edge of the roof is surmounted by smaller rustic tracing of a similar character. This alcove-aviary should be well backed-up by thick-growing trees of considerable size, and the plantation should be of sufficient depth to prevent it being seen through, or the effect of a dark back-ground to the structure would be destroyed, and the spell of seclusion—the great charm of the scene—would be broken.

An additional interest might be imparted to this secluded spot, by the introduction of a large but excessively simple tazza, containing gold fish; into this a gently bubbling fountain should convey a continual supply of fresh water. This tazza should be almost of the dimensions of a miniature pond or basin, while its slight elevation on a low stand, as designed, would give it a novel and architectural character, in keeping with the other dressings of the scene. The small fountain in the centre might be made to issue from an opening of miniature rocks, raised slightly above the level of the water, and covered with water-loving Ferns and Mosses. But the exterior of the tazza should be kept freshly cleaned or painted; for wherever animal life, in whatever form, is the object to be petted and cared for, an appearance of daily attention, and perfect order and cleanliness are the most agreeable adjuncts to all arrangements for the purpose. The stand of the tazza is intended to be surrounded at some little distance with a low cement coping, within which some low-growing profusely-flowered plant is intended to grow,—such as Thrift at some seasons, double Daisies at another, or annual dwarf Lobelia at another,—which would partially break the formality of the coping, without destroying its symmetrical effect.

An Aviary and Alcove of this kind might be approached from the house by a *covered* path if thought advisable, in which case, the entrance from such a path should be from the back, so as not to disfigure the open approach; and in that case a door in the back of the Alcove should lead to the covered path, which might pass through without interference with the close shrubbery, which should effectually shroud the back of the structure.—H. N. HUMPHREYS.

On the subject of Bowers, we append the following hints and sketches supplied by another correspondent :—

It sometimes happens, when trees are cut down a few inches from the ground, that they send up shoots all round the stump. These shoots grow to a greater or less height, according to circumstances, and in some cases even attain a size little inferior to the original tree. It is difficult to prevent these shoots pushing up from a tree-stump, which thus often becomes a source of annoyance on a lawn or pleasure-ground, while the labour of uprooting it is grudged. One mode of overcoming this evil, or rather of converting an object of annoyance into an object of utility and ornament, is

FIG. 1.—TREE STUMP PREPARING FOR A BOWER.   FIG. 2.—THE SAME MORE ADVANCED.

illustrated by the following sketches. Fig. 1 shews the stump of a tree (Ash) with the young branches grown up round it; and Fig. 2 illustrates the fashion in which these branches may be made to form an elegant canopy to one of the most natural of Rustic Seats—the stump of the tree; which may, however, be provided with a soft cushion if required. The branches need simply to be tied together by means of wire; and if a few plants of Ivy and Brier, with one or two of the more choice climbing Roses are planted around the base, the whole would soon become very compact and beautiful. The wires should not be tied tightly, lest they should cut the branches in the course of time; and perhaps, for this reason, ordinary string ties would be preferable.—DELTA.

ON THE GERMINATION OF CLUB-MOSSES.

GREAT obscurity has hitherto prevailed on this subject, the opinions of different authors who have experimented and written on it presenting many discrepancies. Recent researches, by M. Hofmeister and M. Mettenius, have revealed some very curious facts respecting the mode of development of the new plants in those species which are now included under the generic group of *Selaginella* : such as the old *Lycopodium denticulatum, helveticum*, &c., in which the spikes bear spores of two kinds, large ones in small number at the base of the fruit-spike, and small ones in large number in all the succeeding sporangia.

From the researches just alluded to, it appears that this tribe exhibits phenomena resembling, to a certain extent, those recently made known in the germination of Ferns, only they are more recondite here. and escape all but the most searching investigation. It seems that the small spores of the *Selaginellæ* do not produce new plants, but have an office analogous to that of the pollen grains of the flowering plants, effecting a fertilization of a germ produced by the large spore. The changes which these small spores themselves undergo are as follows:—At a variable, but often a long period after they are sown, the coat bursts, and a delicate inner coat protrudes a little ; this also becomes ruptured, and from it emerge very minute cellular vesicles which have been produced in its interior, and each of these bursts to allow the exit of one of those mysterious, actively moving, spiral filaments, such as we find in the "antheridia" of the other Cryptogamous plants. According to M. Hofmeister, these bodies are not set free until more than five months after the spores are sown, in *Selaginella helvetica*.

The other kind of spores is very much larger than the "pollinic" spore, and is the true reproductive body, analogous to the ovule of flowering plants. The changes which it exhibits are very remarkable, and it requires very minute microscopic dissection to trace them. At the time these large spores are shed from the sporangium, an exceedingly delicate layer of cellular tissue is found inside the thick coat, at the upper end. This layer of cells is analogous to the delicate little green leafy body produced by the Fern spore when it germinates; but here it is formed *inside* the spore. After a time we may discover upon it structures closely resembling the "pistillidia" or "archegonia" of the other Cryptogamous plants, and when these have become perfect the outer coat of the spore cracks just over them and folds back in triangular flaps so as to lay them bare. It is supposed that fertilization now takes place by one of the spiral filaments coming in contact with the germ-cell contained in an "archegonum." At all events, the germ-cell of one of the "archegonia" is soon after found enlarging and dividing into several cells, and growing down into the centre of the spore. Here the embryo enlarges still more, and gradually acquires form, exhibiting a leaf-bud and a nascent rootlet, which, by their increasing size, burst the spore and make their way out, in which stage they may be recognized by the naked eye as closely resembling in appearance a little Dicotyledonous plant, springing from its seed ; having a descending, thread-like root, and a slender stalk bearing two little leaves with a bud between them.

Through the kindness of Mr. Moore, I had an opportunity of verifying much of the above in some spores of *Selaginella denticulata* and *S. stolonifera*, which germinated in one of the houses at the Chelsea gardens, in the beginning of the past winter. I found the structures described in the large spores, and traced the gradual development of the young plants from them ; but I only found the burst empty coats of small spores, not having hit upon any in a sufficiently early stage. A curious fact connected with this is related by M. Hofmeister; as already stated, the spores are often a long time germinating, but the large and small ones differ in their periods ; thus the small spores of *S. helvetica* produced their spiral filaments in about five months, while the large spores, sown at the same time, did not exhibit "archegonia" until six weeks later. And all experiments of sowing both kinds of spores together, or large spores alone, were fruitless ; the only way in which the large spores could be made to germinate, was by keeping a living and freely fruiting plant growing under the glass shade in the pot in which the spores were sown. As the small spores ripen gradually from the bottom to the top of the spike, a succession of them is thus afforded, some of which produced their filaments at the exact time required. The spores of *Selaginella Martinsii*, and other tropical species germinated in a few weeks after sowing. These points should be attended to by those who cultivate these plants. They indicate also a possibility of obtaining hybrids by sowing the large spores in pots containing growing plants of other species, isolated by being covered with a bell-glass.

The species of *Lycopodium* proper, to which our indigenous *L. clavatum*, *inundatum*, &c., belong, only produce one kind of spore, and these small. M. Hofmeister states, that he has not succeeded, after repeated trials, in causing any of them to germinate. He considers it probable that they produce a "prothallium" (that is, the cellular structure found inside the large spore) on which, as on the germinating Fern, both "antheridia" and "archegonia" are produced, consequently that they are androgynous instead of monœcious.—ARTHUR HENFREY, F.L.S.

New Garden Plants.

IMPATIENS FASCICULATA, *Lamarck.* Fascicle-flowered Balsam. Oider Balsaminaceæ (Balsam tribe).—A tender annual of little beauty. The leaves are lance-shaped and toothed, the flowers blush-coloured, their interior petals spreading like two broad wings, and the long filiform spur tinged with green. It comes from Ceylon, and seems extensively distributed over the Indian continent. It is the *Impatiens setacea* of Colebrook; *I. heterophylla* Wallich; *Balsamina fasciculata*, De Candolle; and *B. heterophylla*, Don.

ECHINOCACTUS LONGIHAMATUS, *Galeotti.* Long-hooked Hedgehog Cactus.—Order Cactaceæ (Cactus tribe). —A very handsome, as well as curious, succulent greenhouse plant, nearly globose in figure, with deep furrows, and having clusters of strong spines, the central ones four inches long, flattened, deflexed, and hooked at the end. The flowers are large and bright yellow. It is from Mexico, and flowers in July. It has been also named *E. hamatocanthus.*

PORTULACA THELLUSONII, LEYSZIL. Leysz's Purslane.—Order Portulacaceæ (Purslane tribe).—This is a very desirable variety of Thelluson's Purslane, differing only in having the flowers double. The colour being a bright carmine, it must be a very showy annual. It was raised by M. Leysz of Nancy.

CENTROSOLENIA GLABRA, *Hooker.* Smooth Centrosolenia. Order Gesneraceæ (Gesnerwort tribe).—A smooth prostrate epiphytal herb, with opposite obovate-lanceolate leaves, and axillary white flowers, about as long as those of the scarlet Achimenes. It is a native of the West Indies, and has been introduced to Kew by Mr. Purdie.

DRYANDRA NOBILIS, *Lindley.* Handsome Dryandra.—Order Proteaceæ (Protead tribe).—A very handsome greenhouse evergreen shrub, the thick, hard leaves of which are a span long, and deeply pinnatifid with recurved lobes; they are deep green above and white beneath, and have a very elegant appearance. The flowering branches are terminated by a large yellow head. Mr. Drummond sent it from the Swan River colony. It flowered at Kew in May 1851.

CONRADIA NEGLECTA, *Hooker.* Neglected Conradia.—Order Gesneraceæ (Gesnerwort tribe).—A dwarf stove herb, with large obovate oblong leaves, and axillary flowers (the colour of which is not stated) seated down among the leaves. It is from Jamaica, and has been raised at Kew.

LINDENBERGIA URTICÆFOLIA, *Lehmann.* Nettle-leaved Lindenbergia.—Order Scrophulariaceæ (Linariad tribe). —A weed-like annual plant, with ovate leaves, and solitary axillary flowers rich yellow, with a deep red spot within the throat. It is an Indian plant, and was sent by Dr. Hooker to Kew. It is the *Stemodia ruderalis* of Vahl.

AZALEA INDICA CALYCINA, *Lindley.* Long-calyxed Chinese Azalea.—Order Ericaceæ (Heathwort tribe).— A coarse-looking variety of Chinese Azalea, having the habit of the more vigorous varieties of that plant, and large loose flowers of a purplish rose-colour, spotted with red. It is remarkable for the long segments of its calyx. Mr. Fortune found it in China, and sent it to the garden of the Horticultural Society, where it flowered last year. It is not of much importance.

DENDROBIUM ALBUM, *Wight.* White Dendrobe.—Order Orchidaceæ (Orchid tribe).—A neat stove epiphyte, with erect jointed stems, oblong elliptic acuminate leaves, and large pure white axillary flowers, growing in pairs. It is stated to be near *D. aqueum.* It is an Indian species, and has been introduced by Messrs. Veitch.

ACACIA COCHLEARIS, *Wendland.* Cochlear Acacia.—Order Fabaceæ (Leguminous plants).—The *Mimosa cochlearis* of Labillardiere. It is a fine greenhouse shrub, with narrow sharp-pointed phyllodes, and balls of yellow fragrant blossoms on stalks shorter than the leaves, two or three springing from each axil. It is from the west coast of New Holland, and has been raised in the garden of the Horticultural Society. Flowers in the early months of the year.

OLEARIA GUNNIANA, *Hooker fil.* Mr. Gunn's Olearia.—Order Asteraceæ (Composite plants).—A daisy-flowered, half-hardy Tasmanian evergreen shrub, growing to a moderate size. De Candolle called it *Eurybia Gunniana.* The leaves are neat, oblong, with sinuately-toothed margins, and the flower-heads an inch and a half across, have a white ray, and yellow disk, and are very freely produced in autumn. Against a wall, it will endure our milder winters; but a reserve should be kept under protection.

ZAMIA CALOCOMA, *Miquel.* Beautiful-headed Zamia.—Order Cycadaceæ (Cycad tribe).—A fine addition to a very interesting group of stove shrubs, having trunks of less or greater size, crowned by a tuft of pinnated fronds. In this case, the trunk is described as ten inches high, by four and a half inches diameter at the base, somewhat conical in form, and crowned by the erecto-patent lance-shaped fronds, which are nearly two feet long, smooth, with dense, very numerous (65-70 pairs), linear-falcate subacute pinnæ. It is allied to *Z. tenuis.* The plant is of West Indian origin, and is cultivated in the nursery of M. Van Houtte of Ghent, and in the Botanic Garden of Amsterdam.

MAXILLARIA PUNCTULATA, *Klotzsch.* Dotted Maxillaria. Order Orchidaceæ (Orchid tribe).—An epiphyte with greenish-yellow flowers, having a three-lobed yellowish lip, which is spotted at the edge with purple. A native of Brazil, and cultivated in the German gardens.

EPIDENDRUM WAGNERI, *Klotzsch.* Wagner's Epidendrum.—Order Orchidaceæ (Orchid tribe).—A small-flowered stove epiphyte from Guatemala, introduced to the German gardens. The flowers are pink, in pendulous racemes.

Passiflora alata superba

PASSIFLORA ALATA SUPERBA.

FLOWERING specimens of the superb Passion-flower represented on the accompanying plate were forwarded to us early in January last, under the name now adopted, by Messrs. Lucombe, Pince, & Co., of Exeter, from whom we learn that the plant, first introduced to England by Mr. Henderson of the Wellington Road Nursery, was originally obtained from M. Meillez, of Lille, in France. It is described, by both Mr. Pince and Mr. Henderson, as being a much freer bloomer than *P. alata*, to which it is closely related, and of the general characteristics of which it largely partakes. Indeed, Mr. Pince describes his plant as being "literally covered with flowers, blooming upon short spurs as well as on the long shoots, and perfuming the whole house." It is, no doubt, a variety of garden origin, and probably a seedling from *P. alata*, but we have not ascertained its exact parentage.

Though unable to describe the habit of the plant from personal observation, we can bear testimony to the extreme beauty of the blossoms, and to the noble foliage which it produces. In the specimen sent to us the stem was quadrangular, with the angles slightly winged. The leaves were large, ovate, almost cordate at the base, slightly acuminate, attached by petioles which are furnished with one or two pairs of glands. The flowers are very showy, large, axillary (on the short lateral shoots produced from the axils of the upper leaves). The pedicels terete, and bearing an involucre of three ovate bracts, which are fringed with a few (one or two pairs) glandular teeth towards their base. The outer series of segments of the corolla or sepals are green externally, and of an ochreous-carmine within; the inner series of segments or petals are externally rose-crimson, tipped with greyish-blue, and on the inner surface deep carmine. The coronal filaments are purple, barred below crosswise with white, and in the upper parts mottled with white and purple. It is a most desirable stove climber.—M.

Among stove climbing plants, this is certainly one of the most beautiful, and well deserves extensive cultivation. As pot plants, the large varieties rarely succeed well; but this being a very free blooming kind, probably would, if properly managed. Planted, however, in the corner of the bark bed, in the plant stove, they succeed admirably, and will cover, in a short space of time, an immense area of trellis. The Passifloras delight in a rich porous soil, such as two parts turfy loam, one leaf mould, and one turfy peat, with an abundance of charcoal and gritty sand. Previous to planting, the station for the plants should be thoroughly drained; for though the plants delight in plenty of moisture, both to the roots and foliage, they do not like it in a stagnant state. The best time to plant out is in March; and the stronger the plant is at the time, the greater the success that will attend it during the first season. The Passifloras, like all climbing plants, flower the better for not being too strictly trained; indeed, they should be allowed to ramble a little, and the branches to hang in loose festoons. The only pruning is to cut the young wood boldly back at the close of the flowering season. With the roots planted in a little heat, on a tank, or in the plant stove, and the branches trained into the greenhouse, many of the Passifloras will flower beautifully in the greenhouse or conservatory in the summer months; and thus they may be viewed in a much more enjoyable temperature than in the damp plant stove. Before the plants commence growth in the spring, remove as much of the old soil from around the roots as possible, and replace it with proper compost. Liquid manure may also be applied occasionally. Through the growing season, Passifloras are propagated by cuttings of the half-ripened wood in sandy loam, the pots being placed in a brisk bottom heat.—A.

THE CULTURE OF ALPINE PLANTS.
THE PRIMULA.

THE genus Primula is an important one in Ornamental Gardening; and, indeed, the natural order to which it belongs is pre-eminently distinguished for the beauty and variety of its cultivated plants. Primula affords some of the prettiest things for flower-garden decoration that are at present in the hands of cultivators. The species, *P. auricula*, in its highly improved condition, maintains its character as a standard "florists' flower;" while, in its unsophisticated form, it appears as a charm-

L

ing spring ornament of every garden border. The same remark is applicable to the Polyanthus, the origin of which is traced to the common wild Primrose of our woods (*P. vulgaris*), which has likewise given birth to a race of most beautiful " double Primroses." *P. sinensis*, in its numerous varieties, is one of the very best winter-flowering green-house plants that we possess; and long as it has been universally cultivated, its claims to attention are now coming more prominently into notice than they ever did before. It is the *Alpine* Primulas, however, that now merit our attention.

As in the case of many other plants, the gradual increase in the number and variety of this family, by successive introductions of new species, has led to a corresponding extension of the taste for their cultivation—so much so, that in some parts of the country we now find the Alpine Primulas no longer intermixed with miscellaneous collections of Alpine plants, but occupying a separate frame specially devoted to themselves. This is the way in which they ought to be treated to be grown satisfactorily; they form a most interesting collection, and present a gay appearance at an early season of the year, when gardens in general are bleak and barren, while the different species exhibit sufficient diversity, both in their foliage and flowers, to give the collection a most agreeable and refreshing variety of character, such as is unknown in many families of cultivated plants.

The frame for Alpine Primulas ought to be so placed, in regard to aspect, that the plants may freely obtain the benefit of the morning sun, but be completely sheltered from the scorching rays of afternoon. The treatment of stage Auriculas is, in many points, applicable to the culture of Primulas in general, which should occupy a cold shady situation throughout the hot season, and be carefully tended in regard to watering.

Whatever may be the merits or demerits of the " one-shift system," as a general system of culture, we regard it as a good rule of guidance in the treatment of Alpine plants; few of these succeed well if their roots are much interfered with, and frequent re-potting is therefore to be avoided, if strong, healthy, well-established plants are desired. The re-potting of Primulas (when necessary) may be done in the autumn, but a systematic yearly re-potting is by no means desirable. They succeed well in good maiden loam, with a small addition of *very* well decomposed leaf mould, and a little sand, if necessary, to give lightness and porosity to the other materials. Primulas, in general, like strong soil, but some of them will even succeed in very sandy soil, the plants, however, becoming weak.

Primulas are not fastidious in cultivation; soil is a matter of less consequence than may at first thought appear. The true secret of their successful culture is only to be obtained by a careful study of their habits; and a knowledge of the natural history of those species which grow wild in our own woods and pastures will afford important aid in the acquisition of this kind of knowledge.

The plants should be removed to the frame before the approach of winter, the pots being plunged in sand or some other porous material which affords facility of drainage, as perhaps nothing is more injurious to this family, in general, than a superfluity of water, to which cause alone the majority of cases of failure in their culture may be traced. Whenever the weather is mild, at whatever season, the sashes ought to be thrown off. In watering the plants after a day of heat and drought, it will be found advantageous to keep the sashes on for the night in order that the plants may benefit by the humidity, but where they are removed to a cool shaded situation for summer quarters, this will of course be unnecessary. Dry and bitter winds, as well as sudden changes to a low temperature, ought to be jealously guarded against by closing the sashes, especially during the spring season, when they are frequent, and when the plants are in a flowering condition.

Attention to the progressive development * of the plants, and the suiting of their circumstances thereto in the different stages, will be found to be the successful mode of treating the Alpine Primulas, as it is with Alpine plants in general. We therefore enter into no minute detail of seasonal operations, as these must be guided in a great measure by circumstances, which will vary in the case of each grower. Winter is a trying time for some of the species; keep them *drier* than Alpine plants are generally kept at that season, and as they often die down to the ground, do not throw out the pots, for their roots still retain life, and will push forth new and vigorous shoots on the return of spring.

* The term is not used in the " Vestigian " sense.

It is important to keep this in mind, as weak plants seem to be especially liable to die down in this manner, and are often thrown out as dead. The inexperienced grower is apt to deluge his plants with water, when he sees them exhibit a tendency to lose their leaves. This is the very worst thing that can be done; water must be withheld as much as possible, and it is a difficult matter indeed to kill Primulas by drought in the winter.

Primulas are readily propagated by division of the roots immediately after spring flowering, or in autumn. They ought not to be disturbed in early spring. The young plants should not be allowed to flower for some time, as it weakens them; and all autumn flowering, of even well-established plants, ought to be guarded against. They may also be propagated by seeds; many of the species produce these freely, and they all come truer from seeds than our wild Cowslips, Oxlips, and Primroses, which would seem to be all capable of being raised from the seeds of one another.

Few Alpine plants are better adapted than the genus Primula for cultivation amid the smoke of a city. Outside the window at which these remarks are penned, *Primula scotica* and *P. farinosa* are spreading out their leaves as robustly, and pushing up their flower stems as freely, as they did in their native wilds, whence they were removed not two years ago. More through accident than design, the soil in the seed-pan which contained them was allowed to get completely dry throughout the winter. No sooner was water applied in March, than they, along with *Saxifraga hirta*, pushed forth vigorously.

One of the most recent additions to the genus Primula is *P. sikkimensis*, which we owe to the labours of the indefatigable Dr. Hooker in Sikkim-Himalaya. He styles it "the pride of all the Alpine Primulas, inhabiting wet boggy places, at elevations of from 12 to 17,000 feet, at Lachen and Lachlong, covering acres with a yellow carpet in May and June." Sir William Hooker, in the *Botanical Magazine* (t. 4597), describes it as the *tallest* Primula in cultivation, and very different from any species hitherto described. It may possibly prove quite hardy and suitable for the herbaceous border; but it will for many years be too rare and interesting a beauty to be regarded otherwise than as a first-rate Alpine. Mr. Smith styles it as a "free growing" species. With us it died down to the ground last winter, and revived again with the genial warmth of April.

In a genus like the present, where every species is an object of beauty and interest in the eyes of the cultivator, it is difficult to make a *selection* of what the nurserymen call "approved sorts." Setting aside the whole race of florists' Primulas (Auriculas, Polyanthuses, and Double Primroses), together with those suitable for flower-border decoration, we enumerate twenty kinds well worthy of attention, and which will be found to exhibit the leading features of form and colour belonging to this attractive family. Those marked with an asterisk are particularly interesting:—

P. capitata.	* P. involucrata.
P. ciliata purpurata.	P. marginata major.
P. cortusoides.	P. minima.
* P. denticulata.	* P. Munroi.
P. elatior cærulea.	P. nivalis.
P. farinosa.	P. pusilla.
P. farinosa alba.	P. scotica.
P. helvetica.	P. sibirica.
P. hirsuta.	* P. sikkimensis.
P. integrifolia.	* P. Stuartii.

In recommending the plants to be at once potted in large-sized pots, we would not be understood to advocate a practice having a tendency to render facilities of thorough drainage less perfect. Drainage is a vital point in the cultivation of these plants, and it ought to be kept in view that the larger the pot is, the greater the necessity for good drainage. These, like most other Alpine plants, do well in shallow pots, the value of which in horticulture generally is too little known. They allow of the free horizontal development of the roots, which is decidedly more natural than that allowed of by the pots usually in use. *Depth* is not necessary for most plants, but the free spread of their rootlets is essential for their well-being. It is not to be expected that a plant can continue in healthy vital action when its rootlets are concentrated at one point within the narrow bottom of a flower-pot, an occurrence which the pot, in its usual form, is certainly peculiarly well fitted to induce.—G.

EPIDENDRUM REPLICATUM.

THIS very pretty species of Epidendrum was exhibited at one of the Chiswick Fetes last year, by S. Rucker, Esq., of Wandsworth, to whom we are indebted for the opportunity of figuring it. The pseudobulbs are crowned by the ensiform or narrowly - elongate lance-shaped leaves, from between which proceeds the flower scape, four feet long, the upper half forming a large branched panicle. The flowers, though not gaudy, are very pretty, and being numerous, they render this species ornamental. The sepals are cuneate-spathulate, with a mucro dull yellowish brown; the petals are spathulate, narrowed below, mucronate above, of the same ground-colour as the sepals, and marked with a large chocolate-coloured blotch at the broad apex. The lip is white, veined with purple, three-lobed, the two lateral lobes large, oblong-ovate, appressed to the column at the base, spreading above; the middle lobe is cordate-acuminate, folded together backwards, and having a waved margin.

It is a stove epiphyte, and requires the same kind of treatment as other tropical orchidaceous plants.

Our figure represents one of the branches of the flowering panicle in its naturally pendent position, and of the natural size.

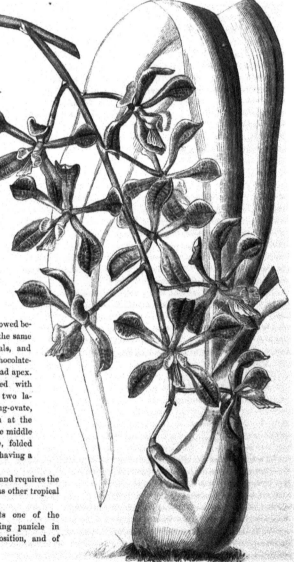

THE CULTURE OF FUCHSIA SERRATIFOLIA.

IT is somewhat extraordinary, yet notorious, that this princely Fuchsia, although grown in most plant establishments, is more noted for leaves than for blossoms; at least, I have seldom seen it in the perfection of which it is in reality capable; that is to say, a majestic shrub of some eight to ten feet high, possessing a full, bold, and prepossessing outline, and laden with its gorgeous tubes from the surface of the soil to the very points of every shoot.

We have two or three huge plants in tubs or large pots here, answering fully the above description, and one has been equally fine for three years; thus proving a settled and durable habit. Now, in my opinion, this plant, in its general treatment, is a pretty good illustration of the old adage, "killed with kindness." It is notorious to most of our practical men, that no inconsiderable portion of our plants, derived from climes where solar light, heat, moisture, &c., exist in a somewhat different ratio to each other as compared with Britain, are, in spite of the advancements of modern science, and the most earnest practice, compelled to assume a kind of anomalism or contrariety of character which does not belong to them in their native clime. Hence our "leggy" plants, or "drawn," as gardeners term them.

The subjecting some plants to an undue excitability, too, at improper periods,—plants which really enjoy a periodical rest in their own climate,—is another fertile source of weakly or over-leafy specimens; and the plant in question is, as far as I have observed it, an instance of this. It frequently happens that gardeners in the country, whose main business is to grow the substantials of a family the year round, are both short of structures and short of heat to what buildings they do possess. The necessary consequence is, that numbers of plants which, in the plant-houses about the metropolis, are taken as much care of in winter as in summer, are by such men "crammed away" in the back parts of vineries, where, it is almost needless to observe, they are sure to suffer neglect, not by choice but necessity. Now, it turns out that this kind of treatment, exceedingly injurious to many a plant, is as well suited to others; and if gardeners in general, thus situated, could be prevailed on to give lists of those things (from the experience of years) which had been successfully cultivated under such necessities, it would at once show what plants had naturally been injured with kindness, and would even teach our plantsmen a lesson.

The fine plants I have here alluded to have, indeed, been annually subjected to this kind of treatment, at first through necessity, and now through choice and system. Whilst they were a novelty, I used to keep them warm (as gardeners say) all the year, and the only reward was abundance of the most luxuriant foliage; but few blossoms. Their present condition and treatment is this:—The large specimens are composed of one strong and woody main stem, and several subordinate ones; all, however, of sound and matured character: that is to say, wood of some four or five years old, firm, and possessing a shelling character of bark, which appears as though it would fain ape that of some of our timber trees. When profuse blossoming is past, which, with us, happens about Christmas, they are allowed to sink into a kind of vegetable dishabille, which would greatly alarm any young gentleman taking his first lessons in horticultural matters; they are supplied with water in a most niggardly way, thrust away into any corner in-doors, where frost and a coaxing temperature are alike unknown, and the consequence is, they cast almost every leaf. And now, I have no doubt, the necessary amount of solidification becomes confirmed, through the total absence of all exciting or stimulating causes; there is no expenditure of the vital action for many weeks, and our rustic, uncouth, and ill-used Fuchsia wakes, in due time, like a giant refreshed. I must now beg the reader to take a kind of magical bound over some six or eight weeks, when a thorough reversal of practice takes place. They are now tumbled out of their tubs or pots with little ceremony; a portion of the loosened soil dislodged, and re-potted in the very same box or pot again; in fact, what gardeners term a partial disrooting is practised. Thenceforward, the plants are "set to work;" they are introduced to any warm corner in any house which happens to be at liberty; perhaps the Peach-house, or it may be a Vinery, only taking care to secure not only warmth but atmospheric moisture. The plant now is speedily all activity; for, of all the plants of a partially deciduous character, this Fuchsia appears to me the most excitable after a sound rest.   .

From this period they are coaxed into a most liberal growth by all available means; the chief conditions requisite being the usual appliances of warmth, light, and atmospheric moisture. In a short time they become so prolific in suckers, side shoots, &c., that thinning-out has to be practised; and this is so managed as that a due succession of blossoms is secured from the tub or box to the very apex. Long before Midsummer they are blossoming abundantly, and means being taken previously to "harden them off," they are henceforward set out in the flower-garden, in a light and sheltered situation. I may here mention that, from the moment the trees blossom freely, liquid manure is constantly plied, weak and clear. Such is the course of culture which produces them in the highest perfection from Midsummer until Christmas; and little more need be said.

It may here be observed that no plant is more impatient of frost, in whatever stage, especially when in full blossom. The patron of this noble tree must consequently lay his account with a perfect immunity from this gardening meddler. Towards the middle of September, therefore, we get our prime pots in-doors, or else cover, on the least suspicion. As to soil, one-half strong turfy loam, and the other half compounded of leaf soil, cow manure (old), and heath soil, will grow them in the highest perfection, taking care to drain them well.—ROBERT ERRINGTON, *Oulton Park.*

CULTURE OF THE SIKKIM RHODODENDRONS.

THE very general interest excited by these plants, from which the hybridizer may hope for a very great addition to our present splendid hybrids, may render a few remarks on what I have found to be a good method of treating them not without interest; the more so as I have heard from various quarters that they are considered "miffey," that is, apt to die off during the dormant season. I do not doubt but that this has in a great measure been caused by over-anxiety to grow them on into large plants by the aid of a strong heat, thereby inducing a tenderness of constitution which proves fatal to many of them when removed to a colder place to rest during the dormant season. Having lost only four plants out of nearly four hundred, I think I am qualified to speak from experience. My seeds were sown early in June, 1850, in shallow pans of peat, well drained; they were placed on the front stand of a vinery, then in the process of colouring the fruit, and as that involved the admission of a great amount of air, of course the temperature was not much above the average of summer weather. As soon as the plants had made two leaves, they were very carefully pricked out at one inch apart, some in shallow pans, and some in four-inch pots, which latter, in the upshot, produced the strongest plants. After standing in a shady part of the vinery for a few days, they were returned to the front stand, and remained until the first week in October. Some had made six and eight leaves, but the majority only four; by this time also most of both pots and pans were covered with a close short moss all through the plants, which, however unsightly, and indicative, as many would say, of bad treatment, I judged best to leave undisturbed, and therefore removed them to a cold pit, where they received only the ordinary treatment as regards covering, and more than once had to submit to several degrees of frost. Here they remained until early in February, 1851, having received scarcely any water through the winter. At that time they were removed to a fresh started vinery, and after a few days I commenced by potting the largest singly in small sixties, the next size three in such a pot, and the smallest six or eight in a six-inch pot, and the whole were placed on shelves of the vinery. Of course the rooting process was anxiously watched, and as soon as the fibres began to show, they were shifted into a size larger pot, and eventually by the end of June they were nearly all potted singly in pots of various sizes. At this time the question of their future disposal became urgent, and we reasoned that as hothouse plants they were useless, and we could only find greenhouse and conservatory room for one or two of a sort. The greater part must eventually be trusted to the tender mercies of our uncertain climate, and it was agreed to educate them for that purpose. The whole were, consequently, transferred to a portion of a new cold pit, kept close for a few days, and then gradually hardened so as to bear full exposure, and they were only protected from heavy dashing rains. By the beginning of October they were dormant, and looked very strong and healthy. *R. Aucklandii* had grown to nearly a foot, *R. Dalhousiæ* and *R. argenteum* six inches, *R. niveum* and *R. Falconerii* to about three inches, with large woolly reticulated handsome foliage; the rest averaged from one to three inches. *R. ciliatum* is a perfect gem as to foliage, which is close, compact, dark green, and looks as hardy as a Ponticum. *R. Edgworthii* is another very distinct foliage, so also is *R. campylocarpum*; indeed, they all promise to introduce a new feature in the way of foliage. When dormant, I wedged in some damp moss very tightly into all the interstices between the pots, in which state they remain, and are now, with the exception of four, started into a strong and healthy growth; I give them a constant circulation of air, and very often full exposure, and do not intend to let them have any artificial heat again. I am quite aware that by hard forcing there may be much larger plants, but will they stand as fair a chance when submitted to all the vicissitudes of our weather, which the greater portion of them must eventually come to? I think not.—JOHN COX, *Redleaf*.

THE FRUCTIFICATION OF LICHENS, AND OTHER CRYPTOGAMS.

THE development of the fructification of Lichens has been lately brought under the notice of the Botanical Society of Edinburgh, by Wyville T. C. Thomson, Esq., who defines the *spores* as being ultimate germinating cellules, the product of the division of the compound granular cell which is the result of the union of the conjugating cells in cryptogamous plants; *sporidia* as compound granular cells, the product of the union of conjugating cells; *proto-sporidia* as the simple cells of Lichens, in which the two conjugating cells are afterwards formed; *gonidia* as free cellules, derived from, and part of, the cellular tissue of the parent plant, capable of continuing, to a certain extent, their development when free from the parent, without the intervention of the true generative act of conjugation (the analogues of free buds or bulbils in flowering plants); and the *pro-embryo* in Ferns and other Cryptogams as the cellular expansion formed by the development of the gonidium, and containing the conjugating cells. This pro-embryo, then, corresponds to the ordinary cellular expansion of Lichens. The fronds of *Lecanora tartarea*, a crustaceous Lichen, holding a middle place between the foliaceous and the pulverulent species, show first a mass of elongated, more or less filiform cells, mostly empty, delicate, and of a light grey colour; and resting immediately above these are groups of rounded cells filled with bright-coloured chlorophyll, scattered in small irregular patches, or as isolated cells among the grey tissue. Above the green cells is another layer of transparent tissue, closely resembling that below it. In *Lecanora* we have, above all, a layer of somewhat flatter cells, forming an imperfect epidermal covering. The green tissue appears to represent the living and actively vegetating part of the Lichen—determining by its development the form of the frond, and giving origin to all the other tissues. The green cells termed gonidia frequently accumulate in masses, burst through the cuticular layer, and appear as a green powder on the surface of the plant. In this state the single gonidia are capable of continuing the powers of cell development at a distance from the parent, forming round themselves the grey hygrometric tissue; and, like the parent plant, producing at length true reproductive organs. This is by no means a solitary instance of the formation of these from developing cells in the vegetable kingdom. We have in the Ferns an instance of another order propagating through gonidia. In the Ferns, cells, long called spores, are found within modified leaves, or parts of leaves. These cells, when placed in favourable circumstances of heat and moisture, develop, by nuclear division, a small cellular expansion (still part of the parent plant, as no process of cell conjugation has intervened), called the pro-embryo. On this pro-embryo two cellules, of different character, appear; an union takes place between the different cells, and the product is an ovoid body, the sporidium. Within this sporidium by nuclear division, spores are produced, only one of which comes to perfection, the others proving abortive. The spore is developed, in situ, feeding upon the pro-embryo, as upon a cotyledon, and forming the new Fern. Sections made through the apothecia of *Lecanora* at various stages of growth, show, at an early stage, a hollow sphere of delicate rounded cells (perithecium), surrounding a number of elongated filiform cells (paraphyses), arranged vertically in a rounded mass. Advancing a little farther in development, the cells of the perithecium above the centre of the mass of paraphyses have given way, and among the paraphyses a few flask-shaped, delicate cells (asci), are visible, closely resembling paraphyses distended, and filled with mucus or cytoblastema. Shortly the fluid contents become slightly granulated, and the granules eventually aggregate into cytoblasts. Round these cytoblasts, delicate rounded cells are formed, which take at length an ovoid form, and we may generally easily perceive within them two free nuclei. Round these nuclei two secondary cells are developed, which gradually increase in size, so as nearly to fill up the parent cell. They become filled with densely granular chlorophyll, and finally the two cells conjugate; that is to say, the walls of both cells give way, and the granular contents amalgamate, nearly filling up the parent cell. The result of this conjugation is a large compound granular cell. Watching its further progress, we observe the granules becoming more and more distinct and defined, till at length the mother-cell bursts, and the contained cellules escape; at the same time the ascus gives way, and the cellules are dispersed as spores, to originate new individuals. Mr. Thomson considers the conjugation of cells as being in all orders of plants the type of the generative act.

SCIENTIFIC GLEANINGS.

THE variegated-leaved variety of *Hydrangea japonica* is a novelty deserving of cultivation in collections of curious plants. It differs from the typical plant simply in the variegation, the leaves having an irregularly-defined white border. M. Van Houtte has recently published a very excellent figure of it, in the *Flores des Serres*. It is a vigorous plant, without the diseased appearance sometimes borne by variegated plants, and especially those in which the variegation is marginal.

Potentilla striata formosissima is a beautiful new garden variety of a now favourite race of hardy border flowers, of which many seedlings, of a very ornamental character, are in cultivation. This was raised by M. Ch. Van Geert, of Anvers, from seed collected indiscriminately from *atrosanguinea*, *Applebyana*, *Hopwoodiana*, *Menziesii*, *Russelliana*, and *insignis*. Its parent is supposed to be *insignis* fertilized by *Russelliana*. The flowers are large, bold, yellow, much blotched, streaked and veined with crimson. It will be a very ornamental plant, and, of course, quite hardy.

Captain Cook's Araucaria (noticed under the name of *A. Cookii* at p. 13) has been figured in the *Botanical Magazine*, by Sir W. J. Hooker, under the name of *A. columnaris*, which name he has restored in accordance with the botanical law of priority, the "specific" name of *columnaris* having been that first applied to the plant. It was called *Cupressus columnaris* by Foster, from its column-like appearance. The tree is most nearly allied to *A. excelsa*; and, like it, will no doubt prove tender, though a very elegant plant.

It is difficult to give a clear and well-defined idea of *Beauty* in horticulture. Lessing, Wathley, and others, have given definitions more or less ingenious; but beauty, considered as far as it is in relation with the art of gardening, does not always show that harmony in its parts which many theorists believe. Cast your eyes on this plant, whose stem is so frail and fruit so heavy,—on this Rose, whose buds bend down the feeble branch by which it is supported; is there any harmony of parts? No! And this leads us to acknowledge the fact that beauty can also exist without harmony of parts. Beauty exists in all kinds of form; but, perhaps, most frequently in the round form. A straight line in a landscape may please the eye, but a curved line is always agreeable. Plantations of trees scattered over the mountains, descending to the valleys, and dispersed in varied masses, is more acceptable to our view, as a forest, than a monotonous level wood.—*La Belgique Horticole.*

S. T. Rosenberg del. & Imes.

Printed by G. F. Stafford, London.

Castrolobium pyramidale

GASTROLOBIUM PYRAMIDALE.*

THIS is one of the most decidedly distinct species of *Gastrolobium* which has come under our notice for some time past, and as to form it into a fine specimen it will require peculiar treatment, a few remarks on that subject may not be out of place. It is a strong free-growing plant, but like many plants of that character, it is liable to run away, or as cultivators term it become "leggy;" and hence, to form it into a compact specimen, it must be grown freely, and cut down repeatedly, until a good foundation or bottom is formed. Now in forming a good bottom of a plant various schemes are resorted to; with some plants frequent stopping of the young shoots will cause the plant to become bushy, but with others, as it only leads to enfeebled growth, frequent stopping of the young shoots is neither advisable nor necessary. In such cases the best method to pursue is to encourage the plants to grow as wildly and unrestrictedly as possible, and then when they are properly established to cut them boldly back to the lowest bud that is likely to produce a shoot. Under such treatment they will produce strong vigorous shoots, and such cut back two or three times will form first-rate specimens. It is thus that fine bushy plants of the *Hovea Celsi*, and other hard-wooded plants are procured, and this in a great measure is the secret of success in the management of most of the upright growing plants seen in such rude bushes at the metropolitan exhibitions. We have seen a single stem of *Hovea Celsi*, when cut close down, throw up sixteen shoots, some of them four feet high, and form in one season a specimen such as most cultivators might justly be proud of. The subject of our present notice would no doubt succeed under similar treatment, but then as it is a new plant not out of the hands of Messrs. Henderson, we must wait some time before we can get a strong plant to cut down. However, those who can afford to buy two plants may try to train or stop one into proper form, while the other may be allowed to run wild, as we have before directed. The soil most suitable for Gastrolobiums is rich turfy peat broken small, and intermixed with charcoal potsherds and gritty sand, but this kind, being a strong grower after it is thoroughly established, may have a sixth or eighth of nice mellow turfy loam added to the compost. Start the plants into active growth in February, and keep them by a moist atmosphere and a temperature of from forty to fifty degrees, growing as vigorously as you can until July. The plants should then be placed in a sheltered situation in the open air, and be gradually inured to the full sun, to which they may be exposed until they are housed for the winter. Shift the plants as they require more pot-room, but be cautious not to over-pot late in the season. This class of plants is liable to the attacks of red spider and sometimes thrip, but if each plant is placed upon its side and syringed with clean water, they may be soon cleared of such pests. The plants should be laid upon the grass, or a clean mat, while they are being syringed, and upon no account should they be syringed in the house, or many of the insects may rise again and attack the plants.—A.

This magnificent greenhouse shrub has been raised by Messrs. Henderson of the Edgeware Road, from seeds forwarded by Mr. Drummond from the Swan River colony. It will become a most valuable exhibition plant, from its bold, striking habit, and the size and very rich colour of its numerous blossoms. Our drawing was made in the latter part of April in the present year.

It forms a very handsome evergreen shrub, of pyramidal habit, growing four or five feet or more in height, the branches stout and erect, more or less woolly, and densely so in the young state. The leaves grow in whorls of three, and spread horizontally; they are oval-obtuse, sometimes rotundate, one and a half to two and a half inches long, terminated by a short rigid mucro, densely woolly on both surfaces when young, but becoming at length smooth on the upper side; they are stalked, the petioles being about half an inch long, and densely woolly. The stipules are three-fourths of an inch long, setaceous, becoming recurved, at first brown and woolly, but soon shrivelling and becoming

* *Gastrolobium pyramidale*, n. sp.—Young branches and leaves, stipules, peduncles, bracts, and calyces, densely tomentose; stipules long setaceous recurved; leaves stalked, in whorls of three, one and a half to two and a half inches long, oval-obtuse or rotundate, mucronate, at length smooth above; racemes axillary, densely capitular, the peduncles somewhat shorter than the leaves; bracts dark brown, the lower trifid, the upper obovate mucronate; calyx teeth brown, the upper and lateral pairs oblique; pedicels shorter than the calyx; ovary subsessile villose.—M.

black, but not at once cast off. The inflorescence is axillary, the racemes forming dense globular heads, on woolly peduncles, which are somewhat shorter than the leaves, and have nearly the same horizontal direction. The bracts are caducous, dark brown, and shaggy, those at the base of the raceme trifid, with the lateral lobes longest, the upper ones obovate mucronate. The flowers are shortly stalked; the calyx bell-shaped, with five teeth, of which the pair forming the upper lip are slightly broader, and, as well as the next opposite pair, are obliquely ovate acuminate, the lower tooth being equal; the calyx is permanently shaggy, with loose hairs, which are dark coloured on the teeth, and much longer on the upper side of the two oblique pairs than on the lower. The corolla is large, bearing a proportion to the broad foliage and stout habit, and is of a deep rich órange-yellow, marked with dark maroon; the standard is sub-rotund, emarginate, (five-eighths broad, one-half inch deep), clear orange-yellow, with a small horse-shoe rayed band of reddish brown around a small yellow base; the wings are oblong-spathulate (three-eighths long), deep yellow, covering the boat-shaped, maroon-coloured keel. The style slightly exceeds the stamens, and is twice as long as the calyx. The ovary is two-ovuled, subsessile, villose, half as long as the calyx.—M.

---+---

CAN LARGE SPECIMENS OF HARD-WOODED PLANTS BE GROWN IN SMALL POTS?

IT is now about nine years since I first called attention to the growth of plants upon the large or "one shift system," as it was at that time very inappropriately called. How far the art of cultivation has improved since, the metropolitan exhibitions fully testify; for though there may be many who deny the practicability of the plan, the large shift system has answered in the hands of good gardeners, and even bad ones must have profited by it. My object, however, in this essay, is to direct the attention of cultivators in an opposite direction, and to enquire whether it is not possible to grow specimen plants in pots much smaller than those generally used, and to some extent considered indispensable. We all know that some years back Pelargoniums and Calceolarias were grown in large pots, at least in pots very much larger than those allowed at the present time. But were the plants finer than they have been since growers have been confined to eight-inch pots? Though not a grower for exhibition at that time, I think I may unhesitatingly assert that Pelargoniums were never shown in finer condition than during the past season, for some of the specimens produced by Mr. Cock, of Chiswick, were matchless, and, as was remarked at the time, he "quite eclipsed himself." I recollect, some years back, when Mr. Cock used to show magnificent plants, but very deficient in bloom; but in small pots no person has bloomed them more superbly, not only for quantity, but also for quality, of flower. The same might also be said of all the leading growers, for, though some may have had a "miss," the majority of exhibitors have presented Pelargoniums in very creditable condition. Now the question naturally presents itself,—How has this been accomplished? Why, by using composts in a highly concentrated form, by feeding, in addition, with manure water, or, in a word, by putting as much food into a small pot as used to be contained in a large one. This is the secret of success with soft-wooded plants, and can the same result be attained with hard-wooded ones? With those who have not studied the subject, the question will be answered in the negative, at once, and they will "whistle me down the wind" as a simpleton for proposing it; but others, who look beyond the surface of things, if they look to their own collections, or to the collections of neighbours, may possibly recollect plants that have been growing in small pots for a number of years, and yet, at the present time, have not a very discreditable appearance. Many of the London exhibitors will recollect a large specimen of *Erica ampullacea*, which Mr. Bruce, gardener to Boyd Miller, Esq., used to show in fine condition every season. That plant was grown in a pot considerably smaller than was generally considered necessary, and I think, the last time I saw the plant at Chiswick, Mr. Bruce told me it had not been shifted for either five or seven years. The large Heaths shown seven years back by Mr. May, gardener to E. Goodhart, Esq., were remarkable for the smallness of their pots as compared with the size of plants, yet some of these plants are still alive, and form not the least conspicuous objects in the noble collections annually produced by W. Quilter, Esq., of Norwood.

It is rather remarkable that these plants were not only grown in small pots, but they were also grown in finely-sifted soil; for as Mr. May gave the smallest shift possible when he did shift, he was compelled to use fine soil; but apart from the necessity of the matter, I believe he had not, nor has not any objection to sifted soil for plant-growing. I am not supposing the plants are going to grow as well in small pots as in large ones—that is quite another matter; but my object is to show, both by precept and example, that very admirable plants may be grown in small pots, and that, I think, will be an object gained by the amateur cultivator, who has not conveniences for growing large specimens, but who, at the same time, would be delighted with really well-grown small ones.

Of course, it cannot be denied that soft-wooded plants have an advantage over hard-wooded ones, in being annually cut down, shook out of the old soil, and disrooted, whereby they have a fresh start and fresh soil every season; but they also present a much larger surface of foliage to the evaporating influence of the atmosphere, and hence require much greater attention in watering. Some of my large specimen Pelargoniums, on hot, dry days in summer, require watering three or four times between morning and night, to prevent their drooping; and I think I may safely say, a large specimen in an eight-inch pot will suck up four to six quarts of water in twenty-four hours, and hence must evaporate at the same rate. Hard-wooded plants, though presenting a smaller evaporating surface, will require less attention and less watering, but at the same time, if the foliage is to be kept green and good, they must never know the actual want of water. The leading requisites in the growth of plants in small pots are properly prepared composts, good potting, and an occasional supply of manure-water; and these desiderata I will consider under separate heads.

First, then, Soil. This, for hard-wooded plants, consists of peat, procured from upland situations; and, in selecting it, great judgment is necessary, for it is not sufficient to say procure it from Wimbledon Common, Epping, or Wrotham, for though peat of the finest possible quality may be found, it is not unusual to see great rubbish carted from each of these places; therefore, select with care, for it is better to spend a few hours in selecting good soil, than in carting home that which is worthless. The best time to procure soil is in the autumn, and it should then be placed in ridges, and in such a manner that while the rain is penetrating the mass, the air has free access between each turf. Thus prepared, it will be fit for use in a few weeks; but if it can be prepared for twelve months before using, it will be so much the better—indeed, those who intend to grow plants properly, must always keep a good stock of properly aerated soil on hand. Peat soils differ in texture; some is hard, as that from Wimbledon and Wanstead, while that procured from Wrotham, in Kent, and Spring Park, near Croydon, is light and spongy, but very rich. In the light peat, plants grow very vigorously for a time, especially if it is used in a rough state, but it soon gets sour, and the plants die off almost without a moment's notice. In the hard peat, on the contrary, plants grow moderately, but that is poor, and hence, if the plants suffer for the want of water once or twice, the leaves turn yellow, and assume a sickly appearance, from which it is difficult to recover them. I therefore recommend the hard and soft peat to be used in equal proportions, selecting it with the greatest care, and rejecting every portion which does not appear perfectly clean and healthy.

Break the soil into small pieces not larger than a hazel nut, and pass the whole through a sieve with half-inch meshes, and take care to make every portion pass through. Then add sand and charcoal and potsherds broken small sufficient to secure the porosity of the mass, and have some of the material standing by so that an additional quantity may be added to such plants as require it. Quick growing, soft-wooded Heaths do not require so much sand as the *aristatas, obbatas*, and the like. Some of the more free growing New Holland plants will be benefited by having a little nice mellow turfy loam added to the peat and sand. Pimeleas of all kinds, but more especially the fast-growing ones delight in loam, so do Polygalas and Bossiæas, and even Boronias are not injured by a little of it. Leaf mould I rarely use, not even for soft-wooded plants, as it is full of insects, and unless formed of good clean leaves is rarely what it ought to be.

The use of rough turfy soil has been carried to a wild extreme, and has caused the death of more plants than any other thing I know of, for though the plants may grow vigorously for a time, the rough soil, as decomposition proceeds, is sure to become a sour soapy mass, in which the roots perish the first time they get a little too much water. Mechanical action, which was the object of the use of rough soil, may be attained in other ways, and it is much better to depend upon pot-sherds and charcoal broken small and mixed with sand through the mass, to secure porosity, than upon the interstices between large lumps of soil. If the soil is broken small it is the same through-out, and not a stratum of soapy sodden soil in one part of the pots and a sand heap in others, and hence the roots make steady and regular progress.

Now, what is good potting? A few years back we should have been told it consisted of tumbling the soil into the pots in as large lumps as possible; but, in the preceding remarks, I have shown that this was an error which I believe most gardeners have learned to avoid. The first requisite in good potting is properly prepared composts; the second, clean porous pots; and the third, soil made as firm as it can be by the use of the fingers and thumb, but without resorting to the ramming system of com-pression. As the object of these remarks is especially to direct attention to the growth of plants in small pots, of course it will be desirable to commence with the plants in a young state, and hence they should be selected while they are in three-inch pots, taking care to pick out those of sturdy and vigorous growth, and with plenty of healthy roots. The stem of a good plant should be short and thick, the branches sturdy and evenly distributed, the roots fresh and vigorous, enveloping the ball in great abundance, but not matted together. When a plant is in this state, pot it immediately into one a size larger, taking care to make the soil firm, but never elevating the ball above the rim of the pot.

After potting, the young plants should be placed in a cold frame or pit, be shaded during bright sunshine, and receive sufficient water at the root, and a light sprinkling overhead in the afternoon of every warm day. Of course care will be taken to keep the plants clear of insects, mildew, and dead foliage, and as cleanliness is the stepping-stone of success in plant management not an atom of extraneous matter of any kind should be allowed to accumulate either upon the plants, the pots, the soil, or the glass. As the plants progress in growth take care to stop and regulate the branches, and also, if you have courage to do so, denude them of their flowers for the first season, which will add much to their strength. When the new pots get full of roots assist the plants with a little WEAK liquid manure about twice a week, but be cautious in its use, and on no account apply it except to plants in free growth. The best manure water for all choice plants consists of sheep or deer dung and soot, in the proportions of four pecks of the former to one peck of the soot, mixing the whole with boiling soft water into a paste, and then filling the tub up with a hogshead of soft water. Keep this stirred daily for a week, and then throw in two or three lumps of quick lime, which will make the water quite clear. If it can be so managed the water should be drawn off by means of a tap, and it must be used in the proportion of one gallon of manure water to five gallons of soft water. Pits and frames may sometimes be sprinkled with this manure water, as the ammonia evolved will be found very beneficial to the plants. However be cautious, enough is as good as a feast, and great speed is not always progress in plant management. Shift the plants as they require more room, until they get into six-inch pots, after which it will be necessary to resort to liquid manure to make up for large quantities of soil, and then for free growing plants it is an experiment worth trying whether very weak liquid manure should not be used at all times in the growing season. In speaking of growing in small pots I propose that the largest sized pot should not exceed thirteen inches, or, as they are generally called, No. 8's. In pots of that size I am sure very hand-some plants might be grown, and will be when proper pains are taken, and cultivators once take the trouble to try how much they can attain in a small space.

When the plants get of pretty good size, and the pots are full of roots, no doubt they may be much assisted by protecting the pots from the scorching rays of the sun by a cover of some kind, such as placing each pot within a larger one, or by hanging a shade along the front of the pots. One of Mrs. Lawrence's late gardeners once suggested to me the propriety of having a separate shade for each pot, composed of oiled canvas, calico, or something of that kind, and though pots in petticoats may seem rather ridiculous things, I am not quite sure that such a plan might not be adopted to some extent with advantage. However, I throw these crude notions on the waters of public opinion, satisfied that if I can only induce cultivators of hard-wooded plants to make the experiment they will soon produce plants as matchless in form in small pots as they have hitherto done in large ones. The Pelargonium growers looked upon small pots as quite out of the question; to grow large specimens in them was an impossibility, but time has answered their doubts, and success has crowned their efforts.—W. P. AYRES.

New Garden Plants.

ACANTHOSTACHYS STROBILACEA, *Klotzsch*. Cone-flowered Acanthostachys.—Order Bromeliaceæ (Bromelwort tribe).—A stove perennial, with long narrow curved scurfy spiny leaves, and a long simple mealy scape, surmounted by a cone of yellow flowers, in orange-coloured prickly bracts, a pair of long channelled leafy spathes growing at the base of the inflorescence. It is a Brazilian plant, and is cultivated in the continental gardens.

ACACIA SQUAMATA, *Lindley*. Scaly Acacia.—Order Leguminosæ, § Mimoseæ (Leguminous plants).—A remarkable erect - growing shrub, branched, and having the appearance of being leafless. The branches are slender, terete, flexuose, somewhat glaucous. The leaves are of the form and thickness of the branches, stiff, slightly divergent, about an inch long, bearing in their axils a scaly bud. The branches thus *appear* to consist of a series of terminal buds seated in the forks of dichotomous branches; the apex of the leaves is slightly recurved and mucronate. The racemes are short, and bear two or three globular heads of deep yellow flowers; these spring from the axils of the leaves, and issue from the bud of boat-shaped brown membranous scales. This interesting plant has been introduced by Mr. Drummond from the Swan River, and has been raised and blossomed by Messrs. Henderson, of the Pine-apple Nursery. Like the other Acacias, it blooms in early spring.

HAKEA MYRTOIDES, *Meisner*. Myrtle-like Hakea. — Order Proteaceæ (Protead tribe).—A rather pretty evergreen greenhouse shrub, with myrtle-like foliage, and red flowers nestled among the leaves. It grows a foot and half high. Native of the Swan River settlement, and introduced by Drummond. It flowers about February.

HAKEA SCOPARIA, *Meisner*. Broom-like Hakea.—Order Proteaceæ (Protead tribe).—A greenhouse shrub from Swan River. It bears long slender quill-like leaves, and sessile axillary heads of pale yellow flowers.

PENTARHAPHIA VERRUCOSA, *Decaisne*. Warted-stemmed Pentar-

ACACIA SQUAMATA.

haphia.—Order Gesneraceæ (Gesnerwort tribe.)—A neat stiff shrubby stove evergreen shrub, the oval leaves of which are bullate (blistered), and the flowers tubular, downy externally, and coloured scarlet. It comes from Cuba, and was introduced by Linden. Schiedweiler proposed to call this plant *Conradia verrucosa,* but Dr. Lindley's genus Pentarhaphia has the priority.

BESCHORNERIA TUBIFLORA, *Kunth.* Tube-flowered Beschorneria.—Order Amaryllidaceæ (Amaryllid tribe).— An Agave-like cool greenhouse plant from Mexico, cultivated at Kew. The leaves are radical, and eighteen inches to two feet long. The scape rises four feet, and bears a many-flowered erect raceme. The flowers are drooping, brownish-purple externally, green within. It blossomed in February, 1852.

TRICHOPILIA ALBIDA, *Wendland.* White Trichopil.—Order Orchidaceæ (Orchid tribe).—A stove epiphyte. Compared with the other species of Trichopils now known, this is of little value. The flowers are pale, the sepals and petals are yellowish, and the lip white, with a blotch of crowded yellow ochre-coloured spots. It is allied to *T. tortilis,* but the pseudo bulbs are longer, and the petals scarcely twisted. It comes from Caraccas, and has been flowered at Birmingham during the past year.

CYCNOCHES MUSCIFERUM, *Lindley.* Fly-bearing Cycnoches.—Order Orchidaceæ (Orchid tribe).—An interesting stove epiphyte, not, however, very showy. It looks like a diminutive form of *C. barbatum.* The plants bear an upright loose raceme of pale-coloured flowers, minutely speckled with brown ; and their resemblance to some kind of fly is striking. It is from Columbia, and had been obtained from Mr. Linden by Messrs. Rollison, with whom it blossoms in February.

LENNEA ROBINIOIDES, *Link, Klotzsch,* and *Otto.* Robinia-like Lennea.—Order Fabaceæ (Leguminous plants). —A greenhouse bush, three feet high, with pinnated distichous leaves, and pendulous axillary racemes of flowers as large as those of the Judas-tree, and of the same colour. It blossoms in May. It is a Mexican plant, and is grown in the Berlin gardens.

ODONTOGLOSSUM EHRENBERGII, *Klotzsch.* Ehrenberg's Odontoglot.—Order Orchidaceæ (Orchid tribe).—A very pretty dwarf stove epiphyte, resembling *O. Rossii.* It is of very dwarf, compact habit, and has white flowers, the sepals of which are banded with brown, and the lip acuminate. A large mass of it would have a very pretty appearance. It is Mexican, and was found by M. Ehrenberg on an Oak-tree, near San Onofro, on the banks of the Zimapore.

DENDROBIUM BIGIBBUM, *Lindley.* Bigibbous Dendrobe.—Order Orchidaceæ (Orchid tribe).—A very pretty epiphyte from tropical New Holland, introduced by Mr. Loddiges, with whom it flowered in January last. It has long fusiform stems, bearing near the end a few long narrow acute leaves, and terminated by an erect raceme of three or four rich purple flowers, which Dr. Lindley compares with those of *Bletia verecunda ;* the sepals are oblong acute, the petals broader, and roundish, and the lip has a kind of double chin at the base. It is allied to *D. Kingianum* and *D. elongatum,* but is much handsomer.

RYTIDOPHYLLUM OERSTEDTII, *Klotzsch.* Dr. Oersted's Rytidophyllum. — Order Gesneraceæ (Gesnerwort tribe).—A stove subshrub, of epiphytal habits, with oblique oblong leaves, and greenish hairy flowers spotted with purple, an inch and a half in length, with a bent swollen tube. It is a native of Central America, and was introduced by M. Warczewicz to the German gardens.

PASSIFLORA SICYOIDES, *Schlechtendal.* Sicyum-like Passion-flower.—Order Passifloraceæ (Passion-flower tribe). —This is the *P. odora* of Link and Otto. It is a slender hairy climber, with three-lobed leaves, and sweet-scented flowers, having a white corolla, and a coronet variegated with red. It is a native of Mexico, and was introduced by the late G. Barker, Esq., of Birmingham, with whom it first flowered in 1839.

NOVELTIES AT THE LONDON EXHIBITIONS.

THE inaugural Floral *fête* of the metropolis, held at Chiswick on the 9th ult., proves, at least, that plant culture is not at all on the decline. As a whole no finer exhibition was ever seen. To particularize :—the Azaleas were gorgeous, the Orchids varied and magnificent, the miscellaneous plants perfect in all respects, the Pelargoniums and pot Roses in considerable muster, and " well done," though the Roses were hardly expanded ; whilst *versus* the senseless objections which have been made to the new mode of showing florists' flowers in pots, there were Heartsease, which it did one's heart good to see, plants bearing each from a dozen to a score of magnificent flowers. These matters were varied by some finely-grown groups of exotic Ferns from Syon, and the garden of H. B. Ker, Esq. ; by variegated-leaved plants, especially a beautiful *Cissus* called *marmorea* or *discolor,* recently obtained from Java, from Messrs. Rollisson's Nursery ; by a fine pyramidal-grown Pelargonium, of a new light-coloured bedding variety called *citriodorum grandiflorum,* from Mr. Ayres ; and by a beautiful collection of *Anœctochilus* and other variegated Orchids, from C. B. Warner, Esq. Fruit was exhibited in tolerable profusion for the season, and of about average quality.

The novelties claim a more detailed enumeration. Foremost was a new plant allied to Thunbergia, which came from Mysore in British India, and was produced by Messrs. Veitch; this plant, the *Hexacentris mysorensis* of Dr. Wight, is a stove-climber, with woody stems, elliptic-oblong acuminate three-nerved leaves, and pendulous racemes of very curious flowers, which stand upwards from the pendent axis which supports them, and are enwrapped at the base by a pair of large oblong rich red-brown coloured bracteoles; the corolla is funnel-shaped, with an oblique limb reflected backwards on each side as in *Mimulus cardinalis*; this part is yellow, with the tips of the segments of a rich reddish-brown. Altogether, from the position and colouring of the flowers, it is a most remarkable-looking plant, adapted for training on rafters, or on trellises which will display its peculiar flowering habit. Next to this in interest was a small species of Azalea, introduced from the North of China by Mr. Fortune, and believed to be nearly hardy; this, which was exhibited by Messrs. Standish and Noble, is well called *A. amœna*, and is a fit associate for the compact-growing brilliant-flowered *A. obtusa* which was obtained from the same source a few years since by the Horticultural Society; the colour of the flowers is a pleasing rosy-purple, but the peculiarity is that the calyx is corolloid, so that there seems to be one flower within another as occurs in the common hose-in-hose primrose. It will be invaluable as a breeder independently of its own peculiar beauty. Messrs. Standish and Noble also had a small plant of the purple variety of the Himalayan *Rhododendron lepidotum*, and two varieties of a striped Chinese Azalea (*A. vittata*), which, though pretty, are of less importance. Among the Rhododendrons produced, was one called *sulphureum*, from Mr. Lane, which bore fine trusses of primrose-coloured flowers free from the dingy indistinctness which is so common among what are called "yellow" hybrid Rhododendrons.

M. Van Houtte sent a prettily variegated species of *Aplelandra* [?], in which the curved veins which spring from the midrib on each side are marked by a broad white line; and with it was a hybrid *Water Lily* with rose-coloured flowers. A very pretty *Tetratheca* called *ericifolia*, a stiff shrub with drooping rosy flowers, not new, but lately reintroduced; the compact growing *Gastrolobium calycinum*, a very showy species, with glaucous opposite oblong carinate cuspidate leaves, and spikes of opposite orange and brown flowers issuing from between large membranous bracts; a white flowered variety of *Impatiens platypetala*; and the pretty *Pultenæa ericifolia*, a desirable exhibition plant, figured in the *Gardener's Magazine of Botany* last year, were all contributed by Messrs. Henderson, of the Edgeware Road.

Besides their *Hexacentris*, Messrs. Veitch sent plants of two new hardy evergreen trees, which in the mature state are said to be very ornamental. These are *Fitz-Roya patagonica* and *Saxe-Gothea conspicua*. In the young state in which they were produced the former is an elegant cypress-like plant, the latter too much like a yew. They had also some nice pots of their new annual *Collinsia multicolor*, in the way of *C. bicolor*, but more highly coloured, and *Streptocarpus biflorus* bearing much larger flowers than *S. Rexi*, two on a stalk, but otherwise similar. A *Boronia*, named *Mollinii*, from Sir J. Cathcart's garden, appeared to be not different from that cultivated under the name of *B. spathulata*. Messrs. Rollisson showed *Caraguata lingulata*, a spineless pine-apple-like plant, having a spreading head of crimson bracts, and the curious *Ataccia cristata*. Mr. Cole, gardener to H. Colyer, Esq., of Dartford, had an Ixora, known in nurseries as *I. aurantiaca*; and appearing to be intermediate between *coccinea* and *crocata*. A promising blue-flowered *Libertia* was sent by Mr. Hally, of Blackheath.

Messrs. Veitch had a fine new Dendrobe, *D. clavatum*, a species with oblong lanceolate leaves along the stems, and deep orange-coloured flowers, having a yellow lip with dark eye-like spots; *D. albo-sanguineum*, a very handsome species, exhibited last year; and also a finely-branched *Aerides* from Moulmein, in the way of *A. affine*. A pretty variety of *Cattleya intermedia*, with the upper half of the central lobes of the lip purple, came from Mr. Shaw of Cheltenham. Mr. Ivison sent a good plant, of the handsome yellow flowered *Oncidium sessile*; and a pale worthless *Trichopilia*, probably a bad variety of *T. coccinea* (*T. marginata*) came from Mrs. Lawrence's garden.

The Royal Botanic Society's Exhibition in the Regent's Park took place on the 19th ult., and was honoured by the presence of her Majesty and the Prince Albert. The exhibition was very similar in all respects to that at Chiswick ten days previous, but time had somewhat altered the Azaleas for the worse, and the Roses and Pelargoniums decidedly for the better.

Many of the same new plants were present at both places, namely—Messrs. Veitch's *Hexacentris mysorensis, Collinsia multicolor, Streptocarpus biflorus,* which latter proves a very ornamental species and *Fitz-Roya patagonica ;* M. Van Houtte's variegated *Aphelandra,* and hybrid *Nymphœa ;* accompanied however, on this occasion, by a brilliant orange half shrubby composite with zinnia-like flower-heads named " *Conoclinium*" *aurantiacum ;* Messrs. Standish and Noble's *Azaleas vittata* and *amœna :* Messrs. Rollisson's *Caraguata lingulata* and *Cissus marmorea,* the latter, however, in beautiful state, proving this to be a most charming variegated plant for an orchid house, climbing vigorously, and having the oblique elongate-ovate foliage richly marbled with purple, dark velvety green, and gray. The following were additional :—*Hemiandra pungens,* a showy labiate with awl-shaped pungent leaves, and large delicate lilac flowers spotted with rose, and *Gastrolobium gracile,* a slender plant with yellow pea flowers in heads, from Mr. Colyer's garden at Dartford. A graceful New Holland species of Pultenæa, with coppery red blossoms and fine taper leaves, under the erroneous name of *Gompholobium Brownii,* from Messrs. Jackson of Kingston. *Sarauja cauliflora,* a tall shrub with a crest of large elliptic-lanceolate leaves, and small white lily-of-the-valley-like flowers on the older parts of the stem, from Messrs. Rollisson. *Hoya Paxtoni,* a neat growing species,˙like *H. bella,* but the flowers having a rather paler central star, and the leaves broader at the base and more elongate ; and *H. suaveolens,* a slender rooting-stemmed kind, with oval acute leaves, and umbels of minute whitish papillose flowers ; together with *Tropæolum Hockerianum,* a species with entire peltate leaves, and moderate sized yellow flowers with dark blotches, from Messrs. Henderson of St. John's Wood. *Gastrolobium calycinum* and *G. trilobum,* two very showy yellow-flowered papilionaceous shrubs, from Messrs. Henderson of the Edgeware Road. *Trollius chinensis,* one Mr. Fortune's introductions, a hardy perennial with deep orange globe-cupped flowers remarkable for the length of the nectaries ; and four fine varieties of *Moutan,* one having bright rose-red flowers, from Messrs. Standish and Noble. *Calodracon nobilis,* a very ornamental foliaged plant, with broader leaves and a denser more compact habit than the species commonly known as *Dracæna terminalis,* was sent by Messrs. Rollisson. A good plant of the *Hoya Paxtoni* was also sent by Mr. Over, gardener to — McMullen, Esq., of Clapham.

The only new Orchids of any importance were the Javanese *Phalænopsis Lobbii,* a species intermediate between amabilis and rosea, the flowers being whitish with a rose-coloured lip ; and a species of *Dendrobium* having something the habit of *macrostachyum,* and flowers greatly resembling *nobile.* These were both sent by Messrs. Veitch of Exeter.

These exhibitions, though they now leave little or nothing to be desired at the hands of the cultivator, do most urgently call for some improvement on the part of the managers, as to the manner in which the objects are displayed. Plants with striking and elegant foliage, such as Palms, large-growing Ferns, the variegated *Dracænas* and *Calodracons, &c.,* or with ample massive foliage, such as some of the hothouse species of *Ficus* and others ; or of such exotic aspect as *Cannas, Musas,* &c., ought to be largely introduced, and some plan devised by which the present mode of staging collections might be altogether abandoned, and grouping for effect only, adopted instead. We throw out the following as a hint to those concerned. The element of competition cannot probably be dispensed with, and it would therefore be necessary to adopt some plan under which the prizes might be duly allotted. Now to effect this, why should not the plants (which should bear the exhibitor's private mark) be set temporarily in competition groups where convenient, and their merits adjudicated early in the day—say by eight o'clock, or so that this might be completed by nine. This would leave ample time for the arrangement of the plants, which, under the direction of persons of taste, should be afterwards disposed on the stages with a view to produce the highest effect of which the materials at hand are capable? It appears to us that very little forethought would, with very little difficulty, reduce some such scheme as this into good working order; and no one surely can doubt the effect on the beauty of the exhibition if it were properly—that is, tastefully—carried out.—M.

~
in
he

la-
tal
o ;
ike
ind
in
ing
ety
wi-
t, a
ew
ime
ith
der
bat
de;
ute
res
od
ru.
rdy
our
alo-
hic
ood
.
ate
of
ile.

the
ner
ge-
as
x.,
ms
he
ed
lly
ate
ed
ve
be
als
ty,
on

1 Cyclamen ibericum   2 Cyclamen Atkinsii

CYCLAMEN ATKINSII AND CYCLAMEN IBERICUM.

IF there be a group of plants, of limited extent, and possessing every quality which should, and indeed, does, render them favourite objects of cultivation, and which therefore ought to be well known, and easily recognized, but which more than any other, have their nomenclature involved in difficulty and confusion, it is that of the Cyclamens. So it ever has been, and so it remains: for the most recent *resumé* of the species is not less free from the prevailing mysticism than the descriptions which have preceded it. This has no doubt arisen from their having been examined in a dried state, in which many of their pecularities are lost sight of; and the only hope which remains of the question being satisfactorily settled is, that some cultivator may collect all the forms that are known, and submit them for examination, while fresh, to some competent authority.

Something of this kind, we are glad to know, is being attempted by Mr. Atkins of Painswick, to whom we are indebted for the accompanying illustrations of *C. Atkinsii*, and the forms, represented at *a* and *b*, in our figure, of *C. ibericum*. Mr. Atkins has for some years paid considerable attention to the family, and now possesses a very extensive collection of them, which he is annually extending by means of hybridization. The origin of *C. Atkinsii* is thus explained to us:—

"After many ineffectual attempts," writes Mr. Atkins, to produce a good cross between *C. coum* or *C. vernum*, and *C. persicum*, combining the *neat habit* of the two former, with the colour and larger petals of the latter, having at the same time the foliage *dark*, yet relieved with a lighter band, or marbled, I at length succeeded in raising the hybrid now figured, from seeds produced by a variety of *C. coum*, impregnated with *C. persicum*, and this, I have every reason to believe, I shall be able to perpetuate, and thus introduce a new and most interesting feature into this beautiful family of plants. Amongst the seedlings, it was found that every plant deviating in the marking of the foliage from the seed-bearing parent, produced white or blush flowers, whilst those retaining its plain dark leaf, have invariably bloomed with different shades of the colour of that species."

CYCLAMEN ATKINSII AS EXHIBITED BY MR. ATKINS.

This account of its origin perfectly explains its appearance, it being, in fact, exactly intermediate between its parents as to size and form, and to some extent even in colour. The specimen which our vignette represents was exhibited last March, before the Horticultural Society, with about seventy fully expanded flowers, and bears full evidence of the success of Mr. Atkins' mode of culture, which, we

* *C. Atkinsii* (hyb; ♂, persicum ♀ coum).—Leaves ovate obtuse, cordate at the base with overlapping lobes, subcrenate, zoned with pale green, dull purple beneath; calyx teeth lance-shaped acute; tube of the corolla globose, mouth scarcely angular, petals broadly obovate acute; stamens included, style equalling the tube.—M.

N

understand, is different from that generally practised, and which we hope, when some doubtful points shall have been cleared up, we may be permitted to make public.

Our figure of *C. ibericum*,* a beautiful, but little known species, was made, in January last, from Messrs. Rollison's nursery at Tooting, aided at *a* and *b* by blossoms from some of Mr. Atkins's more vigorously grown plants, which were communicated along with the hybrid *C. Atkinsii*. Its affinity is with *C. vernum*, but it differs altogether from that species in its foliage.

In *C. Atkinsii* the leaves are large (two and a half by two inches), ovate obtuse cordate at the base, with a deep sinus the sides of which overlap, dark glossy green, with an irregular pale zone within the margin; the under surface is liver-coloured, or dull purple. The flowers are elevated on longish verrucose stalks, and are of a French white, marked with a deep crimson ovate blotch at the base of each segment; the calyx consists of five acute lance-shaped pubescent segments; the corolla has a short globose tube, and a limb of five broadly obovate segments nearly seven-eighths of an inch long; the mouth of the tube is nearly circular, the angles being indistinct; the stamens are included, but the style equals the tube. The flowers are scentless.

C. ibericum produces flat heart-shaped leaves, having an open sinus, and the margin very slightly sinuate-dentate or entire; they are deep green, with an irregular heart-shaped belt of pale greyish-green some distance within the margin, the veins sunken on the upper face, prominent and green beneath, on a dull reddish purple ground. The flowers vary in colour; in some, they are pale rosy, or flesh-coloured, in other plants, deep rose-colour, in some they are white; but in all cases they are marked with a broad ovate spot at the base of the segments, which spot is either purple or crimson, and is extended in the centre as far as the mouth, which, in the front view, thus shows five purple bars or spots; the bases of the segments are curved outwards at the margin, the mouth thus becoming pentangular, with concave sides. The calyx lobes are acutely lance-shaped; the tube of the corolla is ventricose, the segments of the limb either roundish obovate or oblong obovate. The stamens are quite inclosed, and are slightly exceeded by the blunt, simple stigma, which is somewhat exserted.—M.

THE BEAUTIFUL IN GROUND-SURFACE.

ARTISTS and men of taste have agreed that all forms of acknowledged beauty are composed of *curved lines*. The principle applies as well to the surface of the earth as to other objects. The most beautiful shape in ground is that where one undulation melts gradually and invisibly into another. Everyone who has observed scenery where the fore-ground has been remarkable for beauty, must have been struck by this prevalence of curved lines; and every landscape gardener well knows that no grassy surface is so captivating to the eye as one where these gentle swells and undulations rise and melt away gradually into one another. Some poet, happy in his fancy, has called such bits of grassy slopes and swells " earth's smiles; and when the effect of the beauty and form of outline is heightened by the pleasing gradation of light and shade, caused by the sun's light variously reflected by such undulations of lawn, the simile seems strikingly appropriate.

A flat or level surface is considered beautiful by many persons, though it has no beauty in itself. It is, in fact, chiefly valued because it evinces art. Though there is no positive beauty in a straight or level line, it is often interesting as expressive of *power*, and we feel as much awed by the boundless prairie or desert, as by the lofty snow-capped hill. On a smaller scale, a level surface is sometimes agreeable in the midst of a rude and wild country, by way of contrast, as a small level garden in the Alps will sometimes attract us astonishingly, that would be passed by unnoticed in the midst of a flat and cultivated country. Hence, as there are a thousand men who value power, where there is one who can feel beauty, we see all ignorant persons who set about embellishing their pleasure-grounds, or even the site for a home, immediately commence *levelling* the surface. Once brought to this level, improvement

---

* *C. ibericum*, " Goldie."—Leaves exactly heart-shaped, with an open sinus, entire or very slightly sinuate-toothed, zoned with greyish-green, purple beneath; calyx teeth lance-shaped acute; tube of the corolla ventricose, mouth pentangular, with lunate sides; segments of the limb roundish obovate or oblong-obovate; stamens shorter than the blunt, simple stigma, which is included or very slightly exserted.—M.

can go no further, according to their views, since to subjugate or level is the whole aim of man's ambition. Once levelled you may give to ground, or even to a whole landscape, according to their theory, as much beauty as you like: it is only a question of expense. This is a fearful fallacy, however;—fearful oftentimes both to the eye and purse.

It is not less fearful to see a fine varied outline of ground utterly spoiled by being graded for the mansion and its surrounding lawn, at an expense which would have curved all the walks, and filled the grounds with the finest trees and shrubs, if the surface had been left nearly, or quite, as nature formed it. Not much better, or even far worse, is the fancy many persons have of *terracing* every piece of sloping ground—as a mere matter of ornament,—where no terrace is needed. It may be safely said, that a terrace is always ugly, unless it is on a large scale, and is treated with dignity, so as to become part of the building itself, or to be supposed, more properly, to belong to it than to the grounds—like the fine architectural terraces which surround the old English mansions. But little gardens, thrown up into terraces, are devoid of all beauty whatever,—though they may be rendered more useful or available in this way.

The surface of ground is rarely *ugly* in a state of nature, because all nature leans to the beautiful; and the ceaseless action of the elements goes continually to soften and wear away the harshness and violence of surface. What cannot be softened is hidden and rounded by means of foliage, trees, and shrubs, and creeping Vines, and so the tendency to the curve is always greater and greater. But man often forms ugly surfaces of ground by breaking up all natural curves without recognizing their expression, by distributing lumps of earth here and there, by grading levels in the midst of undulations, and raising mounds on perfectly smooth surfaces; in short, by regarding only the little he wishes to do in his folly, and not studying the larger part that Nature has already done in her wisdom. —A. J. DOWNING, *in Horticulturist (U. S.)*

THE LINNÆA BOREALIS.

WE have received the following communication from the author of the series of papers on *The Culture of Alpine Plants*, at present in course of publication in these pages:—

In my paper on *The Culture of Linnæa borealis*,[*] I casually alluded to what seems to be a somewhat prevalent belief, that the Linnæa is not a cultivable plant. If the *rarity* of its cultivation were any proof of this, then the belief would be justified, for it is one of those plants we seldom meet with even in good collections of Alpines. I did not dwell upon this point; but since my remarks were written, a poem has appeared in Chambers's Edinburgh Journal on the *Linnæa borealis*, which has a decided tendency to foster the erroneous idea of this interesting plant not being capable of cultivation, and therefore it may be advisable to offer one or two observations on the subject. I rejoice that Linnæa has at last been introduced to the realms of poesy, and I should be the last man in the world to pick holes in a poet's fancy; but I fear the present one may have a practical influence on practical men, to avert which is the object of these remarks.

The poem is prefaced by an apt text from "Rambles in Sweden and Gottland," by Sylvanus, to amplify and illustrate which is its object:—" Linné selected a tiny wild-flower that he discovered, of exquisite beauty and delicious odour, to bear his name,—*one that refuses to exchange the silent glen and melancholy wood for the more gay parterres of horticulture.*"

THE LINNÆA BOREALIS.

'Tis a child of the old green woodlands,
  Where the song of the free wild bird,
And swaying of boughs in the summer breeze,
  Are the only voices heard.

In the richest moss of the lonely dells
  Are its rosy petals found,
With the clear blue sky above it spread,
  And the lordly trees around.

In those still, untrodden solitudes
  Its lovely days are passed;
And the sunny turf is its fragrant bier
  When it gently dies at last.

But if from its own sweet dwelling-place
  By a careless hand 'tis torn,
And to hot and dusty city streets
  In its drooping beauty borne,

* Garden Companion, pp. 34—5.

Its graceful head is with sorrow bowed,
And it quickly pines and fades ;
Till the fragile bloom is for ever fled
That gladdened the forest glades.

It will not dwell 'neath a palace dome,
With rare exotic flowers,
Whose perfumed splendour gaily gleams
In radiant festal hours :

It loves not the Parian marble vase,
On the terrace fair and wide ;
Or the bright and sheltered garden bowers
Smiling in gorgeous pride.

But it mourns for the far-off dingles,
For their fresh and joyous air,

For the dewy sighs and sunny beams
That lingered o'er it there.

O lonely and lovely forest flower !
A holy lot is thine,
Amid nature's deepest solitudes,
With radiance meek to shine.

Bright blossom of the shady woods !
Live on in your cool retreat,
Unharmed by the touch of human hand,
Or the tread of careless feet :

With the rich green fern around your home,
The birds' glad song above ;
And the solemn stars in the still night-time
Looking down with eyes of love !

LUCINDA ELLIOT.

It seems harsh and unkind to restrain our sympathy from the beautiful sentiment that prevails and forms the poetic burden of these pretty verses ; but it behoves the *Garden Companion* to expose its fallacy, and to claim the Linnæa for a garden flower.

It is enough for me to state that I never yet saw an instance of this plant failing in cultivation, where reasonable care was bestowed upon it ; the simple directions indicated at page 34 will enable any one to grow it with success. Not only does it grow and flower in cultivation, but it does both in a most satisfactory manner, and certainly flowers *more profusely* in the Alpine frame than I have ever seen it do in its native haunts ! It even seems to flourish amidst the smoke of a city ; but my experience of it, in this respect, is not sufficiently extended to enable me to speak with entire confidence. The American form probably grows even more freely than the Scotch plant.

For these reasons, let me urge cultivators whose attentions are directed towards the Alpine flora, to extend the cultivation of one of the neatest Alpine shrubs known to science, one of the most interesting of vegetable productions, and one of the most easily cultivated plants that was ever introduced to the Alpine frame.

For the benefit of botanical readers, I may observe that several parasitical fungi grow occasionally upon the leaves of *Linnæa borealis*. One of these—*Sphæria Dickiei*—is figured and described in the "Annals of Natural History" (April, 1852).—G.

SCIENTIFIC GLEANINGS.

ACCORDING to Martius, the fine Palm, Moriche (*Mauritia flexuosa*), Quiteve, or Ita Palm belongs, as well as Calamus, to the group of Lepidocaryeæ or Coryphineæ. Linnæus has described it very imperfectly, as he erroneously considers it to be leafless. The trunk grows as high as twenty feet ; but it probably requires from 120 to 150 years to reach this height. The Mauritia extends high up on the declivity of the Duida, north of the Esmeralda mission, where I have found it in great beauty. It forms, in moist places, fine groups of a fresh shining verdure, which reminds us of that of our Alder groves. The trees preserve the moisture of the ground by their shade, and hence the Indians say that the Mauritia draws the water round its roots by a mysterious attraction. By a somewhat similar theory, they advise that serpents should not be killed, because the destruction of the serpents and the drying up of the pools or lagunes accompany each other ; thus the untutored child of nature confounds cause and effect. Gumilla terms the *Mauritia flexuosa* of the Gauranis, the tree of life—arbol de la vida. It grows in the mountains of Ronaima, east of the sources of the Orinoco, as high as 4000 (4263 English) feet.—*Humboldt's Aspects of Nature.*

Mr. Berthold Seeman, the naturalist of Her Majesty's ship Herald, who has just commenced the publication of the plants collected during the voyage, thus gives his experience of the Mangosteen :—
" One of the finest productions of Singapore, the Mangosteen, was nearly out of season, and could only be procured in small quantities ; but neither these samples, nor those afterwards obtained off Sumatra, came up to the high expectation which I had formed as to their taste. I am glad, however, to have met with the fruit. It enables me to compare it with its two rivals, and I may now say I have tasted

'the finest fruits in the world,' in those localities in which they are supposed to attain their highest perfection,—the Pine Apple in Guayaquil, the Chirimoya on the slopes of the Andes, and the Mangosteen in the Indian Archipelago. Perplexing as must always be the office of a Paris, when on either side such high claims are advanced, yet, I think we may, in this case, without offence to the advocates of the other, assign 'the apple' to the chirimoya. Its taste surpasses that of all other fruits, and Hænke was quite right when calling it a master-piece of nature."—*Hooker's Journal of Botany.*

At the Edinburgh Botanical Society's Meeting, last May, Dr. Murchison exhibited some curious specimens of Extract of Tea, prepared in the form of lozenges by the Chinese. These lozenges were of various forms, and had impressed upon them mottoes in Chinese characters, and the figures of different insects, musical instruments, and other objects. They had been brought from Pekin in the year 1812, and were stated to be used by the Chinese when travelling; when introduced into the mouth, they were said to dissolve slowly, preventing thirst, and proving very refreshing. Though it was forty years since they had been brought from China, they still retained a very perceptible flavour of Tea. Dr. Murchison presented the specimens to the Museum of Economic Botany, at the Royal Botanic Garden, Edinburgh.

The Taban (*Isonanda Gutta,* Hooker), formerly so plentiful in Singapore, has long since been extinct. It must ever be an object of regret, that on the first introduction of the Taban Gum, its proper name was not promulgated. Now, everybody in Europe and America, speaks of Gutta Percha, when, in fact, all the time, they mean the Gutta Taban. The exportation of the indigenous Gutta Taban, from Singapore, commenced in 1844, but as early as 1847 all, or at least, most of the trees had been exterminated. That at present shipped from the place is brought in coasting vessels from the different ports of Borneo, Sumatra, the Malayan Peninsula, and Jahore Archipelago. The difference existing in its appearance and property is owing to the intermixture of Gutta Percha, Jeletong, Gegrek, Litchu, and other inferior Guttas, in order to increase the weight. Though far from extinct in the Indian Archipelago, Gutta Taban will every year be more difficult to obtain, as the coast region is pretty well cleared, and a long transport from the interior must, by augmenting the labour, increase the price of the article. The quantity of solid Gutta obtained from each tree varies from five to twenty catties, so that taking the average of ten catties, which is a tolerably liberal one, it will require the destruction of ten trees to produce one picul. Now the quantity exported from Singapore to Europe, from January, 1845, to the middle of 1847, amounted to 6918 piculs, to obtain which 69,180 trees must have been sacrificed. How much better it would be to adopt the method of tapping the tree, practised by the Burmese in obtaining the Caoutchouc, than to continue the present process of extermination.—*Seeman in Hooker's Journal of Botany.*

THE MIXED FLOWER GARDEN.

IT is much to be regretted that the rage for novelty often leads to the neglect of plants which, from having been in the country many years, and a variety of other causes, are partially gone out of repute, and are only met with here and there, where the rage for massing has not excluded the mixed flower garden. The beauty of some of these neglected plants is in no way inferior, and often superior, to such as have only novelty to recommend them. No place of any pretension should be without a mixed flower border; and as there are few places in which it would be desirable to keep up a *collection* of plants without regard to their intrinsic merits for beauty and adaptibility for decorative purposes, therefore a *selection* of good things would be infinitely preferable. I propose to offer to the amateur readers of the *Garden Companion* a few remarks on a selection of plants adapted for producing very good effects in a mixed arrangement; which arrangement, in my estimation, contains many charms; and although I am equally alive to the grandeur of the effects produced by an harmonious arrangement of colours in large masses, as exemplified in the bedding system, yet I can quite as well appreciate the intrinsic charms of individual plants in a mixed arrangement. If, too, I may judge from the expressions of admiration, and the particular inquiries of many persons, particularly ladies, with whom I have had the honour to converse on the subject, I should say that the feeling is becoming more disseminated, and will eventually play sad and deserved havoc with the exclusive attention which at present it is the fashion to bestow on bedding plants.

Whenever a new plant is brought into notice, the question which appears to arise spontaneously to every tongue is—Is it adapted for bedding purposes? as though, forsooth! bedding purposes were the *sine qua non* of excellence and desirableness. Take, for example, the *Dielytra spectabilis*, one of the most beautiful of the many plants lately brought into prominent notice, but which, if Paxton's *Botanical Dictionary* is correct, was introduced into this country from Siberia in 1810, just forty-two years ago. One hardly ever takes up a gardening periodical without finding some allusion made to this so-called new plant, which is most deservedly allowed by every one to be charming, graceful, unique, and what not; yet no sooner has it began to display its charms, when an outcry is raised as to its capabilities for bedding, a purpose for which it will not be well adapted; for although as hardy as any of the fumeworts, and to a certain extent continuous-flowering, the best of its beauty is over before that of bedding plants comes on. No. For the mixed flower garden it is invaluable, but for the production of a definite effect in bedding arrangements, quite out of place.

Before proceeding to give a detailed list of good things adapted for a mixed arrangement, I will beg to call attention to a few plants which, from their intrinsic merits and beauty, I have often been surprised are not more generally cultivated. For example: the *Sternbergia lutea*, a most beautiful bulbous plant, a native of the south of Europe, and introduced in 1596. Its season of flowering is from the end of September until it is positively killed by the frost, which must be unusually severe before it will give over throwing up its tulip-like flowers of the purest yellow. The bulbs are just now gone to rest, and the present is a good time to plant it. The Sternbergias are handsome hardy bulbs, seldom met with in ordinary collections. Another bulbous plant of the same family, and also a native of the south of Europe, is the *Pancratium maritimum*, introduced 1597. This striking and unique plant is deserving of the highest commendation; it is perfectly hardy, flowers abundantly in June, and is very seldom met with. The *Trillium grandiflorum* is also a plant seldom seen, but is one of the best of the tribe, and, when in flower, has generally produced an inquiry as to its name and origin, being often considered as a new plant, although it was introduced from North America in 1799. *Leucojum vernum* is another very rare and beautiful plant, highly deserving of more extensive cultivation. This was introduced from Germany in 1596, is perfectly hardy, and easily increased by offsets from the bulbs.

Amongst the many beautiful varieties of Narcissus, which will hereafter claim attention, I cannot forbear to particularize the *Narcissus minor*, or, as it is sometimes called *Ajax minor*, one of the very earliest of spring flowers, seldom passed without being praised for its beauty. This is often taken for a new plant, although it was brought from Spain in 1629. Enough for the present; in a future paper, I propose to offer a select list of good hardy perennial, herbaceous, and bulbous plants, suitable to all who desire only a selection of the best.—C.

VARIEGATED ORCHIDS.

PERHAPS there are no objects throughout the whole vegetable kingdom more delicately beautiful than the metallic veined foliage of the small group of insignificant-flowered Orchids, of which *Anœctochilus* may be taken as the type. Formerly one or two kinds only were known in cultivation, but now their number is so far increased that a group of them becomes an exceedingly interesting and attractive feature. Unfortunately they require a high temperature, and thus their cultivation is limited to those who can provide them with a strictly tropical climate.

They are grown in a mixture of light fibrous peat (Shirley peat carefully selected, is the most suitable near London), and sphagnum moss cut up very fine; three parts of sphagnum are used to one part of peat, and a few small potsherds are mixed in the moss; the pots also must be thoroughly drained. The plants should be kept up even with the top of the pots, and the soil should be packed about them rather lightly. They are then to be plunged in moss at the hottest part of an orchid-house or a damp stove. In winter they require very little water, but in summer when they are grow-ing freely, and there is a full command of heat, water may be used with freedom.

The temperature in winter should be from 65° to 75°, and in summer from 70° to 90°. The plants are best covered with ample bell-glasses, which should be wiped dry every morning; and the plants should be frequently *slightly* smoked with tobacco, to keep them free from insects.

The following are the kinds now in cultivation, with the names by which they are known in the nurseries :—

Anœctochilus setaceus. The leaves beautifully and closely netted with lines of gold-colour, on a rich velvety brown-green surface. There is a variety similar to this, with the veins a few shades lighter.

Anœctochilus xanthophyllus (*A. setaceus pictus*). The leaves with a broad bar of gold-colour down the centre, and marked on each side with netted lines of the same on a dark-green ground.

Anœctochilus intermedius. Intermediate between the two preceding, having a smaller bar down the leaf, but otherwise marked with golden meshes on the dark velvety green surface.

Anœctochilus striatus. This has narrow lance-shaped foliage, marked with a bar of gold through the centre, upon a dark-green ground.

Anœctochilus Lowii (*Cheirostylus marmoratus ; Dossinia marmorata*). This has very robust foliage, of a rich dark mottled velvety bronzy-green, marked with fine transverse lustrous golden lines. Another variety of this differs in being a few shades lighter in colour.

Anœctochilus Lobbianus (*A. latimaculatus*). The foliage of this is of a rich green, the midrib silvery, and the rest of the surface marked with fine transverse silvery lines.

Physurus argenteus (*A. argenteus*). The leaves green, thickly netted with silvery lines.

Physurus argenteus pictus (*A. argenteus pictus*). Green, with a wide central silvery bar, and otherwise netted with silvery lines.

The beautiful *Cissus marmorea*, recently introduced by Messrs. Rollisson from Java, would be a most appropriate climber for a house in which these variegated orchids were kept, the shady and still atmosphere of such a situation being favourable to the development of the beautiful markings of its leaves; and along with the New Holland Pitcher Plant (*Cephalotus follicularis*), and the Fly-trap (*Dionœ amuscipula*), these form a most interesting group.—THOMAS BROWN, *Tooting Nursery.*

RURAL POESY—THE VALES OF WEVER.*

————————— " By yonder stream,
Where oak and elm along the bordering mead
Send forth wild melody from every bough,
Together let us wander ; where the hills,
Cover'd with fleeces, to the lowing vale
Reply ; where tidings of content and peace
Each echo brings."—AKENSIDE.

POETRY is not among the subjects which it is proposed to treat of in the *Garden Companion*, but Nature-loving poets occasionally give birth to poems which we have no doubt will interest our readers. " The Vales of Wever" is of such a character, a loco-descriptive poem, whose purpose it is to depict some cherished scenes, and in which special allusions to many of the natural history produc-tions giving those scenes their beauty, and a commentary of running foot-notes, are introduced. Our attention has now been drawn to the work by an esteemed botanical correspondent, who writes :— " The accompanying poem is by a very venerable friend of mine, who died last June at the advanced age of 80 years. Last Christmas (1850) I had the pleasure of spending a few days with him at his residence, Twyford, on the banks of the Trent. He was particularly attached to the study of Botany, and his herbarium was rich in specimens of native plants, many of which, though collected upwards of sixty years since, were in a beautiful state of preservation. His Mosses and Seaweeds were really splendid. I saw him for the last time in the month of April last, at the seat of his brother-in-law, Sir Francis Darwin, who is the only surviving son of the celebrated Dr. Erasmus Darwin, author of " The Botanic Garden." These interesting facts form a sufficient warrantry for our entering the realms of

* The Vales of Wever, a Loco-Descriptive Poem, in three Cantos. By John Gisborne; Esq. *Second Edition.* London: Whittaker and Co. 1851.

poesy on this occasion; and indeed we should show ourselves unworthy of the title assumed by the *Garden Companion* were we to exhibit a total want of poetic taste, for, however good a gardener, he makes but a poor *companion* who is insensible to the influences of poetry.

The beauty of Mr. Gisborne's depictions can, of course, only be fully appreciated by those intimately acquainted with the localities. However, it would appear that in the most minute details, his descriptions accord with the individual appearances of Nature in the localities described. Our author had apparently a most enthusiastic passion for trees, and he portrays "the huge Oak," and its associated objects, just in the way that a naturalist would do, apprising the reader in a foot-note that many of the cliffs in the dales appear rifted by the Oaks which have forcibly inserted their roots and trunks between them; and some of the trees seem to support the disjointed strata of stone with their elbowy roots and excrescences:—

> "First the huge Oak, with dusky charms,
> The suns meridian rage disarms;
> Proud o'er the beetling crag he bends,
> With bold contortions heaven ascends;
> His delving roots abrupt recoil,
> Or struggle through the flinty soil;
> Chill twilight shrouds his trunk below,
> And glory slumbers on his brow."
> 　　　　　　　Canto I., 99—106.
>
> * 　 * 　 * 　 *
>
> "Yon Oak, whose tottering trunk displays
> The tarnished pride of other days,
> Still wreathes his shatter'd head with green,
> With charm of contrast aids the scene.
> Oft have I linger'd to survey
> That trunk, with age enamell'd grey;
> O'er his rent bark pale Lichen bends,
> And Moss her folds of velvet blends,

> Where insect nations range unseen,
> And mine the arborescent screen;
> Weave with nice skill the spider fold,
> And cradle embryo young from cold.
> With what fell art the spider spreads
> His glistening snare, mechanic threads;
> Redundant meshes bright unfurls,
> And round each bud ingenious whirls.
> Ye insect armies, who delight
> To skim the realms of breezy night,
> Or twinkling through the noontide glare,
> With busy murmurs fill the air;
> If floating on the zephyr's breath, 　 *
> Ye rush within these webs of death,
> From his dread ambush darts the foe,
> Enraptur'd with the cries of woe,
> Swift glides along his tremulous toil,
> And riots o'er his struggling spoil."
> 　　　　　　　Canto I., 233—57.

Again the Oak is noticed in connection with Rousseau. In a field at a small distance from Northwood stands a cluster of Oaks, commonly called the *Twenty Oaks*, which form a circle, disclosing between their trunks a beautiful prospect. To this silent retreat Rousseau used frequently to retire, during his residence at Wootton, and some of the stones may still be seen which formed his seat.

> "Lo! where those Oaks encircling meet,
> There Genius formed his rural seat.
> Oft in calm solitude the sage
> Composed his fascinating page,*
> Or bending on the turf survey'd
> With nice regard each flower and blade;

> Or mark'd gay nature's liberal smile,
> Admir'd Britannia's temperate isle;
> Yet thought on Gallia's lovelier vales,
> Her brighter founts, her softer gales;
> Thought on her *chains* with Freedom's sigh,
> And the patriot kindled in his eye."
> 　　　　　　　Canto II., 79—90.

We had marked other passages for quotation, some of which might have better shown the author's *power*, but we have given enough to show the style of the poem. We cannot conclude, however, without observing, that the author deeply felt the manifestation of the power of the Supreme Being in all the works of nature, and aptly quotes a sublime passage from the writings of Dr. Blair:— "In the midst of your solitary musings, lift your eyes, and behold all Nature full of God. Look up to the firmament and admire his glory. Look round the earth, and observe his presence everywhere displayed. If the gay landscape or the fruitful field present themselves to your eye, behold him smiling upon his works. If the mountain raise its lofty head, or the expanse of waters roll its tide before you, contemplate in those great and solemn objects his power and majesty. Nature, in all its diversities, is a varied manifestation of the Deity. If you were to take the wings of the morning, and dwell in the uttermost parts of the sea, even there you would find him. For in him you live and move. He fills and animates all space. In the barren wilderness as in the peopled region, you can trace his footsteps, and in the deepest solitude you may hear a voice which testifies of him."—I.

　　　　* Letters on Botany. By J. J. Rousseau.

G. P. del Conte

Printed by Brannony & Penn

Aotus Drummondii

AOTUS DRUMMONDII.*

THIS very fine Swan River shrub has been raised by Messrs. A. Henderson & Co., of the Pine Apple Nursery, from Mr. Drummond's seeds, and promises to be one of the most desirable of greenhouse shrubs for exhibition or decorative purposes. Our figure was prepared from Mr. Henderson's plants in April last; since which time we have received from Messrs. Knight & Perry, of the Exotic Nursery, Chelsea, another form of it, differing only in being somewhat larger in all its parts. This was also raised from Drummond's seeds, and is, we presume, one of those natural variations which are so frequently met with among seedling plants.

The habit of this *Aotus Drummondii* is remarkably good, being stiff-branched and spreading. The branches are pilose, with short spreading hairs, and clothed with scattered sub-opposite or sub-whorled leaves, which are linear-acute at both ends, and are stalked, the petioles being also pilose. The upper surface of the leaves is plane, smooth, excepting a few scabrous elevations near the revolute margin; the lower surface is smooth, with a prominent midrib, on which occurs a few short scattered hairs. They are half an inch or more in length (in Messrs. Knight & Perry's plant fully an inch), the larger about one-eighth wide. From the axils of the leaves spring the flowers, either solitary, or more frequently two or three together, borne on hairy pedicels scarcely so long as the calyx. The calyx is bell-shaped, two-lipped, with nearly equal teeth, those of the upper lip being erect and largest, those of the lower lip reflexed, all pilose externally and smooth within. The flowers are clear bright yellow, the roundish standard only being marked at its base by a small rayed zone of bright red; the wings are oblong, slightly exceeding the paler yellow keel. The stamens are slightly longer than the slender tapering style, but inclosed by the keel. The ovary is villose, and bears one ovule.—M.

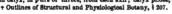

ON THE RESPIRATION OF PLANTS.

THE idea generally entertained of the respiration of plants is, that it is a process by which carbonic acid is decomposed, and oxygen evolved in a free condition, as a gas, into the atmosphere, this operation going on most actively under the direct influence of the sun's rays. But it has long been known that there exists also in vegetable life a process by which carbonic acid is set free, as it is in the respiration of animals, and this process, observed most distinctly in plants removed from the sun's light, is one respecting which much obscurity still prevails. In drawing especial attention to this process as occurring so generally in plants or parts of plants devoid of chlorophyll, I remarked,† some years ago, that from its evidently general occurrence it must be a true vital process, and not merely a result of a destructive or decomposing action of oxygen upon the vegetable tissues and their contents.

Some very interesting experiments have been recently published by M. Garreau, of Lille, which throw much light upon the conditions of this exhalation of carbonic acid from living plants. He finds that it takes place not only in the absence of the sun's light but in the full sunlight, and simultaneously with the evolution of oxygen, the much greater quantity of the latter, together with the process of reabsorption of the evolved carbonic acid under such circumstances having disguised this fact in the experiments of most previous observers.

M. Garreau placed branches, and other portions of living vegetable structures, under conditions in which he could fix any carbonic acid set free (by means of solution of caustic baryta), and thus remove it completely from the liability to be re-absorbed by the green parts of the plants under the influence of sun-light, and the result of numerous trials, was to show that leaves exhale carbonic acid during the day, both in the sun and in the shade, and that the quantity increases in proportion to the temperature in which the plant is kept.

To show the simultaneous occurrence of the two phenomena one branch of a living plant of

---

* A Drummondii, *n. sp.*—Branches pilose, rigid, spreading; leaves scattered, or somewhat whorled, stalked, linear, acute at both ends, slightly scabrous above near the revolute margins, with a few hairs on the prominent nerves beneath; pedicels shorter than calyx, in pairs or threes, from each axil; calyx pilose, the teeth nearly equal, those of the lower lip reflexed.—M.

† Outlines of Structural and Physiological Botany, § 207.

Fagopyrum cymosum was introduced into a glass flask securely closed, and connected with a caoutchouc bag containing 200 cubic centimetres of carbonic acid. After six hours exposure to the sun-light only 75 centimetres of gas remained, the rest had been absorbed by the plant. At the same time another branch of the same plant, of equal size, was introduced into a closed flask provided with a quantity of solution of baryta, to absorb any carbonic acid given off, and at the end of the six hours the baryta had absorbed eleven centimetres of carbonic acid. Other experiments showed that this carbonic acid is given off in greatest abundance by germinating seeds, next in proportion by buds, and least by the leaves; and that the amount of carbonic acid is given off most abundantly, weight and surface being equal, from organs which contain the greatest quantity of the nitrogenous cell-contents.

This last fact is of great interest since it seems to connect this process of evolution of carbonic acid most closely with the respiration of animals, for it is well-known that the nitrogenous or proteinous cell-contents, the *protoplasm* of Mohl, or *endochrome* of some authors, is the real living part of the cell, the cell-wall composed of cellulose being rather a kind of shell or case. For we see that all the phenomena of development depend upon it, and moreover, what is still more striking, it is this matter that exhibits all those phenomena of locomotion which have been observed in plants, namely, the circulation of the cell-sap, as it is called, in *Vallisneria*, *Chara*, the hairs of *Tradescantia*, &c., and in the zoospores, or moving reproductive bodies of the Algæ, which are composed entirely of nitrogenous matter when moving freely in the water, and only acquire a cellulose coat afterwards.

From these and similar considerations M. Garreau proposes to restrict the name of respiration to that process in which carbon is consumed, and carbonic acid given off, as in animals, and to place the other process, in which carbon is fixed and oxygen given off, among the nutritive processes. This would indeed appear to be the most philosophical way of arranging these phenomena of vegetation, but at the same time we are still so imperfectly acquainted with the import of these processes, and the details of their operation, that it would perhaps be wise to leave our terminology untouched until the analogies and differences of the nutritive operations in plants and animals have been more completely elucidated.

The experiments of M. Garreau are published in the "Annales des Sciences naturelles" for 1851, in Vol. XV., No. 1, and Vol. XVI., No. 5.—ARTHUR HENFREY, F.R.S., F.L.S., &c.

CULTURE OF CYCLAMENS.

THE Cyclamen is a genus of plants which unfortunately may be placed among the neglected ones, for, though in some places it may receive proper care, such instances form the exception rather than the rule. Mr. Atkins, the fortunate raiser of the beautiful variety described at page 89, has devoted more attention to Cyclamens than perhaps any other man in this country, and, at the present time, possesses one of the finest collections in Europe, which he manages with singular success. We regret we cannot give Mr. Atkins's system of culture, as that gentleman has some experiments in progress which he cannot make known until they are completed. Among Metropolitan growers Mr Myatt, senior, of the Manor Farm, Deptford, is certainly one of the most successful, having on several occasions had plants with two hundred expanded flowers at the same time, and every winter and spring he has a small house filled with this beautiful plant, the flowers of which find ready sale to the bouquet-makers in Covent Garden Market.

The Cyclamens, for the most part, are Alpine plants, and in their native state are found growing upon the debris of rocks and vegetable accumulations. Where they grow spontaneously, large patches of ground may be found covered with their tubers, which only require to be taken up at the proper time, that is, when the growth is completed, to be immediately fit for potting.

In this country Cyclamens are best treated as cold frame plants, as to grow them to perfection they require considerable shade in the growing season. They are increased sometimes by division of the roots, which is a bad plan, but generally by seed, which healthy plants produce in tolerable abundance, more especially if artificial impregnation be resorted to. The seed should be sown directly it is ripe and as early in the season as possible, using large shallow pans and a rich compost for the purpose, and covering the seeds not more than one-quarter of an inch deep. Place the pans in a gentle moist heat, water slightly, and take care that the surface of the soil does not become dry. As the young plants progress supply them liberally with water, and give plenty of air to make them strong. If a large quantity is grown, it will be best to prick the young plants out on a prepared bed, under a frame, and the frame should be thus prepared :—First place a good depth of draining material upon the ground (a snug warm corner), and then, over that, a foot or eighteen inches deep of properly fermented dung, or dung and leaves. When the heat has to some extent subsided, place the frame upon it, place a stratum of cinders or cinder-ashes over the entire surface, and then fill the frame to within four inches of the glass with rich compost, consisting of mellow turfy loam and peat, or thoroughly decomposed leaf-mould, in equal proportions, to which sufficient gritty sand may be added to make the whole mass light and porous; place this in the frame, and when it is warm proceed to prick the young plants out, taking them up as carefully as possible, so as not to injure the roots.

The plants should be placed in rows three inches apart, as, if you wish to make the most of them, it is advisable not to remove them until the end of the second year, at which time the largest will be blooming bulbs, and the others quite of a marketable size. Supply the plants plentifully with water after they are established, and shut the frame up warm every afternoon; but when the growth is completed, gradually decrease the water, and withdraw it altogether as the foliage begins to die off. Through the winter the frame must be kept quite dry, and be protected by proper covering in severe frost.

In the second season the plants will start of their own accord, then remove the surface soil and top-dress with fresh compost, to which one-eighth of perfectly decomposed cow-dung may be added. Sprinkle the plants twice or thrice a-week until they get into proper growth, and then, if the weather is suitable, give a good root-watering, and continue to water plentifully, using weak liquid manure occasionally until the season's growth is completed, then dry off as in the preceding season, and take up the tubers.

When grown in pots the same rules must be observed, namely, a vigorous growing season, and a season of rest, and the plants should be potted early in the autumn, so as to get them thoroughly rooted before they are introduced for blooming. The Cyclamen will force a little in a moist temperature; but, if the plants are potted as they show symptoms of starting into growth, but little forcing will be necessary, as a succession of flowers may be had throughout the winter and spring months.—A.

NEW AND RARE PLANTS.

CISSUS DISCOLOR.[*]—This plant, which is now exciting so much interest among cultivators, on account of its exceedingly beautiful foliage, is a native of Java, and was found in the low moist valleys, in the interior of the Island, having for its companions the far-famed Upas-tree (*Antiaris toxicaria*); several monster Arads; two species of *Amorphophallus,—campanulatus* and *giganteus,*—whose tubers measured eighteen inches in circumference, those of former having flowered since their introduction; numerous species of *Ficus*, one of which has leaves like the common willow; another, a pretty little creeping sort, has something the habits of *F. repens*, but the leaves are more coriaceous, of a dark glossy green, and in form nearly falcate; and also the *Fagræa auriculata*, the flowers of which are white, and in form and size resemble those of the old *Solandra grandiflora*. The Upas does not appear to be possessed of such active poisonous properties as have been frequently attributed to it, the taking off a branch, and chopping up the leaves in the hand, not producing any sensible injury, but its virulent properties might no doubt show themselves if taken internally.

The *Cissus discolor* reached England in the autumn of 1851, and proves to be a free-growing

 Cissus discolor, Blume Bijd., 181; *C. marmorea*, of gardens.

fibrous-rooted evergreen stove-climber, having the old stems nearly round, and covered with a slightly verrucose bark of a grey colour. The young shoots are slender dark red, and deeply channelled. The joints are furnished with a pair of blunt scales, pale green in the centre, and margined with pink. The tendrils are inserted opposite the leaves, and when fully grown are about six inches long, unequally divided near their extremities and of a transparent rose colour. The leaves are alternate, cordate at the base, serrated, acuminate, with the veins reticulated; the larger ones seven and a-half inches in length, by three and a-half inches at the widest part, but the medium-sized ones are about six inches

CISSUS DISCOLOR.

by three; the petiole is from two to three inches long, channelled, and of the same colour as the young shoots. The under surface is a dark reddish purple, and on the upper surface the colours are disposed as follows:—First, there is a velvety band with an undulating margin down the centre, of a rich violet purple, covering one-third of the entire surface, widest at the base, and gradually tapering towards the point of the leaf; from this ramify smaller bands down the side ribs, olive green, and becoming beautifully interlaced at their extremities. The spaces between these ribs are raised, giving the leaf the appearance of having been embossed, and, in colour, resemble a lustrous pearl, stained (especially next the central band) with granulated purplish lake. The entire leaf, including the serratures, is surrounded with a well-defined narrow belt of lake. When the leaves become old the ribs are all margined with grass green, and the spaces between them "silvery grey." As the plant is a tolerably quick grower, and consequently has leaves in all stages of growth at the same time, this rather adds to, than detracts from, its merits as an ornamental plant, by increasing the variety of colour.

However many vegetable beauties may still flourish unseen in the almost impenetrable forests and jungles of the East, certainly the *Cissus discolor* is by far the most striking variegated plant that has hitherto been seen in this country. The peculiar "metallic" hue of the leaves, when viewed as a whole, is not to be found elsewhere, except it is among the endless colours of the Humming Birds.

It may be urged that as those plants which have highly coloured, or otherwise, handsome foliage, have generally less attractive flowers, and are consequently of little importance for decorative purposes; but let any who has not done so try the experiment of arranging their plants (whether in the stove, green-house, or conservatory). not so as to form an uninterrupted mass of flowers, but with a proportionate number (not less than one-third) of plants having ornamental foliage regardless of their flowers interspersed, and the improved effect will be apparent. They impart that rich tropical appearance to a collection which is at once appreciated by a person of taste, and the foliage of the majority being persistent, they are equally attractive at all seasons.

The *Cissus discolor* is a plant of easy culture, and will be found to grow well in equal parts of light turfy loam and peat, adding a little leaf soil, with sufficient coarse gritty sand, to keep the compost porous. Let it be well drained with large crocks, covering them over with rough turfy peat. Drainage made with the crocks broken small, soon becomes choked up. It is worse than useless for any plant after it has been removed from a three-inch pot.

This plant requires a high temperature, and must therefore be placed in the hottest part of the stove or orchid house, and shading must be particularly attended to on bright days. This latter is essentially requisite in order to produce that intensity of colour which makes it so charming. Most plants require strong solar light to bring out their colours to perfection, but the one under consideration is an exception, which is readily accounted for by tracing the plant to its natural habitat, where the sun is scarcely able to dart his fiery rays through the dense mass of luxuriant vegetation by which it is surrounded, but whose burning heat, acting on the saturated moss-clad soil, causes a thick vapour to exhale, which is highly congenial to vegetable life, but far otherwise to the botanical rambler, who may prolong his stay among these unhealthy shades.

The plant is admirably adapted for training up a pillar, or on the end walls, or divisions of the stove. If trained up the rafters the young shoots must be allowed to hang down, or the effect would be partially destroyed by the surface of the leaves turning to the roof, instead of facing the observer's eye. It is also equally suitable for pot culture, and in this case any trellis may be used that taste may suggest; probably one of upright pillar-like form will be found to be as suitable for displaying its varied tints as any that may be devised.

As the autumn approaches, the supply of water must be gradually diminished, and the plant kept rather dry from November till February, allowing it only just sufficient water to keep the roots healthy. This partial rest will enable it to start into growth with renewed vigour in the following spring, when the former treatment may be resumed. It has not yet flowered, and is at present only in the Tooting Nursery.—H. BUCKLEY, *Tooting.*

TETRATHECA ERICÆFOLIA.—We are obliged to Messrs. Henderson of the Pine Apple Nursery for the means of illustrating this pretty greenhouse shrub, originally introduced in 1820, but long since lost, and now reintroduced by the agency of Mr. Drummond. It is an evergreen sub-shrub, with erect branches, bearing linear heath-like leaves, which, on the more perfectly developed portions of the plant, grow five or six in a whorl, but are sometimes scattered; they are revolute, with scabrous margins. From the axils of the

TETRATHECA ERICÆFOLIA.

leaves towards the end of the branches the nodding flowers are produced, so as to form leafy spikes of blossom; they consist of a calyx of four ovate acutish sepals, and a corolla of an equal number of oblong obtuse pinkish-lilac petals; the anthers are dark-coloured, tipped with yellow, and open by a tubular orifice at the apex. The flowers have a very agreeable scent, resembling that of *Cyclamen persicum:* and, altogether, this is a greenhouse shrub deserving of extensive culture. It belongs to the order Tremandraceæ.

NOVELTIES AT THE METROPOLITAN EXHIBITIONS.

THE June *fêtes* of the Horticultural and Royal Botanic Societies were held, the latter on the 9th, the former on the 12th ult., in both cases under very unfavourable conditions of weather. Indeed, so thoroughly wet an exhibition-day as that of the Royal Botanic Society we never remember to have seen; and this was the more to be regretted as the display of American plants, which has this year been very fine, was at the time in full beauty. The Horticultural Society's day, though more favourable, was so cold and cheerless as to very much limit the attendance. As to the objects of exhibition, both Societies were well supplied, though there was lacking the freshness of May. Thus the miscellaneous groups, the Azaleas, the Orchids, and Roses, were not so fine as on the former occasions, while on the other hand, the Heaths were decidedly improved, and the Pelargoniums also were better developed. There were again some finely-grown Pansies in pots, and very creditable Pinks exhibited in a similar way. The display of fruits presented nothing extraordinary.

The novelties produced at the Regent's Park included some interesting plants. There was from Messrs. Henderson, of the Pine Apple Nursery, the very fine *Gastrolobium calycinum*, which promises to be a first-rate plant when brought under proper cultivation; and along with it, from the same source, a slender yellow-flowered bushy *Gompholobium* called *Bidwillii*. They also sent a very pretty novel *Stylidium*, bearing rosulate tufts of radical spathulate leaves, and pyramidal racemes of pink flowers of conspicuous size. *Munronia javanica*, a sweet and free-flowering dwarf white-flowered meliaceous stove shrub, came from Messrs. Rollisson of Tooting. Messrs. E. G. Henderson & Son sent the *Pentarhaphia verrucosa*, a pretty stiff shrubby Gesnerwort, with small leathery leaves and scarlet flowers; and also a coarse stove perennial, with cream-coloured axillary gesneraceous flowers, called *Nantylocalyx bracteatus*. The fine *Franciscea eximia* was produced, but not in good condition. Indifferent plants of the very pretty *Linaria reticulata*, accompanied by a paler-flowered variety, and *Armeria Welwitschii* from Portugal, came from Mr. Stark, of Edinburgh.

In addition to these, there were the *Calodracon nobilis*; a fine species of *Ficus* called *imperialis* and *Jacaranda Caroba*, the two latter from Messrs. Rollisson, and all plants remarkable for their foliage. The most remarkable new Orchid was *Dendrobium clavatum*.

At Chiswick, the finest novelty was unquestionably a species of *Lælia*, called *purpurata*, from Messrs. Backhouse of York, remarkable for the rich deep colouring of its lip, which is purple, paler, and veined towards the tip, the tube-like base yellow with purplish veins; the sepals and petals are flesh-coloured; it is from St. Catherine's. *Cleisostoma?* *crassifolium*, an insignificant plant, came from the same source; also a Californian *Diplacus*, with nankeen-coloured flowers, which had been previously bloomed in one or two collections near London during the last autumn and present spring. Messrs. Standish and Noble sent a very pretty scarlet-flowered Chinese Lily, *Lilium sinicum*, in the way of *L. concolor*; and along with it two splendid evergreen Berberries, *B. Beallii* and *B. trifurca*, both having very large leathery pinnated foliage of the richest green, and expected to prove hardy

Among the Cacti produced at this exhibition was one from Mr. Green, called *C. crenatus grandiflorus*, a very striking kind, with creamy white flowers, the sepals being yellow and brown externally; its stems are very broad, flat, and crenated. Messrs. Rollisson had a remarkably fine tuft of the Venus' Fly Trap, *Dionæa muscipula*, exhibited beneath a large bell-glass.

We noticed one or two fine seedling Fuchsias exhibited by Mr. Turner. One of these, *Model*, has very large flowers with bright coral-red well reflexed sepals, and a fine deep purple corolla; another named *Perfection* had the flowers similar, but the plant appeared coarser in habit. There was also a seedling variegated Pelargonium, raised by Mr. Kinghorn, named *Attraction*, the peculiarity of which consisted in the presence of an irregular zone of red and brownish-purple interposed between the green centre and white margin of the leaves; the flowers are cherry-coloured, produced in large trusses. Another useful kind for bedding was shown, the Titness Ivy-leaved, which has deep rosy crimson flowers. At the Regent's Park, where Mr. Kinghorn's Attraction was also shown, there were two others of the ".scarlet" class with horse-shoe marked foliage, both likely to be useful for the flower-garden; these were Miss Emily Field, with pinkish-white flowers, and Kingsbury Favourite, with the flowers a delicate salmony-rose.

Among the most striking of the novelties recently presented to the National Floricultural Society, the following may be mentioned :—*Fuchsia Glory*, from Mr. Smith, Hornsey; it has large flowers, and well reflexed sepals of a rich coral-red, with fine deep violet purple corolla. *Pelargonium odoratissimum punctatum*, from Mr. Ayres of Blackheath, one of a promising new class of bedding flowers; this variety has scented foliage, and deep maroon spotted flowers on a pale lilac ground, and is a cross between the fancy and the scented-leaved classes. *Calceolaria Heywood Hawkins*, from Messrs. A. Henderson & Co., a dwarf free-flowering half-shrubby yellow and brown variety, promises to be useful in the flower garden.

WALKS AFTER WILD FLOWERS.*

THIS, which is the title of a book we desire to introduce to the notice of our readers, tells us that it comes from the Sister Isle; and the author, who dates his preface from Cork, explains that the "Bohereens," or "little roads," in which his walks after wild flowers were principally pursued, were the green lanes of the vicinity of that city. But although local in its subject, these "Walks" are calculated to excite an interest in all who enjoy the pleasures of natural history gossip, since they have been the inducement to the collection of a number of very interesting facts and anecdotes, combined and digested into a most entertaining and pleasingly-written little volume. The plan adopted is that of a series of letters devoted to the popular description, and the antiquarian and poetical illustration of the Irish native species of the orders Ranunculaceæ to Cruciferæ inclusive, as enumerated in the British Flora; but although this systematic outline is adhered to, there is scarcely any other trace of scientific technicality, and the greater part of the letters are occupied with those points which are interesting to all. When we say that the author's references range from Sir John Mandeville to Burns, and from the Library of Useful Knowledge to Shakspere, we give some idea of the variety of his reading, and the comprehensiveness of the fields in which he has gleaned, and we willingly bear testimony to the taste with which he has selected. We have not often seen a little work better calculated to excite a taste for the observation of nature; and while in this respect it is admirably fitted for the young, it contains very much that will be read with equal pleasure by those of all ages who delight to while away a leisure hour in instructive chit-chat.—H.

THE PARTERRE OF VARIEGATED PLANTS.

IF the present age is distinguished for one thing more than another, it is for the searching scrutiny with which every object brought forward is examined. While great discoveries in art and science are being revealed, we are constantly warned by signal failures against entertaining too sanguine expectations. The mind thus becomes disciplined into that circumspection which best comports with prudent action; and, as inquiry proceeds, many objects which had long been overlooked, or lightly treated, undergo a rigid investigation. During the last few years many common subjects, formerly neglected by horticulturists, have been introduced to notice, and have received much attention both from the practical operative and the learned theorist. Ferns, Mosses, Lichens, Weeping Trees, and American plants, may be instanced; and it appears now very likely that variegated plants will become much more extensively studied and grown as a class than they ever have been.

The immediate cause of the variegation of leaves has scarcely been satisfactorily accounted for, and perhaps it will long remain among the mysteries of nature. It is also a curious fact, that the flowers of many variegated plants are singularly inconspicuous. With respect to the markings of the leaves,

* Walks after Wild Flowers, or the Botany of the Bohereens. By Richard Dowden. London: Van Voorst. 1852.

it has indeed been asserted that plants having foliage with any colour different from the various shades of green, are not in a true state of health, but the result of much experience, is decidedly adverse to such an hypothesis, since the marks of yellow and white and crimson are not only the same in the same variety, but invariably permanent in their duration, and this, too, while the functions of the plants are perfectly regular and complete.

Variegated plants, then, may be very properly considered as a distinct class; and while it is perhaps impossible to account satisfactorily for their peculiarities, their numbers continue to increase. Even many of the common wild plants have been accidentally obtained with beautifully marked foliage.

Variegated plants are seldom if ever successfully propagated from seed, and therefore the surest and best methods of perpetuating a variety having the leaves marked with white, yellow, or red, are by division, by cuttings, or by grafting or budding on a stock of the plain leaved species.

With respect to the flowers of variegated plants, those of the Geranium, Bramble, and many of the small herbaceous genera, are in nowise inferior to those of the true species; while in the case of some exotics, there is a striking paucity of colour, and often of the size of the flower, and this is especially the case with plants that are natives of tropical climates. Nothing, for example, can surpass the rich markings of the leaves of some of the species of *Anœctochilus*, *Physurus*, *Dossinia*, *Cissus discolor*, or even *Maranta*, and one or two species of *Caladium*, as *C. bicolor*, but their flowers are not at all attractive. On the other hand, *Æchmea fulgens*, and *Vriesia speciosa*, form rare examples of a richly-coloured inflorescence accompanying finely-marked leaves in tropical species.

The number of variegated plants of dwarf habit, suitable for growing in pots or the borders, is now considerable, and amateurs having small gardens may derive much pleasure in the culture of a select group. Many species of Alpine plants are to be obtained with variegated leaves. Striking peculiarities in plants are always interesting, and when connected with beautiful colour or handsome forms, their value is much augmented.—P. F. K.

SCIENTIFIC GLEANINGS.

THE following particulars are gleaned from the proceedings of the Botanical Society of Edinburgh, at its meeting on the 10th June:—Mr. M'Nab mentioned a magnificent specimen of the *Lilium giganteum* of Wallich, or *L. cordifolium* of Don's Flora Nepalensis, now flowering, for the first time in Britain, in the Comely Bank Nurseries, from seed originally sent home by Major Madden, collected in the damp shady woods of Kemaon. The plant at Comely Bank is now nine feet six inches high, and in flower. Major Madden states that this gigantic Lily grows at between 7000 to 9000 feet of elevation, in deep black vegetable soil, and averaging from five to eight feet in height, the bulbs being always found on the surface of the soil.

A paper was read from C. C. Babington, Esq., M.A., on a supposed new species of *Eleocharis*. The plant described by Mr. Babington had been picked in the autumn of 1844, by Professor Balfour, at Taynlone, in Cantyre, along with *Scirpus pauciflorus*. Among specimens of the latter plant transmitted by Dr. B., Mr. H. C. Watson had detected the new species to be noticed. The species has been denominated *Eleocharis Watsoni* by Mr. Babington, and is thus described:—Spikes terminal, solitary, oblong; glumes acute, (?) the lowest one somewhat blunt, and surrounding the base of the spike; style bifid; the achene convex on both sides, oblong, very obtuse, with its base slightly attenuated, the angles rounded, and obscurely punctate-striated, the base of the style persistent, broadly depressed; four—six hypogynous setæ shorter than the achene; culms sheathed at the base, the sheath abruptly truncate. Mr. Babington, after remarking on the differences between it and the allied plants, *Eleocharis uniglumis*, *E. multicaulis*, and *E. palustris*, expressed an earnest hope that some botanist would visit the locality in Cantyre, and determine more completely the character of the species, which at present rests on the examination of three or four specimens only.

Chrysanthemums.

1 Golden Drop. 2 La Sapajou. 3 La Ruche. 4 Versailles Defiance

NEW CHRYSANTHEMUMS.

WITH our opening pages we gave a plate of Pompon Chrysanthemums, and we now give a few more gems from the same sources, viz., Messrs. E. G. Henderson and Son, and Mr. Salter of Hammersmith. The kinds now represented are very pretty examples of the Anemone-flowered Pompons, and also Mr. Salter's seedling, Versailles Defiance, a large kind of so much merit that it obtained a certificate of excellence from the National Floricultural Society in the autumn of last year. Mr. Salter is the only raiser of seedling Chrysanthemums in this country, and that only from seed saved in the south of France or Italy; for it is found that Chrysanthemum seed will not ripen in our dripping climate except under circumstances,—those of dry stove heat,—which cannot be afforded as a mercantile speculation. At Welbeck, a few years back, Mr. Tillery succeeded in ripening seed in the Pine stove, but we never heard that anything remarkable emanated from his labours.

The Pompon Chrysanthemums may certainly be classed among the choicest of flowers for winter garniture; for, blooming as they do

" When chill November's surly blast
Lays field and forest bare,"

they come when flowers are doubly welcome and loveable. The improvement that has been made in the Pompon varieties since their introduction is quite remarkable, for if the drawings representing the seedlings of last year, sent over by M. Miellez, of Lille, are to be relied upon, perfection of form is really attained; the serratures upon the end of the petal have almost disappeared in some varieties, which are assuming a broad, full, and hemispherical form. To be perfect, each flower should form at the least two-thirds of a ball, have stout, full, broad, and smooth petals, without either notch or serrature upon them, and these must be symmetrically formed, and then the *florists' beau ideal* of perfection is attained. It must, however, be admitted that, though the rule-and-compass plan of judging flowers is good, there are those who consider these laws too arbitrary for general observance; and we are among those who consider that brilliant colour, with even moderate form, is very preferable to perfect form with indifferent colour. Our standard for a useful and generally saleable plant is fine habit, profuse blooming, and rich brilliant colour, and then if the rule-and-compass plan of perfect form and substance can be added, we ask nothing more; but perfect form without either colour or fine habit of plant is not to be tolerated, except by the rigidly tight-laced in floricultural sophistry.

Of the introductions of this season, which M. Miellez's plate lays before us, we would particularly point to *Lais*, a brilliant crimson maroon flower of exquisite form; *Aramis*, plum colour, tipped with rose, and slightly incurved at the tips; *Graziella*, straw white tipped with cherry-colour; *Jason*, bright canary yellow; *Jonquille*, bronzy golden yellow; *Sathaniel*, bright rose, white centre; *Justine Tessier*, pure white, small; *Rose Pompon*, quilled rosy pink with light centre; *Beauté Toulousaine*, lively carmine or flesh colour; *Tacite*, creamy yellow, tipped with cherry-colour; *President Decaisn*, pale flesh colour, rather large; *Alveoliflorum* is an Anemone-flowered variety, with, if the drawing is correct, bluish lilac rays; *Quassimodo* and *Phœbus* are two pretty and distinct flowers of the yellow section. All the Pompon Chrysanthemums are pretty, but our continental friends run their varieties so close, that in select collections many of them are valueless. Most of these varieties are inclined to grow dwarf and compact, and we think they might be had in very compact bushy specimens in the following manner:—We would procure a quantity of bottomless pots of the 4-inch size, and having planted the stools or old plants in a good rich border, we would, towards the end of July, peg each shoot down horizontally to the surface of the ground, and placing a piece of slate or tile under the point, would place a pot over it, so that the shoot in its after progress could grow upright through the pot. In this state they might remain for a time, but towards the middle we would, taking advantage of a sunny day, strip the leaves from the lower part of the shoot within the pot, give it a slight twist to lacerate the bark, and then fill the pot half full of good rich soil. Into this the branch would root, and, having still the support of the old plant, would grow very robustly. As the plant progressed, the pot might be filled with compost, and it could also be assisted with liquid manure both to the old plant and the young one. Towards the end of September, we should, at intervals of a few days, gradually separate the young from the old plant, pot it at once into an 8-inch pot in rich compost, and plunge in a slight bottom heat in a frame or pit, taking care to shade for a few days. In this way we have no doubt plants as dwarf, perfect, and compact as the Geraniums shown at the London exhibitions might be grown, and the slight bottom heat would enable them to throw fine compact flowers.

With the large kinds it is the fashion of some of the prize growers to plunge the pots containing the plants into large tubs, these tubs being filled with manure or rich compost, into which the plants root, and, consequently, instead of being "grown in 11-inch pots," they have had all the advantage of an 18-inch pot. But what is their fate on the day of exhibition? To keep them from flagging they almost require a man to stand by them with the watering-pot, and, consequently, no sooner is the exhibition over than they are consigned to the rubbish heap. This is prize-hunting with a vengeance, but not plant-growing for the love of plants.—A.

FORCING THE LILY OF THE VALLEY.

AMONGST the delicacies of the early spring bouquet, the Lily of the Valley holds a most prominent place. Its purity, gracefulness, and poetic associations, conspire to make it not only the favourite of to-day, but doubtless will secure it such a position as long as civilization endures. Gorgeousness, dignity, and splendour, belong to Azaleas, Camellias, Roses, &c.; but not one of these popular favourites can supply a twig capable of taking the place of the Lily in the bouquet. That universal favourite, the White Camellia may possibly rival its whiteness, but we seek in vain for the exquisite aroma and delightful simplicity of form, calling to mind the hours of childhood; for who has not, in early days, instinctively sought the Lily of the Valley in some secluded nook?

We have recently heard of "Orchids for the Million," "Bedding Plants for the Million," &c.; and why not Early Flowers for the Million, in these days of cheap glass? Amongst the numerous dainties which the possessor of a glass-house and a hotbed may aspire to, our present pet may be placed; for there is nothing astonishing about its culture. The chief danger will consist in the possibility of "killing it with kindness."

It requires two years to prepare the Lily for forcing, in order to have it in the highest degree of perfection. In all forcing affairs, the first, and by no means inferior, division of the subject is preparation. Now, it is well in Lily forcing to have two sets of plants, the one in the open ground, the other in pots from the commencement. The latter is by far the best for early forcing; the former will produce more exuberant blooms at a later period: the pots producing from the end of November until the end of January; those potted from the soil, from that period until Lilies blossom out-doors.

Large pots are necessary; and those who intend to procure a long succession for the drawing-room will do well to get some shallow pans made for the purpose. Such should be about nine inches diameter, by about seven inches in depth, and would, as I think, look respectable if painted a deep straw colour, and sanded over with large and sparkling grit whilst wet. Such would aid in bringing out the purity of the Lilies.

New plantations may be made any time from November to March. I prefer the middle of February. They love a sound and rich soil, but will succeed in any good garden soil, which retains moisture in a steady way, but not in excess. For pots, one-half strong loam, and the other half composed of very old cow manure and leaf soil, thoroughly decomposed, grows them in the highest perfection. In making new plantations, the ground may be marked out into beds, and my practice is to plant them in circles of about eight inches diameter, the circles fifteen inches apart. The ground being duly prepared, we take an 8-inch pot, and inverting it, stamp circles in the proper places; and these circles are filled with young plants, both in and within the ring. When planted, I cover the whole surface three inches with very rotten manure, as a mulching, and this proves of immense benefit.

Of course, the planting in pots is conducted in a similar way, but the latter should be plunged during the whole of their culture. It may here be remarked that the Lily loves a partial shade. I grow them on a wall border, on the north side, where, although they get a liberal amount of solar light, the soil, from its northern inclination, is kept comparatively cool through the summer. The summer's culture consists in keeping them free of weeds, and in liberal watering, and all blossom buds should be picked from the newly planted stock the moment they appear; indeed, by picking them away the second spring, a much superior " crown " is obtained.

And now as to their forcing : Bottom heat is essential to this part of their culture. In common with other herbaceous things, which store up in their roots the material by which the buds are developed, the root must be forced into action first. About sixty to seventy degrees is the bottom warmth most congenial to them. A plunging medium will be found the best—any fermenting material will do. Like the germination of seeds, some degree of darkness is of material benefit. Any structure which will give the above bottom warmth, with, at the same time, a much moderated top heat, of say fifty-five, is the place for them; and in this respect they class very well with the forcing of Dutch bulbs, their treatment for a while being nearly identical. In such a situation, they should be plunged overhead, covering the crown with six inches of finely-sifted old tan or vegetable mould.

In about three weeks or a month from their introduction to such conditions, they will begin to show their heads above the soil, and here what is termed in horticultural language " cooling down," must be resorted to. They have to be gradually inured to the light, and this is the work of another fortnight or so. Any structure which will afford them a gradually departing shade, with a temperature of fifty to sixty degrees, is the very place for them. And now, for the first time since their introduction to artificial warmth, occasional waterings will be requisite. As before observed, the Lily loves moisture, and weak and clear liquid manure may occasionally be administered. About forcing little more need be added. When the blossoms begin to unfold, any cool greenhouse will suit them; a depressed temperature—minus frost—will but tend to render the blossoms finer; so that whether fancy points to the drawing-room, the boudoir, or the snug parlour, it is all the same: anything but a very *high* temperature.

In conclusion, I may add, that those cultivated in the open soil, for later purposes, must be placed in pots in the middle of November, and, after a thorough watering, plunged overhead in any dry spot out-doors, and then subjected to the same ordeal in their turn. Like most other " rest roots," they produce the finest flowers by a gradual course of forcing, especially whilst the torpid root is acquiring a fresh action.

After forcing, the roots may have a renewal of their vigour by kindly attention, in the way of shelter, top-dressing, liquid manure, &c. I prefer, however, a fresh succession, and plant out the rejected ones in the common borders.—ROBERT ERRINGTON, *Oulton Park*.

New Garden Plants.

NYMPHÆA GIGANTEA, *Hooker*. Gigantic Water-lily.—Order Nymphæaceæ (Water-lily tribe).—A very remarkable Water-lily which has just been figured by Sir W. J. Hooker in the *Botanical Magazine*, in the hope of facilitating its introduction from North-Eastern Australia, where it is found. It is remarkable for its size. The leaves are nearly orbicular, and eighteen inches across. The flowers in the dried state are twelve inches in diameter, with numerous blue petals, and stamens so numerous as to hide the stigma. It is probably the same with an Australian Nymphæaceous plant, of which seeds have been imported under the name of *Victoria Fitzroyana*.

BERBERIS NEPALENSIS, *Wallich*. Nepal Ash-leaved Berberry.—Order Berberaceæ (Berberid tribe).—A remarkably handsome evergreen shrub, probably hardy, but only developing its full beauty under glass. It is very much like *B. glumacea*, and forms a stiff erect stem, with large delicate-green unequally pinnated foliage spreading on all sides; these leaves consist of from three to five pairs of ovate spiny-toothed leaflets. The flowers grow in a long, close, upright raceme, gracefully placed at the top of the stem, and are of a rich bright yellow. The fruit of this species is bluish-purple and oblong, by which latter circumstance it may be known from a nearly-related species, also inhabiting the hills of India, called *B. acanthifolia*, which produces globose fruit. This plant is probably the same as *B. Leschenaultii*. *B. nepalensis* is a native of the Himalayas, and is, according to Dr. Lindley, the *B. pinnata* of Roxburgh, as well as the *Mahonia nepalensis* of De Candolle. It was introduced to the Royal Botanic Garden, Kew.

BILLBERGIA POLYSTACHYA, *Lindley.* Many-spiked Billbergia.—Order Bromeliaceæ (Bromelwort tribe).—A very fine hothouse perennial, probably Brazilian, which was exhibited by M. de Jonghe, of Brussels, at Chiswick, in May last year. Dr. Lindley names it with some hesitation, not having had an opportunity of examining its flowers. Its leaves are channelled, margined with spiny teeth, inflated at the base, and curved back at the point. It flowers from a conical crowded compound mealy spike, on a scape taller than the leaves; its bracts and calyx are crimson, its corolla purple. Altogether it is a very pretty plant.

BILLBERGIA THYRSOIDEA, *Martius.* Thyrse-like Billbergia.—Order Bromeliaceæ (Bromelwort tribe).—A showy Pine-apple-like plant, with erect broad leaves, and a conical head of crimson flowers, issuing from amongst bracts of the same colour. It is a very beautiful stove perennial, and has been imported from Rio Janeiro by M. de Jonghe of Brussels, from whose nursery it has found its way to England.

GASTROLOBIUM CALYCINUM, *Bentham.* Large-calyxed Gastrolobium.—Leguminaceæ § Papilionaceæ (Leguminous plants).—A showy greenhouse shrub, of considerable value as an ornamental plant. The branches are smooth; the leaves are opposite (or ternate) elliptic somewhat keeled, glaucous, and terminated by a long pungent awn; at their base is a pair of spreading decurved spiny stipules. The flowers grow oppositely in terminal or axillary racemes, and are very large, the standard deep orange with a yellow spot at the base margined with crimson; the wings and standard deep crimson; they grow from the axil of a large obovate membranous inflated strongly nerved bract, the nerve being extended into a recurved mucro; the calyx is very large, the upper lip much largest, bifid with very obtuse segments, the segments of the lower lip ovate acute. The ovary is villose and distinctly stalked. This interesting plant has been raised by Messrs. Henderson, from Mr. Drummond's Swan River seeds, and we are indebted to them for the materials from which our figure and description are made.

PHRYNIUM SANGUINEUM, *Hooker.* Red-leaved Phrynium.—Order Marantaceæ (Marant tribe). —This very fine stove plant is known in the gardens as *Maranta sanguinea.* We have seen it in flower in several places, but nowhere finer than with Messrs. Jackson, of Kingston, by whom it was exhibited before the Horticultural Society. Whether in flower or not, the plant is ornamental. It has leaves nearly or quite a foot long, oblong-acuminate, green above, reddish purple beneath, and attached by short petioles. The scape is taller than the leaves, and bears a compact panicle of bracteated flowers, the rachis bracts and sepals all bright red. The petals are white, and about as long as the sepals. It has been received from the gardens of the Continent, and there appears to be no information as to its orgin and native country. It is, at any rate, a very desirable stove herbaceous plant.

LIMATODES ROSEA, *Lindley.* Rosy Limatode. —Order Orchidaceæ § Vandeæ (Orchid tribe).— Messrs. Veitch flowered this very handsome novelty last December. It is a stove terrestrial orchid, with fusiform pseudo-bulbs, oblong lanceolate plaited leaves, and many-flowered scapes taller than the leaves, bearing loosely-arranged large rose-coloured villose flowers; the lip is oblong undivided, rolled up at the base like a Cattleya, and marked at the base of the expanded part with a deep red ring; the sepals and petals are lance-shaped. This genus is nearly allied to Calanthe, and the present species

GASTROLOBIUM CALYCINUM.

is a beautiful addition to this favourite and showy tribe. It was found by Mr. T. Lobb, near Moulmein, and is described as a most abundant bloomer.

ACROPERA FLAVIDA, *Klotzsch.* Yellowish Acropera.—Order Orchidaceæ § Vandeæ (Orchid tribe).—A stove epiphyte, with ovate pseudo-bulbs, bearing at their apex a pair of oblong acuminate leaves, narrowed downwards, and from their base a pendulous raceme of pale yellow flowers, having an orange-yellow lip. Native of Mexico.

LYCASTE BREVISPATHA, *Klotzsch*. Short-bracted Lycaste.—Order Orchidaceæ § Vandeæ (Orchid tribe).—A stove epiphyte, bearing yellowish-green flowers, which have a white smooth lip. It has been flowered by M. Nauen of Berlin, and is a native of Guatemala.

CERASUS ILICIFOLIA, *Nuttall*. Evergreen Holly-cherry.—Order Drupaceæ (Almondwort tribe).—This is a fine evergreen bush or small tree, "apparently as hardy as a Laurel, and having the foliage of a Holly, with the flowers of a Bird-cherry." For all purposes to which hardy evergreen shrubs are applicable, this is one of the most valuable of recent introductions. The leaves are waved and spiny as in the Holly, and from their axils appear short spikes of white flowers, succeeded, according to Hartweg, by fruit resembling a small cherry. It is one of the many useful introductions of the Horticultural Society, and was obtained by them through Mr. Hartweg.

RHODODENDRON CILIATUM, *Hooker*. Fringed Rhododendron.—Order Ericaceæ (Heathwort tribe).—This is one of the earliest of the Sikkim Rhododendrons to produce its blossoms, which it seems to do freely in a very dwarf state, which habit may perhaps be turned to account in cross breeding. That which has everywhere flowered is a pale coloured form, which Sir W. Hooker calls *roseo-album*, and, though making a beautiful figure, has not been considered as in itself of much importance as an ornamental plant. The leaves are very hairy, but become at length smooth above; the flowers are bell-shaped, white, tinged with rose. It has flowered in various instances, so that its dwarf flowering habit seems to be confirmed. The little *Rhododendron lepidotum*, from the same country, which has also flowered very imperfectly, though distinct in character, does not promise to be of much horticultural value.

DACTYLICAPNOS THALICTRIFOLIA, *Wallich*. Thalictrum-leaved Dactylicapnos.—Order Fumariaceæ (Fumewort tribe).—A Nepalese plant introduced by Sir C. Lemon, Bart., in 1834, and flowering towards autumn. It is a hardy perennial, with smooth somewhat succulent climbing stems, growing six to eight feet high, biternate tendrilled leaves, and clustered racemes of large pendent yellow flowers of the singular form common to the race.

CANNA WARCZEWITZII, *Dietrich*. Warczewitz's Indian Shot.—Order Marantaceæ (Marant tribe).—A handsome addition to a race of fine exotic-looking stove perennials. This has ovate or ovate-oblong cuspidate-acuminate leaves, and bright scarlet flowers. The stems, peduncles, pedicels, flower buds, calyx, and bracts, are blood red, covered with a bluish bloom. It is a native of Central America.

OLEARIA PANNOSA, *Hooker*. Clothed Olearia.—Order Asteraceæ § Asteroideæ (Composite plants).—A shrub covered over with a close white felt, excepting on the upper parts of the leaves, which are bright green and shining; they are rather large, elliptic-oblong, and in their axils are produced, on long stalks, flower heads consisting of a single row of white ray florets surrounding a yellow disk. It is a native of South Australia, and is a greenhouse evergreen of little importance.

BEGONIA CONCHÆFOLIA, *Dietrich*. Shell-leaved Begonia.—Order Begoniaceæ (Begoniad tribe).—An elegant little stemless stove perennial, with deep shell-like peltate shining leaves. The flowers are very small, red; the petioles and peduncles also are bright red. It is from Costa Rica, and has been introduced by M. Warczewitz to Berlin. The deeply concave leaves, resembling mussel-shells, are very peculiar.

BEGONIA BULBILLIFERA, *Link* and *Otto*. Bulb-bearing Begonia.—Order Begoniaceæ (Begoniad tribe).—A very pretty bulbous stove perennial, producing at first heart-shaped roundish leaves, red beneath, and on the stems leaves of a more pointed and unequal figure. The flowers are deep rose-coloured and axillary. It is a Mexican plant, and is grown in the Berlin gardens.

CYCNOCHES AUREUM, *Lindley*. Golden Swan Orchis. — Order Orchidaceæ (Orchid tribe). — A fine stove epiphyte, bearing a long pendulous raceme of whole coloured pale, clear yellow flowers. It comes from Central America.

VANDA PEDUNCULARIS, *Lindley*. Pedunculate Vanda.—Order Orchidaceæ § Vandeæ (Orchid tribe).—A small hothouse epiphyte, with distichous two-lobed leaves, and racemes of comparatively small flowers on a very long peduncle; these are yellowish-green, with a deep purple lip hairy at the edges, and as much like hairy insects as those of our Bee and Spider Orchids. It is from Ceylon, and was bloomed last March by G. Read, Esq.

GESNERA PURPUREA, *Lindley*. Purple Gesnera.—Order Gesneraceæ (Gesnerwort tribe).—A very fine tuberous stove plant, allied to *G. Douglasii*. The leaves are whorled, heart-shaped, oblong, and downy. The flowers grow in a whorled panicle, and consist of a long downy tube, with the upper tube straight, two lobed, almost square, the lower lip with rounder and much shorter segments. The colour is purplish-rose, spotted with deeper purple. The origin of this fine plant is unknown, but it is supposed to be a garden hybrid. It is figured in *Paxton's Flower Garden*, t. 76.

CALODRACON NOBILIS, *Planchon*. Noble Calodracon.—Order Liliaceæ (Lilywort tribe).—This, which is the *Dracæna nobilis* of Van Houtte, is a beautiful hothouse shrub, growing erect, with dense foliage of a beautiful rich purple and crimson colour, arranged in broad streaks. It has not yet flowered, but it will be cultivated entirely for its splendid foliage. It is a native of Japan, and appears to have been brought into notice by M. Van Houtte, of Ghent.

ODONTOGLOSSUM ANCEPS, *Klotzsch*. Two-edged Odontoglossum.—Order Orchidaceæ (Orchid tribe).—A small stove epiphyte, with greenish-yellow white-lipped flowers, borne on a two-edged scape. It is from Brazil, and has been flowered in the Berlin gardens.

CALCEOLARIA STRICTA, *Humboldt* and *Bonpland*. Upright Slipperwort.—Order Scrophulariaceæ (Linariad tribe).—A shrubby species with good foliage, on this account, perhaps, useful for hybridizing. The leaves are willow-like, and the flowers are pale yellow. It is a Peruvian species, and has been obtained by Messrs. Veitch, of Exeter.

SOPHRONITIS PTEROCARPA, *Lindley.* Wing-fruited Sophronite.—Order Orchidaceæ (Orchid tribe).—A very pretty, though diminutive, stove epiphyte, with roundish oblong leaves, and short corymbose racemes of rosy purple flowers. It is a native of Brazil.

STENOCARPUS FORSTERI, *R. Brown.* Forster's Stenocarp.—Order Proteaceæ (Protead tribe).—A greenhouse shrub, with obovate retuse evergreen leaves, and umbels of small, apparently white flowers, of little beauty. It was sent to the Horticultural Society, from New Caledonia, by Mr. C. Moore.

CALLICARPA JAPONICA, *Thunberg.* Japanese Callicarp.—Order Verbenaceæ (Verbena tribe).—A soft-wooded shrub, growing two to three feet high, with oblong tapering or sometimes rhomboidal leaves, and dense axillary racemes of small pinkish flowers of little beauty. Introduced from Japan by Dr. Von Siebold, and blossoms in August and September.

CASSINIA LEPTOPHYLLA, *R. Brown.* Slender-leaved Cassinia.—Order Asteraceæ (Composite plants).—A neat growing evergreen shrub from New Zealand, said to be hardy. It forms a compact dwarf bush, with heath-like whitish leaves, and the branches terminate in little corymbs of white flowers.

ON THE BRANCHING OF PALM STEMS.*

THE branches of Palms are either subterraneous or arise, like the ordinary branches of Dicotyledons, above ground. Those Palms which produce subterraneous branches have a rhizome, or underground stem, produced from a horizontal branch of the parent stem; this sometimes turns up after running a certain distance, and comes above the ground; in such cases it gives off another branch at its base, which continues the horizontal growth (just like the growth of the rhizome of *Iris*); this is the mode in which the rhizome of the *Calamus Draco* of gardens is formed.

Branches spring from the axils of the scale-like leaves which clothe the rhizome, and if the latter are crowded the branches break through them. The branches either remain short, forming what is called a *turio*, or stretch out and form *runners*. *Metroxylon Rumphii* has very long ones, but in *Chamædorea elatior* they attain a length of four feet. In this plant these runners often arise from the base of the stem above ground, and dip down into it, rising out of it again at a distance of several feet to form a new stem. The underground parts are clothed with whitish or brownish scale-like leaves, which soon decay.

The branches occasionally given off above ground by Palms mostly arise low down, close to the roots, rarely from the axils of green or decaying leaves higher up on the trunk, and more frequently in young than in old stems. They occur oftenest in *Caryota sobolifera, Diplothemium maritimum, Phœnix dactylifera,* and *Chamædorea elatior;* while the allied *Caryota urens, Diplothemium caudescens, Phœnix sylvestris,* and *Chamædorea Schiedeana* produce no branches. *Phœnix dactylifera* (the Date Palm) is propagated exclusively by these lateral shoots, and never by seeds, because the trees raised from seed are said to yield less fruit; while, on the contrary, the plants of *Borassus flabelliformis,* raised from the stolons, bear smaller fruit. *Areca alba,* a native of the Mascarenhas, often divides into from two to ten branches, springing apparently from lateral buds; these branches grow perpendicularly upwards like the main stem, which then does not grow to the usual diameter; they bear flowers and fruit.

None of these ramifications seem to follow any definite rule, but to result from accidental favourable circumstances, excepting in the African genus *Hyphæne* (the Doum Palm of Egypt), where the trunk sends out a branch from time to time near the summit, the branch repeating this ramification, so that old trunks appear many times forked.—A. H.

A SIMPLE MODE OF GROWING AURICULAS.

A CORRESPONDENT has sent the following account of the mode of treating Auriculas, by which, leaving out of view the nice points which a florist professes to realize, vigorous health is secured, and this somewhat fickle flower may be converted into a lovely spring ornament. For this purpose,

* From *Martius's History of Palms.*

that race of Auriculas, called Alpines, mostly having flowers of bright self-colours—a class which the florists all but ignore—are most admirably adapted.

The details of culture are thus stated :—About the beginning of June the plants are taken out of the pots, and the soil shaken from their roots; the tap root is shortened if needful, and the plants are then re-potted in a compost of equal parts fresh loam and good well-decayed leaf-mould. The pots are set on the north side of a wall, and there remain all the summer, and until the middle of September, with no other attention than that of watering them when they require it. At the season just indicated they are placed in a cold pit facing the south, where they remain till the end of February. They are then top-dressed with the same kind of compost, and replaced in the frame, where they remain until they produce their flowers. At flowering time they are removed to a temporary pit at the north side of a wall, and are covered with canvas frames at night, as well as just when it rains. In cold weather, if any occurs at this season, they are kept close shut.

I am confident the plants are more healthy when thus treated than when grown in the strongly-manured composts which many persons use for this flower; as a proof of this, I never have a sickly plant.

During the winter, as it is necessary that the plants should be kept comparatively dry, it is desirable to set them on boards, or on a trellised stage; and if the frame can be arranged as to secure a thorough ventilation beneath, it will be all the better. Of course very little water will be given during winter.—R. W.

NOTES AND MEMORANDA.

NEW plants, among the recent introductions to our gardens, possess more interest or are likely to prove more valuable than the *Deutzia gracilis*, not only as an ornament for the shrubbery border, but also for pot cultivation. As a plant for early forcing, for the decoration of the conservatory, and also for cutting for bouquets, it will rank among the most useful in cultivation. Like its congeners, it is readily propagated by cuttings of the young wood, which require to be taken when it is in a half-ripened state. If the wood is strong and healthy, it will not be necessary to cut the cuttings at a joint, as they will strike just as freely if a leaf-bud and about an inch below is taken with it, and thus each joint or bud will make a plant. To insure the cuttings rooting quickly, a gentle bottom heat will be necessary, and they must also be covered with a glass, to prevent the undue evaporation of the moisture of the cutting. In cultivation, any light rich soil will be suitable,—such as a mixture of turfy loam, leaf-mould, and gritty sand, and when planted out any enriched garden soil will suit it. As a pot plant it will require much the same treatment as *Wiegela rosea*,—that is, the wood must be thoroughly matured in the autumn, to insure its blooming profusely when forced. We cannot imagine anything much finer, when grown to a good-sized specimen, than this very graceful plant, as by judicious stopping it may be trained into a very compact and elegant form.—A.

We learn from a private letter that gardening is now in the ascendant in Bavaria. Munich had its first exhibition of plants, flowers, and fruit, in April last, and this first essay was most satisfactory. In illustration, we may mention that the Royal Gardens of Nymphenburg, under the care of Mr. A. Heyl, who has studied horticulture in England, produced Heaths which will soon equal the English exhibition specimens. *Dielytra spectabilis* and *Deutzia gracilis* were among the most striking new plants produced. The parliament have voted a large sum for the erection of a new range of plant houses in the Royal Botanic Gardens of Munich; and the King is erecting, close to his palace, a magnificent winter-garden, which is to be erected on the top of a house at an elevation of nearly sixty feet, and will be very large. The "culture-garden" necessarily connected with this structure is completed, and contains many fine span-roofed houses heated with water-pipes.

The *Hardenbergia ovata alba*, a very ornamental greenhouse creeper, recently brought into notice, has been sent to us from the nursery of Messrs. Rollisson, of Tooting. It, in all points, except in the colour of the flowers, resembles the well-known *H. ovata*, but the flowers are white with a green spot on the base of the standard. For the purpose of variety, where greenhouse-conservatory creepers are prized, this may be considered as a desirable novelty, the contrast being good between its dark green broad leaves, and the pure white of its flowers.

Camellia Martinii, raised by Messrs. Jackson, of Kingston, and nicely figured in our contemporary the *Florist*, is deserving of special mention, as being the brightest coloured among the red Camellias at present known, and proving the nearest approach to scarlet. It is, in addition to this, a flower of good properties, well made, and very full of rounded imbricating petals. The *Countess of Ellesmere*, another of Messrs. Jackson's seedlings, is probably the finest and most beautiful light-coloured Camellia in existence, its fine broad, cupped petals, white faintly striped with pale rose, reminding one at once of the famous *Coupe de Hebe Rose*. This variety had a first-class certificate awarded to it by the National Floricultural Society, in April last.

The collection of Aquatic Plants in the Aquarium of the Botanic Garden, at Hamburgh, is in excellent condition. It includes ten young plants of the *Victoria Regia*, eight of *Euryale ferox*, a very scarce and fine annual water plant; together with many species of the genus *Nymphæa*, as *N. cærulea, cyanea, dentata, micrantha, neglecta, odorata, pygmæa, rubra, semiaperta, thermalis,* &c.; besides many other aquatics, which are expected to give a fine show next summer. Mr. Otto, the inspector of the garden, is an ardent cultivator of aquatics. We understand that his foreman, Mr. Loscher, is at present engaged in the preparation of a work on *Victoria Regia*, its history, cultivation, &c., with two plates.

RENOVATION OF CAMELLIA PLANTS.

MOST collections of Camellias contain some tall woody plants, which from some cause produce only a few leaves and flowers at the top of their branches. Such plants, themselves but little prized, may nevertheless, by a process of grafting, be converted into beautiful flowering trees. In this way these old woody plants, which are only fit to stand at the back of a collection, are turned to good account by many of the Camellia growers of Belgium. This practice is not on the Continent a novelty, but it is not so generally made available by English cultivators. On this account a short description of the *modus operandi* may not be unacceptable.

Old plants, from six to ten feet high, and having a straight stem from two to three inches in diameter, are the most suitable for being grafted, in the way about to be described, but others which are more branchy may also be employed. The first part of the operation consists in removing all the branches (supposing the plant to have a long straight stem), so that nothing is left but the naked stem or trunk, which is cut clean off, the top and the summit being pared quite smooth, and covered with grafting clay. Then along a spiral and imaginary line, carried the whole length of the stem, grafts or buds are inserted at the distance of every second inch *in height*. These grafts are tied in the usual manner, and the tree or plant is placed in a narrow upright glass frame, which is made about a foot higher than the top of the stem. This narrow frame or cover is carefully mulched with moss at the bottom, which rests on the soil in the pot, for the purpose of excluding the air. The tree with its glass cover is then removed to a house where the temperature is moderately warm, or nearer that of an ordinary stove than a cool greenhouse.

The method of constructing these covers is very simple, and they are always useful in such cases. The frame-work consists of four upright wooden bars of sufficient strength and height, grooved so as to admit of being glazed, and the top may be covered with a single square of glass. They may be made of any width, but five or six inches will be found to be wide enough for most purposes. By means of these cases the newest and most select varieties may be worked on the old trunks, either singly at the top or several may be distributed over the whole stem, and in this way many different sorts can be grown on one plant.

The tree thus treated will have made vigorous shoots at the end of the second year; but the shoots which may push out on the old trunk must be carefully cut off as soon as they appear.—H.

Tritoma Rooperii

TRITOMA ROOPERII.[*]

IKE all the other Tritomas in cultivation, this is an extremely handsome plant. It is, in some respects, near T. Burchelli, but differs obviously from the figures and descriptions of that species in its densely-compacted sessile flowers, its very conspicuous bracts, and its included stamens. No other described sort seems to approach it. It has been introduced from Kaffraria by Captain E. Rooper, who describes it as growing in marshy places ; and we are indebted to the Rev. T. Rooper, of Brighton, for the opportunity of figuring it from a specimen which flowered last spring, in his African frame. Mr. Rooper has since informed us that it has been flowering in the open air; and he writes:—"A more brilliant flower I have seldom seen ; the upper blossoms are the colour of sealing-wax highly varnished, the lower yellow, and when the sun shines it is scarcely possible to look long at it. The specimen I sent in the winter was flowered in the frame, and did not do justice to the plant. It is easily propagated by offsets, and, I believe, is hardy ; at least, all the protection it had last winter was a broken hand-light." Captain Rooper describes it as tuberous-rooted, and varying to deep red.

It is a half-hardy, or perhaps hardy, perennial, with a fleshy root-stock, terminated by a crown of leaves. These leaves are upwards of four feet long, two inches broad at the base, and tapering gradually to a long point; they are recurvo-arcuate, carinate, striate, smooth on the keel, and having an entire narrow cartilaginous border below, minutely cartilagineo-serrulate above, especially near the apex. The scape is a foot high, leafless, solid, with a few large bracts below the spike, and terminating in a crown or coma of crowded membranous bracts, subtending abortive flowers. The spike is roundish-ovate, the flowers sub-sessile and pendulous, very densely arranged in spiral series. The pedicels are very short, with a bract at the base of each. These bracts are scarious, those of the spike oblong-ovate obtuse, with three to five fuscous nerves ; they are half an inch long, entire, becoming smaller, narrower, and more acute upwards ; those of the crown are oblong-acute, or even acuminate, one to three-nerved, and have glandular serratures. The perianth is tubular, slightly curved, narrowed above the base, an inch and three-quarters long, flame-coloured or orange-red on the upper side, greenish-yellow below, six-nerved, the nerves green ; the limb consists of six short erectish ovate-obtuse segments, the three inner recurved at the apex, the three outer somewhat shorter, and their apices incurved. There are six hypogynous unequal included stamens, with distinct filaments and ovate anthers. Styles three, more or less consolidated in one, the stigmas spirally contorted. Ovary ovate-conical, three-furrowed, obsoletely three-sided, three-celled, the cells many-seeded.—M.

NOVELTIES AT THE LONDON EXHIBITIONS.

S usually happens, the July shows have been deficient in novelties, as well as on the whole less attractive than the earlier *fêtes*. The Pelargoniums at the Regent's Park, and the Heaths and Roses at Chiswick, were the prominent features. At both, especially the former, the miscellaneous stove and greenhouse plants looked "fagged," though there were some striking exceptions ; and at both, also, the Orchids were far inferior to those produced on former occasions. Nothing remarkable has been produced among fruits.

At the Regent's Park, the most noticeable novelty was a narrow-petalled orange-coloured variety of *Rhododendron javanicum*, or perhaps a distinct species ; in this case the tube of the flower was narrow, and the segments of the limb narrower and more reflexed than occurs in the ordinary Javanese *Rhododendron*, more resembling the figures of *R. Brookeanum*. This came from Messrs. Lane, of Berkhampstead. An indifferent plant of a rather pretty blue-flowered stove annual, called *Klugia Notoniana*, came from Messrs. Henderson. There was also a starved example of some South

* *Tritoma Rooperii*, n. sp.—Leaves very long, recurved, carinate, taper-pointed, minutely cartilagineo-serrulate above ; spike roundish-ovate ; flowers sub-sessile, densely crowded in the axils of oblong-obovate scarious bracts, which are obtuse, with three to five fuscous nerves, the upper ones acute or acuminate, one to three-nerved, with glandular serratures, and forming a coma above the developed flowers ; stamens included.—M.

q

African Lachenalia, which appeared to differ in nowise from *L. tricolor*. Among orchids was a small orange-flowered *Dendrobium*, from Mr. Blake, which, if flowered in masses, might prove to be ornamental. *Musa zebrina*, and a species of *Nepenthes*, were contributed by Messrs. Rollisson; the former is a species of Banana with the leaves blotched with brownish purple; the latter a small species of the pitcher-bearing family, which may prove distinct. A very interesting collection of variegated-leaved plants came from the same nursery. There were some good collections of British Ferns in pots.

At Chiswick the principal novelty was *Medinilla Sieboldiana*, from Mr. Cole, of Dartford; this is a neat-growing and apparently a free-blooming species, with pale purplish flowers. Then Messrs. Veitch has a new *Leptosiphon* from California, with pretty sulphur-coloured flowers, orange at the centre, with a red spot at the base of each segment; and with it was a *Collinsia* named *bartsiæfolia*, too like *C. bicolor*. They had also cut specimens of *Dracæna indivisa*, a large-growing New Zealand species with panicles of whitish flowers. Both Messrs. Rollisson and Messrs. Henderson showed *Æchmea miniata*, a very pretty Bromeliaceous plant, with the leaves dull purple on the under surface, and producing rather dense panicles of vermilion-coloured flowers, the petals of which are at first greyish blue, and afterwards change to pink. It is well worth growing. Mr. Carson had a new small-flowered greenish-yellow *Epidendrum*; and a useful, though comparatively small-flowered, white *Achimenes* called *margaritæ*, came from Messrs. Lane. There were some small examples of ornamental evergreen trees. One of them *Abies jezoensis*, and another *Cephalotaxus Fortuni*, are very distinct and elegant, and quite hardy trees; they came from Messrs. Standish and Noble. The other, *Araucaria Cookii* or *columnaris*, is rather tender, but very elegant; this came from Messrs. Henderson. Among other noticeable collections, were some groups of variegated plants from Messrs. Lee, of Hammersmith, and Messrs. Rollisson, of the Tooting Nursery.

The patronage extended to Roses by the two leading societies, has not yet been productive of results such as might have been anticipated. Neither the Rose-garden in the Regent's Park, nor the Rose-house at Chiswick, have so far presented anything of that fairy aspect which one especially looks for in a garden of Roses; and, indeed, it is difficult to conceive how beds filled with tall bare-stemmed standards in the one case, or crowds of small dwarfs of the delicate tea kinds sunk in a dark wooden house in the other, can be expected to bear a very attractive appearance. There is much room for improvement in the trials that have been made in both cases.—M.

LATE MOSS ROSES.

AMIDST the splendour of our exhibition tents of later days, we are, it is to be feared, in danger of losing sight of some of our old favourites. Admitting the extraordinary beauty of many plants of modern introduction, which of them, it may be asked, may be allowed to set aside the Moss Rose, the Lily of the Valley, or the Mignonette? Nevertheless, such is the influence of fashion, and the ardent thirst for novelty, that one really feels as though an apology is necessary in attempting to offer advice about such venerable acquaintances.

My object is to draw attention to the length of period during which the old Moss Rose may be obtained in perfection, by the application of retarding principles, or a process of arrest; and surely no lady would refuse to introduce a Moss Rose in her bouquet, merely because it is out of season; rather the reverse, it may be presumed. I pass by the fact, that the Moss Rose may be obtained, by a forcing process, in January; and that a succession can be thus carried out until the end of May, when in most parts they can be obtained in the open border, and thenceforward until the early part of July, when, unless particular means are resorted to, they fall away speedily.

As I have been in the habit of retarding them for many years, I may detail my practice. The bushes are never winter-pruned, they remain perfectly unmolested in the wood until the bud begins to swell in April, when the shears are passed over them lightly, merely removing the sprouting points. This proceeding checks them for about three weeks, when other buds in succession begin to sprout;

and now it is that the knife is used, and every sprouting shoot pruned back to the first dormant bud. Another fortnight or three weeks must now pass before the incipient buds can commence an effort; but a month or so passes before we again take them in hand; in fact, not until several of the shoots have grown two or three inches. On examining such bushes, it will be found that their eyes or buds do not sprout equally, not having been coeval in point of formation. Some will have advanced three inches before others have fairly sprouted; and now it is that I top or pinch all the more forward ones, merely removing the point, which is generally a blossom bud. This mode of procedure is intended to strengthen the system of the tree, already severely taxed by a waste of its fluids. By the time these matters are carried out it will be nearly the beginning of June, and not a Rose blossomed. From this time, all suckers or great shoots are pinched when about six inches long, and the trees receive a thorough cleansing with tobacco water the moment they are in full growth; and this is repeated, if necessary, in another fortnight. On this cleansing I lay the utmost stress. Thus far as to the branch; we will now proceed to root culture.

I must go so far as to observe, that *special* root culture is particularly desirable with retarded Moss Roses. The drain on their powers by this repetition of late pruning is so severe, as to require more assistance than Roses under ordinary circumstances. It is of much importance to establish them in a sound, deep, and rich soil; indeed, without these conditions, it is vain to hope for success. If the staple of the soil is not good, it should be made so previous to planting. A substratum of half-decayed manure may be planted beneath them, and plenty of manure of a more decayed character mingled with the soil. I prefer planting them in groups of three, at about one foot apart, forming a triangle. They thus produce a more powerful effect than singly, and so bountifully as to justify and reward a high course of culture. When planted I form a hollow or basin around them, somewhat deep and bold, and this is filled with rich manure, only half decayed generally; droppings which have had a slight fermentation. Watering is the next great essential, and this must be carefully attended to in all dry weather, until they have done blossoming; and, as soon as the blossom buds can be perceived, my practice is to use liquid manure, generally guano water, the strength about three ounces to a gallon.

As before observed, the aphides must be constantly destroyed, the beetles and the caterpillars watched for and destroyed. The Rose aphis is, however, their greatest enemy, and no good Roses fit for the bouquet can be produced where these are permitted to ravage the plants. Another good point in culture, I must repeat, is the constantly pinching all suckers and luxuriant shoots when about six inches in length. These divert the sap from the principal shoots; and, moreover, by subduing their rampant propensities betimes, they become most important portions of the bush as to the blossom of future years. Every autumn a fresh coating of top-dressing should be added, of some two to three inches in thickness, and a little of the old surface-dressing scraped away.

It may be observed, in conclusion, that like retardation in fruit trees, a later habit is engendered, which must facilitate the purpose of the cultivator. As an instance of what this practice will effect, I may add, that the retarded Moss Roses here are just commencing to bloom, July 10, although not one yet fit to gather; and I feel assured of having them until the very end of August.—ROBERT ERRING-TON, *Oulton Park.*

PROFESSOR FORBES'S VIEWS ON THE LIFE OF A SPECIES.

THE subject of the life and duration of a vegetable species, and the analogy between it and the life of an animal individual, was recently brought under the consideration of the members of the Royal Institution by Professor E. Forbes; and we shall endeavour in a brief abstract to embody the views which were advanced.

In natural history and geology a clear understanding of the relations of individual, species, and genus to geological time, and geographical space, is of essential importance. Among questionable, though popular, notions on this subject, is the belief that the term of duration of a species is comparable and of the same kind with that of the life of an individual. It is believed by many that a species (using the term in the sense of an assemblage of individuals, presenting certain characters in common and derived from one original protoplast or stock) passes through a series of phases comparable with those which succeed each other in definite order during the life of a single individual—that it has its epochs of origin, of maturity, of decline, and of extinction, dependent upon the laws of an inherent vitality. This notion has two sources—the one direct, the other indirect. It is not an induction, nor pretended to be, but an hypothesis assumed through apparent analogies. Its first and principal source may be discovered in the comparison suggested by certain necessary phases in the duration of a species; with others in the life of an individual, such as,—each has its commencement, and each has its cessation. The second and more indirect source of the notion of the life of a species may be traced in apparent analogies half perceived between the centralization of generic groups in time and space, and the limited duration of both species and individual. But in this case ideas are compared which are altogether and essentially distinct. The nature of this distinction is expressed among the following propositions, in which an attempt is made to contrast the respective relations of individual, species, and genus to geological time and geographical space.

A. The *individual,* whether we restrict the word to the single organism, however produced—or extend it to the series of organisms, combined or independent, all being products of a single ovum—has but a limited and unique existence in time, which, short as it must be, can be shortened by the influence of unfavourable circumstances, but which no combination of favouring circumstances can prolong beyond the term of life allotted to it according to its kind.

B. The *species*—whether we restrict the term to assemblages of individuals resembling each other in certain constant characters, or hold in addition, the hypothesis (warranted, as might be shown from experience and experiment), that between all the members of such an assemblage, there is the relationship of family, the relationship of descent, and consequently that they are the descendants of one first stock or protoplast (how that protoplast appeared is not part of the question)—is like the individual insomuch as its relations to time are unique : once destroyed it never re-appears. But (and this is the point of view now advocated), unlike the individual, it is continued indefinitely so long as conditions favourable to its diffusion and prosperity—that is to say, so long as conditions favourable to the production and sustenance of the individual representatives or elements—are continued coincidently with its existence.

C. The *genus,* in whatever degree of extension we use the term, so long as we apply it to an assemblage of species intimately related to each other in common and important features of organization, appears distinctly to exhibit the phenomenon of centralization in both time and space, though with a difference, since it would seem that each genus has a unique centre or area of development in time, but in geographical space may present more centres than one.

    1. a :—An individual is a positive reality.

    b :—A species is a relative reality.

    c :—A genus is an abstraction—an idea; but an idea impressed on nature, and not arbitrarily dependent on man's conceptions.

    2. α :—An individual is one.

    β :—A species consists of many resulting from one.

    γ :—A genus consists of more or fewer of these manies resulting from one, linked together, not by a relationship of descent, but by an affinity dependent on a divine idea.

    3. a :—An individual cannot manifest itself in two places at once; it has no extension in space; its relations are entirely with time ; but the possible duration of its existence is regulated by the law of its inherent vitality.

    b :—A species has correspondent and exactly analogous relations with time and space—the duration of its existence as well as its geographical extension is entirely regulated by physical conditions.

    c :—A genus has dissimilar, or only partially, comparable relations with time and space, and occupies areas in both, having only partial relations to physical conditions.

New Garden Plants.

LOMATIA FERRUGINEA, *R. Brown.* Rusty-leaved Lomatia.—Order Proteaceæ (Protead tribe).—A fine half-hardy shrub, useful on account of its fine foliage, which when young is ferruginous, and becomes deep green as it acquires age. It grows ten to twelve feet high, and has bipinnatifid leaves six to twelve inches long. The flowers are said to be crimson within and green externally; but these have not been as yet produced in cultivation. Native of South Chili, and introduced lately by Messrs. Veitch.

BORONIA RUTOSMA.—Rue-scented Boronia.—Rutaceæ § Diosmeæ (Ruewort tribe).—Glaucous, much branched; leaves oblong ovate or obovate sessile fleshy, apiculate, one-nerved; flowers in trichotomous corymbose many-flowered cymes, pedicels thickened beneath the flowers; calyx lobes ovate acute; filaments ciliate in the lower half.—M. This very pretty Boronia is known in cultivation as *B. spathulata*, but does not appear to be the species so named by Dr. Lindley, differing obviously in its much branched habit, and its many-flowered corymbose inflorescence. The whole plant has a tendency to trichotomous branching, and thus forms a dense bush, with terete branches scattered with glandular dots, and bearing opposite fleshy glaucous oblong ovate, or obovate apiculate leaves, furnished with numerous transparent dots, and one-nerved. The flowers terminate the branches, forming a kind of corymbose cyme trichotomously divided; the pedicels are about an inch long, thickened at top; the calyx lobes are ovate acute brownish-green, dotted, and traversed by forked nerves. The petals are ovate apiculate patent, twice as long as the calyx, pink, becoming deep rose when dry. The eight stamens are as long as the calyx, ciliate in the lower half, covered externally above with round glands, the anthers attached below the apex. The ovary is seated on a broad hypogynous disk twice its own width, and is dotted, four-celled, terminated by a simple style, with an obscurely four-lobed stigma. The cells of the ovary are two-ovulate, but only one seed seems to be perfected. The plant, both fresh and dry, has a strong odour of rue. We are indebted to Mr. Watson, gardener to Mrs. Tredwell, of Norwood, for the specimen represented by our figure.

BORONIA RUTOSMA.

CENTRADENIA OVATA, *Klotzsch.* Ovate-leaved Centradenia. C. DIVARICATA, *Klotzsch.* Divaricate Centradenia.—Order Melastomaceæ (Melastomad tribe.)—Two stove herbaceous plants from Central America, introduced by M. Warczewitz to the Berlin gardens. The former has ovate leaves, and trichotomous many-flowered cymes of pink flowers. The latter is more straggling with long acuminate leaves, and few terminal white flowers.

ARBORICULTURAL STATISTICS.

WE are indebted to the Rev. H. P. Marsham, of Norwich, for the following statement of a very curious fact connected with the growth of trees, which he has lately observed. Mr. Marsham writes:—

"I have measured for the last four years about thirty trees, of all ages and size, as nearly at the same time of year as possible, viz., between May the 4th and 14th. I have always taken my measure at five feet from the ground, and I have marks upon the trees, so that the measuring tape invariably goes over the same place. Now, it appears that during the last year, viz., from May 14th, 1851, to May 4th, 1852, with very few exceptions, there has been no increase whatever, as will be shown. I should at the same time add, that no branches have been removed, nor has any other known circumstance happened in any way to retard them.

"An Oak (acorn in 1803), whose average increase is two inches annually, has this year no increase.

"A Cedar, about thirty-five years old, whose annual average is two inches; this year only one and a half inch.

"A Cedar, planted in 1747, whose annual average is one and a-half inches; this year no increase.

"*Quercus rober*, planted 1820; annual average, two inches; in 1852, no increase.

"Cork-tree, no increase; annual average, one and a half inches.

"Oak, planted in 1809; no increase.

"*Fraxinus heterophyllus;* no increase.

"Many others of large dimensions, whose average is about one inch, have scarcely increased over a quarter of an inch.

"On referring to my indications of the spring, I do not consider it at all a backward season. Indeed, it appears that trees appeared in leaf, in some cases, even before medium time, and the appearance of birds and insects was n nowise late.

"I inclose the measurement of a very fine Cedar of Lebanon, planted at Stratton Strawless in 1747, taken in the years 1837 and 1850. It is a most magnificent specimen, and, for its age, I should think the finest in England. Its girth in 1851, at five feet from the ground, was twelve feet three and a half inches. It has averaged about one and a half inches increase for the last four years, but this year there is no increase.

"CEDAR OF LEBANON AT STRATTON STRAWLESS, PLANTED IN 1747, MEASURED:—

"In 1837.	In 1850.	Increase.
1st length, 41 ft.: at 20 ft. 6 in. the girth was 11 ft. 2 in.; squared, 2 ft. 3¼ in.; giving a content of 319 ft. 6 in. 4 pts. (No knots in this length).	The girth was 11 ft. 8 in.; squared, 2 ft. 11 in.; giving a content of 348 ft. 9 in. 5 pts.	29 ft. 3 in. 1 pt.
2nd length, 10 ft.: at 5 ft. its girth was 4 ft. 10 in.; squared, 14½ in.; giving a content of 14 ft. 7 in. (Some branches taken off caused a swell).	The girth was 6 ft. 4 in.; squared, 19 in.; giving a content of 25 ft. 0 in. 10 pts.	10 ft. 5 in. 8 pts.
3rd length, 10 ft.: at 5 ft. the girth was 4 ft.; squared, 1 ft.; giving a content of 10 ft. (This was the first length in crown.)	The girth was 5 ft. 4 in.; squared, 16 in.; giving a content of 17 ft. 9 in. 4 pts.	7 ft. 9 in. 4 pts.
4th length, 10 ft.: at 5 ft. its girth was 3 ft. 6 in.; squared, 9 in.; giving a content of 5 ft. 7 in. 6 pts. (Second length in crown.)	The girth was 4 ft. 4 in.; squared, 13 in.; giving a content of 11 ft. 8 in. 10 pts.	6 ft. 1 in. 4 pts.

"The total length of the tree, measuring timber, is 71 ft., and the contents over the bark, in 1837, 849 ft. 9 in.; in 1850, 403 ft. 4 in. 5 pts. Increase in thirteen years, 53 ft. 7 in. 5 pts.

"In 1837.	In 1850.	Increase.
1st wrong, 12 ft. long; squared, 15 in.; girth, 5 ft.; giving a content of 18 ft. 9 in.	1st length of do., 10 ft.; at 5 ft., girth, 6 ft. 8 in.; squared, 20 in.; contents, 27 ft. 9 in. 4 pts. 2nd length, 10 ft.; at 5 ft., girths, 4 ft.; squares, 12 in.; contents, 10 ft. 3rd length, 10 ft.; at 5 ft, girth, 3 ft.; squared, 10 in.; contents, 6 ft. 11 in. 4 pts.= 44 ft. 8 in. 8 pts.	25 ft. 11 in. 8 pt.
2nd wrong, 10 ft. long; squared, 12 in.; girth, 4 ft.; giving a content of 10 ft.	1st length of do., 16 ft.; at 8 ft., girth, 3 ft. 6 in.; squared, 10½ in.; contents, 12 ft. 3 in. 2nd length, 15 ft.; at 7½ ft., girth, 3 ft. 4 in.; squared, 10 in.; contents, 10 ft. 5 in.=22 ft. 8 in.	12 ft. 8 in.
3rd wrong, 12 ft. long; squared, 9 in.; girth 3 ft; content, 6 ft. 9 in.	16 ft.; at 8 ft., girth, 4 ft.; squared, 12 in.; content, 16 ft.	9 ft. 3 in.
4th wrong, 10 ft.; squared, 9 in.; girth, 3 ft.; content, 5 ft. 7 in. 6 pts.	10 ft.; at 5 ft., girth, 3 ft.; squared, 9 in.; content, 5 ft. 7 in. 6 pts.	nil.
5th wrong, 14 ft.; squared, 8 in.; girths, 2 ft.; content, 2 ft. 2 in. 8 pts.	15 ft.; at 7½ ft., girth, 2 ft.; squared, 6 in.; content, 3 ft. 9 in.	1 ft. 6 in. 4 pts.
6th wrong, nil.	4 ft.; at 2 ft., girth, 2 ft.; squared, 6 in.; content, 2 ft.	2 ft.

"The whole contents of wrongs, in 1837, 43 ft. 4 in. 2 pts.; in 1850, 94 ft. 9 in, 2 pts.

"The whole tree contained:—In 1837, 393 ft. 1 in. 2 pts. of timber, which is—9 load 33 ft. 1 pt. In 1850, 498 ft. 1 in. 7 pts. of timber, which is—12 load 18 ft. 8 pts.

"The total increase, in thirteen years, is 2 load 25 ft. 8 pts."

ON THE FORMATION OF WOOD.

FEW questions in vegetable physiology have given rise to more discussion than this, and, after all, as it seems to us, owing to the very imperfect manner in which most of those who have undertaken to offer an opinion have previously investigated the facts offered by nature. Much confusion, again, arises from the misinterpretation of words, and the figurative expressions to which the transcendental physiologists have had recourse in endeavouring to explain their views.

The two theories which are now most strongly put forth in opposition to each other are—1, That the wood grows down from the leaves; and, 2, That the wood is formed in the place in which it is found when complete. Now, the first of these, if taken in its literal sense, is simply an absurdity, because it is directly opposed to the well-established fact, that there exists no free space between the wood and bark, occupied by a viscid fluid or *cambium*, as imagined by the older writers; but, as the simplest in-spection of a *carefully* made section of a dicotyledonous shoot will show, the so-called cambium is nothing but the extremely delicate cellular tissue in which resides the unlimited power of developing into wood internally and bark externally, which results in the production of annual rings. But even if we take a modified view, that the wood of each successive layer is the organic prolongation down-wards of the wood of the shoots formed in the same year, and is directly continuous with that, the fact of the fibres being continuous, as may often be observed, proves nothing as to the mode or direction of growth; for the fibres of wood run down in continuous lines, not because they have grown down in these lines, but because this is the appointed *plan* of their development. We may say roughly, in ani-mal anatomy, that certain vessels, or nerves, *run into* such and such a limb; but we know that this is only a convenient mode of expression, and that it is not intended to indicate that those structures were formed by a gradual budding out and branching, like that of the growth of the branches of a tree. Just so with the fibres we see running down from a branch towards the roots; they are intended to form the medium of connection between the roots and the branches, and therefore are developed in the way best suited for that purpose; that is to say, in the form of continuous bundles of fibres extending down in this direction, and thickest where the activity of the growth of the tree is greatest. There is as much reason to imagine that the projections and buttress-like prominences on the trunks of old trees, under large branches, arise from the large quantities of fluid drawn up through these tracts by the great evapo-ration from the leaves above, as that the cause lies in an elaborated sap of the leaves having descended.

Of the downward course of the sap, and its physiological characters, we know almost nothing be-yond the mere fact of its existence; but the theory of the downward *growth* of the wood, actual mechanical elongation of individual fibres downwards, is negatived by all experiment, for the only experimental facts brought in aid of it are those of wounds on trees, where conditions are set up which do not exist in the regular course of nature; for the cut ends of the fibres of the upper lip of the wound are *set free* to elongate, which never can be the case in an uninjured tree; and, moreover, in these very cases it is never the *ends of the fully-formed fibres* which grow, but the cambium-cells of the ex-treme outer limit of the wood, which develop outwards, and gradually *fold over* downwards, so as to heal the wound by covering it in.

If any further proof of the origin of the wood had been necessary to unprejudiced observers, a paper lately published by M. Trécul, in the *Comptes Rendus* (Feb. 16, 1852), would have removed all doubt. He laid before the French Academy a statement, with an illustrative specimen, which showed, beyond question, that beth the wood and the bark are formed *from the surface on which they lie*, quite inde-pendently of the tissues higher up. In the specimen (of *Nyssa angulisans*, Michx.), it was shown that new layers of bark and wood had formed on the surface of the previously decorticated alburnum, and *below* the decorticated part as well as *above*. We may give the chief particulars of his description:—

The stem, which the author had brought from Louisiana, was deprived of its bark to the extent of about eighteen inches, but nevertheless continued to vegetate. When cut in the month of Sep-tember, it bore leaves and fruit. New layers of wood had been formed above and below the barked surface. In addition to these, others presented themselves on the surface whence the bark had been stripped. On this surface were seen oblong or hemispherical prominences, covered with greyish bark, varying in size from about one-sixth of an inch long and one-twelfth broad, to fourteen inches long and one to two inches broad. The cortical portion coating them, now dried up, might be readily detached, and displayed, after its removal, a more dense tissue adhering strongly to the wood.

The tissue of one of the smallest of these prominences, examined by the microscope, proved to be what might be expected; the outer easily removeable part was bark parenchyme; the inner adherent parts of the new formations were true wood, even containing vessels, this wood being directly con-tinuous with the fibro-vascular bundles on which it lay, while the medullary rays of the stem, in some cases, extended out into these new structures. The new structures did not adhere by their whole surface to the wood, but by the central part, whence the new growth seemed to have radiated, as from a centre, upwards, downwards, and to each side. In one of the largest of the protuberances, on which the ligneous fibres, and the vessels, were highly developed, they were very sinuous in their course and imbedded in a tissue much resembling that of the medullary rays.

The new tissue formed beneath the bark, on the part of the stem *below* the decorticated portion, was less in quantity than that *above* the bare portion, but the woody fibres were *more advanced in their development, and the vessels more numerous* than above, and the medullary rays were larger and more numerous than in the old wood.

Above the barked region the new ligneous tissue formed a *thicker* layer than below, but it was much less advanced in its development. Very few vessels were observed in the young wood, and the cells were smaller than those of the wood of the older part, and they were shorter in proportion to their distance from the older region.

From the facts briefly enumerated here, M. Trécul draws the conclusions, that:—

" 1. The fibro-vascular bundles are not continued without interruption from the extremity of the leaves to that of the rootlets.

" 2. That the diameter of stems may increase without the intervention of ligneous fibres descending either from the leaves or the buds.

" 3. That the tissue of the wood and the vessels are formed *in situ*, as well as the medullary rays."

It will be very difficult for the advocates of the opposite theory to find a satisfactory objection to these propositions.—ARTHUR HENFREY, F.R.S., F.L.S., &c.

ON THE TRANSMISSION OF FOREIGN SEEDS.

MR. M'NAB very recently communicated to the Botanical Society of Edinburgh an interesting notice relative to the transmission of foreign seeds in soil. His opinion is, that the transmission of fruits and seeds in a fit state for germination would be better accomplished by their being packed in soil than by any other known method. This view was fully tested by himself experimentally during 1834, when he brought over the seeds of many of the rarer American Oaks and other trees in boxes filled with soil, while portions of the same kinds of seeds packed, both in brown paper and cloth bags, were in many instances totally useless. The method adopted for the American tree seeds was as follows :— He purchased several strong deal boxes about fourteen inches in diameter, and made of three-fourth-inch wood. He afterwards procured a quantity of soil taken from a depth of eight or ten inches under the surface so as to possess only a natural dampness. A layer of the soil two inches deep was placed on the bottom of the boxes, above which a layer of seeds was distributed ; another layer of soil and then seed, and so on till the boxes were full ; the whole was pressed very firmly down, when the lids were nailed on, allowing no possible room to shake about. When they reached Edinburgh, December, 1834, the seeds and soil were sown over the surface of shallow pans and boxes. During the following spring they grew freely, while of those brought home in the paper and cloth bags comparatively few of the varieties grew, the Acorns being, without an exception, perforated with insects. The kinds which grew were from four to five weeks later in vegetating than those brought home in soil. Acorns brought home in a box of sphagnum moss, after the superfluous moisture had been wrung from it, were equally successful with those in soil. Owing to the success of the above experiment, Mr. M'Nab, some years ago, recommended to the Highland and Agricultural Society, through the late Dr. Neill, to encourage, by means of premiums or otherwise, the transmission of seeds in soil. This was accordingly done, but nothing has resulted from it, notwithstanding that the notice still exists in their premium list. During the summer of 1851, Mr. M'Nab induced his brother, Dr. M'Nab, of Kingston, Jamaica, to send a box of West Indian fruits and seeds, to be put up as described, and which he despatched in August, containing seeds of Granadilla, Gourds, Forbidden Fruit, Shaddocks, Sweet Sop, Sour Sop, Cherimoyer, Sapota, Guava, Lignum-vitæ, Papaw, Alligator Pear, Mango, Ochro, Fustic, &c. The box reached Edinburgh last October ; shortly afterwards, the seeds and soil were sown over the surface of boxes prepared with drainage and soil for the purpose ; and the result was perfectly successful.

1. Munronia javanica
2. Chorozema nervosum

MUNRONIA JAVANICA.

WE have to thank Messrs. Rollisson, of Tooting, for the opportunity of figuring this very pretty and interesting stove plant, to which, indeed, a representation on white paper scarcely does justice. Our drawing was made about the middle of June. The plant forms an erect shrub, growing to the height of a foot. The leaves are impari-pinnate, with two pairs of sub-opposite lateral leaflets, of which the lowest pair is nearly cordate, the upper pair oblong-ovate, with an oblique acute base, and the terminal one much larger, on a longish stalk, and occasionally lobed. The racemes come from the axils of the leaves, and are few-flowered; the pedicels are subtended by minute subulate bracts, and just above their base have an articulation, below which is seated a pair of minute bracteoles. The calyx is divided into five leafy linear-spathulate divisions. The corolla is white, apparently monope-talous, though really considered to be pentapetalous with the claws of the petals connate into a slender tube; this tube is an inch long, nearly cylindrical, with a spreading limb or free portion, consisting of five — rarely three or four — elliptic-lanceolate unequal imbricating lobes, half as long as the tubular part. The filaments are also conjoined into a cylindrical tube, which coheres with the tube of the corolla beyond its middle, and is somewhat shorter than its lobes; this terminates in a rim of ten subulate processes, within which are placed, at the mouth of the tube, an equal number of conver-gent yellow sessile anthers. There is another delicately-membranous interior tube covering the base of the ovary. The ovary is downy externally, with five one or two-seeded cells, and is surmounted by a slender style as long as the staminal tube, terminating in a flattened obscurely-lobed stigma.

Mr. Buckley, of the Tooting Nursery, has furnished the following notes on the Munronia:—

"The *Munronia Javanica* was raised from seeds collected in Java, in 1848, by Mr. Henshall, who states, that it there forms a dense-growing dwarf shrub. It was, at the time he discovered it, covered with its pure white Jasmine-like flowers. The seeds were sown in 1849, and yet so dwarf is its habit, that the largest plant is not more than ten inches in height at the present time. It is one of the few plants which flower at all seasons, and this feature alone renders it worthy a place in any collection. Since the plants were four inches in height they have always had buds or flowers upon them, which is unusual in a slow-growing plant. It produces but few side shoots.

"The leaves, including the petiole, measure eight inches when mature, and consist of two (occa-sionally three) pairs of leaflets, and a terminal one, which is ovate-lanceolate, one inch wide and three inches long, sometimes undulated and lobed, but more frequently entire, convex on the upper surface, with the points drooping; light green and slightly pubescent. The leaves on the lower part are pendulous, and completely clothe the stem and surface of the soil; the upper ones stand erect, with the points drooping. The flower-stems spring from the axils of the leaves, each leaf producing one, and each spike having from five to nine flowers: it is not uncommon to see eight or nine spikes in flower at the same time, and these, standing boldly above the foliage, produce a very pretty effect. The flowers are of the purest white, about one inch across, when expanded. As soon as the flower fades, the pedicel curves downwards, and remains in that position during the ripening of the seeds. The ovary is five-celled, though it rarely happens that more than two or three seeds reach perfection. The seeds are light brown, and shaped like a small univalve shell.

"The general aspect of the plant is peculiarly chaste and interesting; and it will be found espe-cially useful for those who can afford space for a small collection only, as it will not (as is the case with many stove plants) require frequent renewal by propagation, or pruning, to keep it within manageable limits. It is also easily cultivated. The following compost will be found to be suitable for it:—To three parts of Wimbledon, or any similar peat, add one part of light turfy loam, and about one-sixth of silver sand. Drain the pots well in the usual manner. It may be re-potted any time between February and October; but March or April (according to the state of the plant) is the best time, and if re-potted at this season, once a-year, it will generally suffice for it. It appears to enjoy a moist atmosphere, a rather shady part of the stove, and a high temperature. The usual stove treatment will serve for it in the winter.

" It may be readily increased by seeds which are produced in tolerable abundance, and should be sown as soon as they are ripe, as follows :—Take a six-inch pot and fill it half full of draining materials, covering well with turfy peat ; then fill, to within half an inch of the rim of the pot, with finely sifted sandy peat, making the surface firm and even. Sow the seeds evenly, and cover them one-eighth of an inch. The soil must be used in a moist state, and no water should be given for a few days after sowing. Keep them shaded, by placing a sheet of thin paper over the pot ; this will prevent the soil becoming too dry, and will also assist the seeds to germinate. As soon as the young plants are one inch high, place them singly in small pots ; cover them with a hand-light for a few days, and inure them to full exposure in the ordinary stove, by giving them air daily, gradually increasing it."

" There is nothing gaudy about the *Munronia* to recommend it. Still it possesses that beautiful simplicity which will render it a very general favourite. It may be said to have the aspect of a white Jasmine, but divested of its climbing habit, and is perfectly new to cultivators."

Munronia belongs to the order Meliaceæ, and is closely allied to *Turræa*. It is remarkable in having a monopetalous structure, though belonging to a polypetalous group.—M.

CHOROZEMA NERVOSUM.*

MESSRS. Henderson, of the Pine Apple Nursery, Edgeware Road, have been successful in raising this very remarkable species of Chorozema, from seeds sent from the Swan River by Mr. Drummond. It might well have borne the name of *cordatum* had not that been preoccupied ; we have therefore selected one in reference to the remarkable and conspicuous venation of its foliage. It is very distinct and will doubtless prove a very ornamental plant. It bloomed with Messrs. Henderson in April last, and we have to thank them for the opportunity of figuring it. The plant from which our drawing was made is an erect growing shrub, sparingly branched, the branches terete, densely pubescent with short hairs, adpressed on the upper parts. The leaves are alternate, shortly stalked, broadly cordate, cuspidato-mucronate, about as long (half-inch) as broad including the cusp which is one-eight long, somewhat keeled, undulate, deep green and glossy above, paler beneath, the costa very prominent on the lower face, and extended into the sub-rigid cusp ; both surfaces are prominently and conspicuously reticulate veined, (the veins pallid on a dark ground), and the margin is quite entire and thickened. The stipules are small and subulate. The inflorescence consists of short terminal and axillary few-flowered racemes ; the pedicels are axillary to a subulate bract, and having a pair of small bracteoles on their upper part. The calyx is two-lipped, with triangular incurved teeth. The corolla is showy, the standard broadly emarginate, almost two-lobed, coppery-orange colour, having a yellow spot at the base margined with crimson ; the wings are wedge-shaped laterally curved, twice as long as the keel which they overarch, crimson ; the keel is acute, swollen, and incloses the stamens and stigma. The ovary is silky, subsessile, terminated by the hooked style, and contains about six seeds.—M.

This very distinct species of Chorozema will not, we imagine, be found one of the least ornamental of the genus. As with most of the erect-growing species, to grow it into a fine specimen ·will require careful management ; that is, proper care must be taken to get a good foundation, or it will be useless to expect a fine plant. There are two ways of doing this, as has been indicated in preceding pages ; that is, you may either stop and train a plant until you get it to a good bottom, or you may encourage and allow it to grow wildly until the plant has attained sufficient strength to admit of its being cut down almost close to the pot, so as to get a number of shoots from the base of the stem. The Chorozemas being rather shy-rooting plants, more than ordinary attention must be devoted in watering to prevent them having too much, for should the soil become clogged or sodden, success will be quite out of the question. We should, therefore, recommend the soil to be prepared

* *Chorozema nervosum*, n. sp.—Branches downy ; leaves broadly cordate, with a rigid cusp, glabrous, undulated, and somewhat keeled, with entire thickened margins, and prominent conspicuous veins on both surfaces ; racemes few-flowered, pedicels bibracteolate above the middle, shorter than the calyx.—M.

with great care, and only the very best to be used, mixing that intimately with gritty sand, potsherds, and charcoal broken small.

Most of the Chorozemas delight in a gentle moist heat during the growing season; and as they are subject to the attacks of the red spider, and a peculiar species of thrip, great care must be taken that they do not suffer. The best preventive is perfect cleanliness; the best remedy syringing so as to wet every part of the plant, and then dusting the foliage both over and under with sulphur, which may remain on for a few days, and then must be washed off again with clean water. With plants that are subject to red spider or thrips, or even to mildew, it is a good plan to syringe them with water impregnated with sulphur about once in ten days, or a fortnight, during the growing season. Through the winter, also, Chorozemas should be kept rather warmer than ordinary greenhouse plants; indeed these, with *Boronias, Polygalas, Dillwynias, Leschenaultias, Roellias, Pimeleas*, and some similar plants, should occupy the warmest end of the greenhouse, and not be exposed to cold draughts. The whole of the free-growing Chorozemas, to keep them neat and bushy, require to be cut in boldly every season directly they have done blooming, and if they grow very luxuriantly, the young shoots may also be stopped a time or two to make them branch. Several of the kinds will continue to grow through the depth of winter; indeed they progress better at that season, as to actual growth, than at any other. A little clear manure water is beneficial to them occasionally, especially when the pots are full of roots, and frequent syringing and perfect cleanliness must not be neglected.—A.

THE CULTIVATION OF PEACH AND NECTARINE TREES.

HAVING cultivated the Peach and Nectarine for more than twenty years, in various soils and situations, with a success bordering upon perfection, I enter on the subject with no small degree of confidence. I commence with the border, one of the most essential points, and one too often mismanaged. Too frequently all that is thought necessary is to trench the borders to a *good depth*. The borders which I have prepared, and which have produced some of the most beautiful of fruit trees, were made in the following manner:—The width was fourteeen feet; less, I consider, will not do. In the bottom, through its whole width and length, was laid fifteen inches of drainage, sloping considerably from the wall to the front, where ran a main drain to carry off superfluous moisture. The bottom under the drainage was perfectly smooth, in order to give the latter more effect. Where one end of the border is higher than the other, a cross drain must run from between each tree to the main drain in front, for effectual drainage is the greatest point; without it, it is impossible to grow fruit trees well.

The soil I have used is good friable loam, free from manure, not too light; indeed, a stiffish loam will be found to suit the fruit trees admirably, and in it they will flourish on the warm and comfortable bed of drainage. The extreme depth of the soil for the border should not exceed twenty inches, and it should be allowed to settle thoroughly before the trees are planted. This is a point of no little importance, for if the trees are planted too soon, the settling of the border will cause them to be buried too deep.

I recommmend early planting; for I have always found it best. When trees are had from the nursery in the autumn, and laid in until spring, as is sometimes the case, on their removal for their final planting they will be found to have made a mass of fibres, which, of course, must be injured and broken, and against this loss the tree has to struggle for the first summer; if, indeed, it survives it. I prefer half-standard trees, from three and a-half to four feet high in the stem; and so strongly do I recommend this height, that I should rejoice to see dwarf Peaches, Nectarines, &c., banished altogether from gardens. It is a well known fact that the finest fruit is produced towards the ground. This being the case, the principal object must be to well furnish the bottom of the wall with bearing wood of good quality, and keep it so at all times. Seeing that half-standard trees, trained star-form (*Fig* 3), afford the greatest facilities for this object, their decided superiority to the dwarf fan-trained trees must be apparent, as in the latter case the more a tree has grown the more old wood there is along the bottom of the wall.

When the border has well settled down, it is fit for planting. The trees should be placed so as to have three or four inches of their roots above the ground level, as shown in Figs. 1, 2, and 3. I invariably make it a rule to keep the neck of the trees two courses of bricks above what is to be the ground level, and, after planting, litter is put around each tree, so that they are well mulched for the first summer, and continue so until the following spring. If the summer should prove dry, they will require frequent and copious waterings. The following spring, whatever litter remains, as well as the

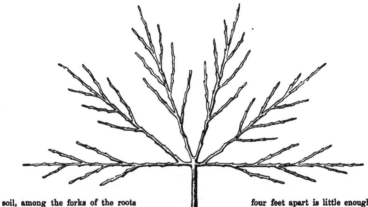

Fig 1

soil, among the forks of the roots will require levelling down to the ground line (Fig. 3), in which state the roots for the future are to be left exposed. Trees planted in this way will be found to flourish much better than if their roots are wholly covered. I plant about twelve inches from the wall, it being advantageous to keep a reasonable distance to prevent the stem getting sunburnt, which it is more than probable may happen if it is set close to the wall. Twenty-four feet apart is little enough for trees on a ten or twelve feet wall, and I have had them cover the whole of that space in four years from the time of planting and produce the most abundant crops. So plentiful indeed have I had them in the third year after planting, that I have sent fruit to the Hall table by the garden sieve full. Six years ago I saw some trees in excellent condition, which I had thus planted fifteen years previously.

I prefer two-year-old headed plants, with five or six branches (such as *Fig.* 1). The head should be clean and healthy, not over gross; the stem should be clean, straight, and healthy. Hide-bound cankery or knotty stocks, and trees with large scars or wounds in the head, should be rejected as likely to gum or canker. The branches forming the head should be, as nearly as possible, of equal strength, as when headed back they will probably then break more regularly. A tree with one or two strong branches at one side, will, in all probability, become a one-sided tree.

I will now explain my mode of pruning and training the Peach and Nectarine. *Fig.* 1 shows a newly-planted tree, to be cut back to two or three eyes, where these appear most likely to break. Not more than two shoots must be allowed to push from each branch. As the loss of a branch would be irreparable, they should receive constant attention, and as soon as the shoots are long enough, they should be steadied by a loose shred, and this care must be continued through the season when requisite, using strong shreds, as the shoots will become of considerable weight. I have had them reach the top of the wall by autumn. All the laterals they produce must be allowed to remain, and the stronger ones tacked to the wall to prevent their being broken by strong winds. The tree, after its season's growth, will have become such as is shown at *Fig.* 2. Notwithstanding the size and strength of wood, it must be again cut back to three or four eyes, according to circumstances ; and when the shoots break the following spring, select the two best shoots from each branch, and such as lay well to the wall.

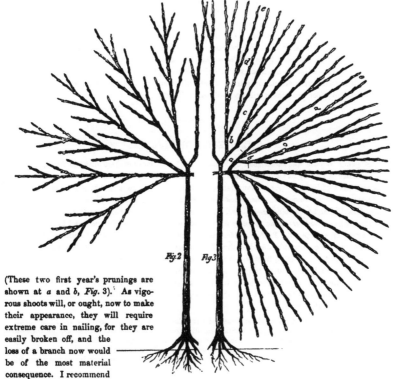

Fig. 2.   Fig. 3.

(These two first year's prunings are shown at *a* and *b*, *Fig.* 3). As vigorous shoots will, or ought, now to make their appearance, they will require extreme care in nailing, for they are easily broken off, and the loss of a branch now would be of the most material consequence. I recommend tacking loosely as soon as the branch is long enough, and to lay it close to the wall as soon after as possible.

The tree will now begin to acquire the form shown at *Fig.* 3. Where the spring growth has attained six or eight inches in length, the shoots are to be topped for the first time, as shown at *c.* In stopping, bear in mind that it must be done as soon as the young branches are of the required length, in the very soft tissue of the points of the shoots, for if the latter are allowed to elongate, and are afterwards topped back in the solid wood, they will not again break freely. In this system of training, this apparently simple point must never be forgotten. The shoots which now break out will be still more liable to break off than the first, if not carefully nailed to the wall. At this and the succeeding toppings, it is more than probable that more branches than are wanted will make their appearance ; two or three more than necessary should be suffered to remain until those that are required are secured, when they must be removed. The growth of the shoots will now be found so rapid as to require almost daily attention in nailing and training. Again, when this growth has attained from ten to fifteen or eighteen inches, the shoots are to be topped. It is impossible to prescribe any special length, as much will depend on the strength of the shoots, what direction they take, and the general formation of the tree; this topping takes place at *d*. The same care and attention as before must now be paid to the new shoots, and when they have grown an equal length they are to be topped again (at *e*). Some trees will be more vigorous in growth than others; but many will require a fourth topping. This I have had to do frequently, and in the following spring, had firm well ripened wood, that cut more like a piece of oak than what is generally seen as peach wood, and the trees were well filled-in with bearing wood. Whilst these various toppings are going on, there are, of course, many vacancies in the trees, which I take for granted are filled up with weaker branches at full length, that the trees may be completely furnished with fruit-bearing wood; and instances will also occur (as seen in *Fig.* 3) where it will not be necessary to lay in more than one shoot at the regular toppings of some of the branches, yet these vigorous branches will require to be topped to bring them into a bearing state. The Peach and Nectarine are the only trees which will submit to this system of summer pruning on the wall; the Apricot and others will not.—THOMAS HATCH.

THE SPECIES OF BEJARIA.

THE genus Bejaria was established by Mutis in 1761, in honour of Don Antonio Bejar, a learned Professor of Botany at Cadiz, and was published subsequently by the younger Linnæus under the erroneous name of Befaria. As garden plants, the Bejarias are elegant shrubs producing a fine effect, in a temperate house, among *Azaleas, Rhododendrons*, and similar plants. Their culture is easy, their foliage beautiful and persistent, their flowers handsome and well coloured; but they are little known. New species have, however, been recently introduced to the gardens of Europe; and hence the following abstract of a paper by Professor Herincq, in the *Revue Horticole*, will be interesting. Some few kinds were long since introduced:—thus *B. racemosa* was obtained from Florida about 1810; *B. glauca* was introduced in 1826, from Venezuela, where it was found growing at an altitude of more than seven thousand feet, and *B. ledifolia* came from the same country in 1846.

Another species was published early in 1849, in the Botanical Magazine, under the name of *coarctata;* but this is quite different from the plant previously described and figured under that name by Humboldt and Bonpland.

Their *B. coarctata* is a shrub of about three feet and a half in height, with glabrous spreading branches, furnished with alternate, glabrous, oblong leaves, generally attenuated towards both extremities, glaucous below, with glabrous petioles; the flowers are purple, and disposed in terminal panicles, their peduncles and calyces covered with dense ferruginous wool. It grows in abundance in Peru in the Paramo of Yanaguanga, at an elevation of from six to nine thousand feet above the level of the sea, in a climate which is cold and misty, where it grows on porphyritic rocks.

[A plant raised in 1846 or 1847, by Messrs. Veitch, and referred to this species by Dr. Lindley (Gard. Chron., 175), is described as having hairy branches, woolly flower stalks, a smooth calyx of 7-8 blunt ovate sepals, a little woolly at the edges, and purple seven or eight petalled flowers, smaller than in *B. æstuans*, and more closely arranged. Mr. Lobb is said to have mistaken it for *B. grandiflora.*]

B. coarctata of the Botanical Magazine, which was received from M. Makoy of Leige, under this name, by the Museum at Paris, differs from Humboldt's plant principally in the extremity of its branches, as well as the leaves, petioles, peduncles, and calyces being clothed with long hairs, which are at first white, then russet, and terminate in a small spherical transparent gland. In this plant we recognize a new species which it is proposed to name *B. Lindeniana* (Herincq), in honour of M. Linden, who, during eleven years of perilous travels through Mexico and New Grenada, has enriched horticulture with a vast collection of beautiful plants.

This plant is a shrub growing more than three feet high, with alternate branches, glabrous below, and at the upper part studded with numerous long glandular hairs. The leaves are alternate, persistent, oblong elliptical, obtuse, slightly mucronate, entire, soft and hairy on both sides when young, thick and somewhat coriaceous when old, and then hairy only on the middle nerve and petiole. The flowers are pale rose, marked with lines of a deeper tinge, and borne at the summit of the branches in compact corymbs as in *Rhododendron;* the peduncles and calyx have long glandular hairs, and the latter is cut into six sharp lobes; the corolla consists of six obtuse, oblong, or nearly spathulate petals; there are twelve stamens as long as the petals, with reddish filaments hairy at the base; the style is terminated by a discoid stigma. It grows in the elevated regions between Carraccas and Merida."

Among the Bejarias that the garden of Paris has received from M. Linden, there is one designated *Bejaria sp. n.*, which appears to come near *B. Lindeniana*, having leaves of the same form and vesti-ture, but the flowers are perhaps different. Other species introduced by M. Linden are the following:—

B. myrtifolia (Herincq); *B. æstuans* (herb. Linden, 775), is a branching shrub, with nearly opposite branches, studded when young with long hairs, not glandular. The leaves are almost verticillate, shortly-stalked, lanceolate-attenuated at the apex, entire, with the lateral nerves rather prominent, at first thinly scattered with hairs, then nearly glabrous, glaucous below. The flowers are of a beautiful bright carmine, arranged in short terminal corymbose racemes, generally furnished with small leaves at the base of the peduncles; the rachis clothed with thick short wool, intermixed with long hairs, not glandular, and which disappear with age; the peduncles are one-flowered, somewhat hairy; the calyx glutinous, hairy at the inferior part, cut almost to the base in very acute segments; the corolla has glutinous oblong petals; the stamens hairy at the base, as long as the petals; the style terminated by a thick capitate stigma. This plant is found on the brow of the mountains of Bogota in New Grenada, where also is found the true *B. æstuans*, with which M. Linden has confounded it. The *B. æstuans*, (Mutis) is a shrub more than six feet in height, having the habit of *Rhododendron hirsutum;* its branches are open, generally opposite, studded with long glandular hairs when young. The leaves are nearly sessile, oblong elliptical, acute, entire, without lateral nerves, downy below, and having a few glandular hairs above when young, then glabrous, almost smooth on the upper face, and with reddish hairs beneath; they are about an inch in length. The flowers are beautiful red, disposed in compact simple terminal panicles; the peduncles one-flowered, very hairy; the calyx large, hairy, cut nearly to the middle into broad and sharply-pointed lobes; the corolla very open, with lanceolate or nearly spathulate obtuse petals, four times larger than the calyx; the stamens hairy at the base, as long as the petals, and shorter than the style. This species, which was the first discovered by Mutis, grows near Santa Fé-de-Bogota, on the chain of calcareous mountains, at an elevation of from nine to ten thousand feet above the level of the sea. [Introduced about 1846.]

B. drymifolium (Linden) is a branching shrub, of upright habit; branches elongated, glabrous. The leaves are oblong, gradually attenuated at both extremities, nearly pointed, green above, paler and nearly glaucous below, with the lateral nerves prominent, perfectly glabrous on both faces, two inches and a half in length, and having rather long petioles. The flowers are pure white, arranged at the summit of the branches in lengthened panicles or paniculated racemes, the rachis clothed with short thick down in a young state; the peduncles downy, one-flowered; the calyx at first slightly downy, then viscous, deeply cut into obtuse lobes, about four times shorter than the petals, the style projecting beyond the petals, terminated by a large capitate and furrowed stigma. It grows in the province of Pampelona, New Grenada, at an altitude between five thousand and six thousand feet. This species, which has some analogy with *B. glauca*, is distinguished from that by its leaves being longer, by the pubescence on the flower-stalk, and by its white flowers. *B. densa* (*microphylla*, Planchon), which we only know from the small specimen at the Museum, appears very like *B. æstuans*, sent by M. Linden himself, but his flowers, instead of being of a brilliant carmine colour, as this is, are rose-coloured.

B. tricolor (Linden). According to M. Linden, this plant has the stems ferruginous, and the leaves smooth. Flowers very beautiful, white and rose, marked with yellow, at the base of the petals. These four latter species have been procured for the French gardens from New Grenada, by Messrs. Funck and Schlim.

[There is in the English gardens another species, the *B. cinnamomea* (Lindley), which is described as a shrub, with downy and hairy branches, furnished with leaves which are covered on the lower side with bright brown wool. The flowers grow in close terminal panicles, and have very woolly and hispid stalks and calyces; the blossoms are purple, apparently smaller than those of *B. coarctata*. It has been found in Peru, on the Andes of Caxamarca, at the height of eight thousand feet, and was introduced into England in 1846 or 1847, by Messrs. Veitch.]

STYLIDIUM AMŒNUM.

THIS novel introduction to our gardens from the Swan River colony, has been raised by Messrs. Henderson and Co., of the Pine Apple Nursery, and was, we believe, collected by Mr. Drummond, who has sent over so many of the fine plants of that country which now ornament our greenhouses and conservatories. The *Stylidium amœnum*, without the gaiety of many New Holland shrubs, is decidedly pretty, and must be a desirable addition to this class of plants. It blooms in June. The *Stylidium nudum* of Lindley is now considered to be synonymous.

It is a herb—perennial, we believe—having at the surface of the soil a rosulate tuft of leaves, which are spathulate, two and a half to three inches long, tapering to the base, shortly acute at the apex,

and terminating in an apiculus; they are paler on the lower than on the upper surface, and have a broken cellular hyaline, scarcely denticulate margin; when fresh they are scattered with transparent dots; the veins are dichotomous, scarcely anastomosing. From the centre of this tuft rises the erect scape, six inches high, terminating in the upper half in a pyramidal many-flowered raceme, below which is a whorl of linear pointed bracts. The rachis, pedicels, and calyx are furnished with hairs tipped by black glands. The flowers are large rose-coloured, measuring five-eighths of an inch in diameter. The pedicels are shorter than the calyx, subtended by small lance-shaped bracteoles. The calyx, besides its gland tipped hairs, is marked with red dots and streaks; its teeth are linear-oblong obtuse, those of the lower lip three in number, narrower than the two forming the upper lip, all being shorter than the ovary. The corolla is three times as long as the calyx teeth; the upper lip consists of four oblong blunt spreading lobes, the lower is very small, with a gland-like deltoid prominence at the base; a pair of short lateral ears, or projections, which become very indistinct in the dried state, and a subulate petal-like point; the throat is furnished with a crown of six clavate processes. The column is flattened at the base, becomes tapered upwards, and is bent twice in the usual way.

STYLIDIUM AMŒNUM.

The Stylidiums should be grown in sandy soil with a preponderance of peat earth, and require to be very carefully drained, for though they like a good supply of water while growing, they cannot endure stagnant moisture. A warm, dry, and airy greenhouse is the best situation for them. Many of them are very pretty, indeed, showy plants; and, in all, the structure of the flower, and the irritability of its column, is so curious, that they have good claim to the small space they occupy.—M.

1 Dichosema subinerme 2. Amygdalus persica flore semipleno

DICHOSEMA SUBINERME.

THIS very beautiful greenhouse shrub, which has been bloomed during the early part of the past summer by Messrs. Henderson, of the Pine Apple Nursery, has at first sight much the aspect of an Aotus, but an examination of its structure shows it to belong to the genus *Dichosema*, previously unrepresented in gardens; and it is, in fact, a species from the neighbourhood of Guildford in Western Australia, which has been described under the name of *Dichosema subinerme* by Dr. Meisner, in the Plantæ Preissianæ. Messrs. Henderson obtained it from Mr. Drummond.

It forms a branching shrub, having slender terete branches, and something the habit of *Chorozema Henchmanni*. The branches are clothed with short, close-pressed, soft hairs, beneath which they are marked by pallid nerve-like lines running downwards from the base of each leaf. The leaves have small roundish hairy stipules at their base, and are linear bluntish, with a thickened costa, and recurved margins, and have pale-coloured transverse veins; when young they are slightly hairy, but they afterwards become smooth. The flowers are solitary, terminating very short, solitary, or twin branchlets, each bearing about a pair of small leaves, produced from the axils of the alternate primary leaves, whence also here and there proceeds a slender spine. The pedicels are shorter than the calyx tube, and bear a pair of small narrow subulate bracts just beneath it, the pedicels, bracts, and exterior of calyx being densely covered with soft spreading hairs. The flowers are very showy, being clear yellow, with a very conspicuous zone of deep rose-crimson at the base of the standard, the prominent wings having also the same red colour. The filaments of the stamens are thickened at the base, and adnate with the tube of the calyx for about one-fourth of its length. The ovary is subsessile, lanceo-late, furrowed above, two-celled, containing six ovules, the style sharply curved upwards, and termi-nating in a small capitate stigma.

We are indebted for our figure and materials for description to the liberality of Messrs. Henderson, which we have had frequent occasion to acknowledge.

The culture of this *Dichosema* will assimilate exactly with that recommended for *Chorozema* at p. 122.—M.

———♦———

THE DOUBLE CRIMSON CHINESE PEACH.

THE double blossomed Peaches of China (*Amygdalus persica flore semipleno*) were among the most useful of the many introductions from that country made by Mr. Fortune during his first journey. The possession by the 'Celestials' of several varieties of double or rather semi-double blossomed Peaches had been long ascertained; but it was not until plants of two kinds, the crimson and white, were obtained and sent to England by the energetic traveller just named, that any of them were known in Europe, in a living state. These have since been distributed by the Horticultural Society, for whom they were obtained, and we have to thank Mr. Glendinning of the Chiswick Nursery—who, by the by, has been particularly successful in their propagation and cultivation—for the opportunity of making the drawing, copied in the annexed plate, from a plant which bloomed finely in his nursery last March.

Besides the semi-double crimson variety represented in our plate, the Horticultural Society obtained, as just intimated, a semi-double white variety of equal beauty. They have both in all respects "the habit of the common Peach tree, except that they are more excitable, in which respect they approach the Almond: and consequently they are better suited for forcing, or for flowering under glass, than in the open air; because although hardy, they suffer from wet cold nights, which brown their flowers and ruin their gay appearance. It is not improbable, however, that seedlings may in time be produced from them in which this precociousness will disappear; for being semi-double, it is expected that they will occasionally ripen fruit." This suggestion of Dr. Lindley is the more likely to be realized, as semi-double Peaches have undoubtedly been brought to produce fruit in the French gardens.

We know of nothing more gay for the decoration of the conservatory in the early spring than well managed bushes of these dwarf double-blossomed Peaches would be; and there is no doubt that as soon as their merits as ornamental plants come to be appreciated, they will find their way into every garden of any pretensions. In the meantime a supply of plants is being produced, in which object Mr. Glendinning has, we believe, been particularly successful.—M.

THE MIXED FLOWER GARDEN.

BULBOUS plants generally are particularly useful as spring flowers in a mixed garden, because, whilst contributing by their gay and showy colours to produce a good display of colour up to June, they have mostly by that time died down, and thus afford room for plants from pots and tender annuals, without which the display in autumn would not be complete.

The edges of all the beds should be planted with the various coloured Crocuses, not a few here and there, but continuous lines in all directions. In geometrical gardens, particularly, a grand effect may be produced by a skilful combination of the different colours, and I do not think a finer sight can be produced than that presented by a garden so arranged on a sunshiny spring day. They die away too, early, and will not in the least interfere with other planting operations. Snowdrops, also, those universally welcome harbingers of spring, should be extensively planted, but not in the open beds; their proper habitat is in small patches, irregularly distributed by the sides of the shady walks, peeping out between the recumbent branches of shrubs, or snugly ensconced in the niches of rockwork, where indeed they grow very large and fine.

The Snowflake, or *Leucojum vernum*, also comes very fine in the niches of rockwork, or little sheltered corners, and is also adapted for patches in the open beds. The tuberous-rooted *Eranthis hyemalis* and *sibirica*, also, do well under the branches of shrubs or the shade of trees, either in patches or distributed over large spaces.

As auxiliaries to these, either in shady places, little odd corners, or in the open beds, the Narcissus tribe deserve particular notice. Those who are in the habit of annually purchasing Dutch grown roots of Prima Donna, Grand Monarque, Soleil-d'or, Double Roman, and Paper white for flowering in pots, should take especial care of the roots after the flowering is over, and plant them out of doors early in October; they will flower in great perfection. In addition plant *Narcissus minor*, *Tazetta*, *majalis*, single and double, *Jonquilla*, *Bulbocodium*, *odorus flore-pleno*, *bifrons*, *tubiflorus*, Sulphur Crown, Double Orange Phœnix, and *Macleaii*. The above will form an excellent selection from this interesting and beautiful tribe of plants—all well worth planting.

The beautiful tribe of Scillas next claim notice. They are most of them very conspicuous and showy spring flowering plants, and may be extensively used, as they will not at all interfere with summer plants. The following are among the best:—*Scilla bifolia*, and its varieties *alba* and *rubra;* with *carnea*, *amæna*, *sibirica*, and *præcox*, all small-growing sorts, flourishing best in light dry soil in sheltered nooks and corners, particularly amongst rockwork. The stronger growing sorts, such as *S. campanulata*, and its varieties *alba* and *carnea*, also *indica* and *Lilio-Hyacinthus*, are well adapted for patches in the open beds.

The genus Muscari affords a fine choice and desirable plants for our purpose. The best are *Muscari botryoides*, and the varieties *alba* and *pallida*, *comosum*, *comosum monstrosum*, *moschatum*, and *macrocarpum*. The Allium tribe also affords a few showy and desirable plants, but due notice should be given to the ladies not to use them in bouquets, or even to handle them, on account of the strong odour of garlic which they emit on bruising: *Allium Moly*, *acutum*, *nigrum*, *umbellatum*, *stellatum*, and *roseum*, are amongst the best. *Erythronium albidum*, *rubrum*, and *lanceolatum*, must not be omitted; they are very useful as edgings to other beds, very showy in flower, and the foliage very ornamental. *Camassia esculenta*, a very handsome bulbous plant, flowers in June, and succeeds best in a shaded situation in peat soil. *Anthericum liliastrum* and *sulphureum*, *Ornithogalum refractum*, *nutans*, *umbellatum*, *montanum*, and *bulbiferum*, are amongst the best of early-flowering bulbs of that description. Add to these *Pancratium maritimum*, and a good collection of the various coloured Hyacinths, and the list will afford a selection of plants calculated to make a grand display up to the end of June, and then to give place to store plants and annuals. The list might be much extended, but I offer a selection of the best.—C.

SCIENTIFIC GLEANINGS.

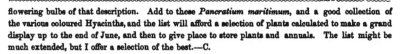

A VARIETY of *Orchis mascula*, supposed to be the *O. speciosa*, Host, has been found in the county of Wicklow, by Mr. D. Moore, of Glasnevin. This plant was discovered last year, and again this year in the county of Wicklow. Koch makes it a variety of *O. mascula*, which it probably ought not to be separated from, the difference being more in appearance than in well defined characters. It is, however, a noble-looking plant, growing nearly eighteen inches high. Some of the flowers in the rachis are imperfect, wanting the labellum, which would appear to be characteristic of the species. Mr. Moore does not find good characters to distinguish it from *O. mascula*, though it differs so widely in general appearance. In regard to the Orchis, Mr. Babington remarks that he does not concur in the opinion that it is the *O. speciosa* of Host. " I believe it," he writes, " to be nothing more than a very luxuriant state of the *O. mascula*. A few days since I found two specimens, exactly corresponding with the Wicklow plant, in the wooded part of the Devil's Ditch, in the county of Cambridge. They possess the remarkable size of Mr. Moore's plant, and the rather acuter segments of the perianth, such as he finds on his specimens. The true *O. speciosa* (which is itself only a variety of the *O. mascula*), has very much more attenuated segments of perianth. It is figured by Reichenbach in his recent elaborate volume upon the Orchidaceæ (forming *Icon. Fl. Germ.*, vols. 13 and 14), and I have lately received a plant which is much more like it than is the Irish plant, from Mr. Keys of Plymouth. Our English *O. mascula* is noted by continental botanists as an obtuse-petaled form of the species. Mr. Moore's plant is far nearer to the continental type of the species."

It appears from Göppert's excellent investigations, that " all the Amber of the Baltic comes from a coniferous tree, which, judging from the remains of its wood and bark at different ages or stages of growth, seems to be a peculiar species, approaching nearest to our white and red Pines. The Amber tree of the ancient world (*Pinites succinifer*) was far more resinous than any conifer of the present period, the resin being deposited, not only as in our present trees, within and upon the bark, but also in the wood itself, following the course of the medullary rays, which, as well as the cells, are still distinctly recognisable under the microscope; and large masses of white and yellow resin are sometimes found between the concentric ligneous rings. Among the vegetable substances inclosed in Amber, there are male and female blossoms of native needle-leaved trees and cupuliferæ; but distinctly recognizable fragments of Thuja, Cupressus, Ephedra, and Castanea vesca, intermingled with those of Junipers and Firs, indicate a vegetation different from that now subsisting on the coasts and plains of the Baltic."—*Humboldt's Cosmos*.

The *Ficus Benjamina* is very remarkable for the profusion of roots, which it throws down from its branches. These, when they reach the ground, become secondary stems, as in the true Banyan tree. Those who wish additional facts to prove that the wood of exogenous trees is formed by bud-roots, have only to look at one of these trees to be fully convinced of the truth of this beautiful doctrine. The main stem of some of them, indeed, I may say of all, does not form one solid mass, as usually occurs in other trees, but is a congeries of thick branching roots, which come down from the lower ends of the large branches, surround the original shoot or stem, and overlay each other in such an open reticulated manner, that daylight can often be seen through a trunk several feet in diameter. It is also curious to observe that the long, horizontal, main branches of these trees have not the conical shape, or at least not so much, as those of the other trees. What is the cause of this? The explanation is very simple. The roots which are sent down from the buds, between the bark and the previously formed wood, in place of reaching the lower part of the branch, are thrown out along the course of it in masses, which resemble enormous horse-tails, and hence the necessity, which the branches of such trees have, for the supports which are formed by these roots when they reach the ground. Instances have been known of these trees, although the main trunk has been totally destroyed, yet continuing to live; its functions being performed, and the whole mass supported by the supernumerary stems formed of the tender rootlets given out by the branches.—*London Journal of Botany.*

The Bejarias, with the exception of *B. racemosa*, a native of Florida, have all been obtained from South America, They are found growing on the high mountains of the torrid zone, in the regions where the thermometer only varies from twelve to fourteen degrees Cent. during the day, and from four to six during the night. They are found in the chain of the Andes, from the southern part of Peru to seven degrees north of Pampelona, where Messrs. Funck and Schlim discovered *B. æstuans* and *B. drymifolia* in the mountains. They are found, again, at 1290 kilometres to the west of the Cordillera of Santa Fe-de-Bogota, and on the peak of the Silla of Caraccas, the summit of which is more than seven thousand feet above the level of the sea. Notwithstanding this great elevation, which indicates a low temperature, it is probable that these plants should always be grown in a greenhouse in Europe. Mr. Pince, of Exeter, hopes, indeed, that they will be found hardy enough for the mild climate of Devonshire. We think, however, with MM. Humboldt and Bonpland, that it will be found more difficult to grow them well in the level plains, than on the alpine districts of Europe. The Bejarias, and the other plants of the Cordilleras, are habituated to a mild temperature, and in that perpetual spring of the elevated regions of this part of America, their health is such that they suffer when they are transported to climates where the air is sometimes intensely cold and very humid, and at other times excessively hot. Generally speaking, the analogy which exists between the climate of certain parts of Europe and that which is proper, either to the valleys of Mexico or the elevated regions of the Andes of Northern America, has been far too much exaggerated. It is neither in England, nor in the south of Europe, that the Bejarias will find that regularity of temperature, and that dry and balmy air which is peculiar to mountainous regions. According to MM. Humboldt and Bonpland, *Bejaria æstuans*, *B. coarctata*, and *B. grandiflora*, grow at a height at which the barometer is very much lower than on the hills of Eastern Florida, where *B. racemosa* thrives. We cannot therefore hope to see the cultivation of these plants successful in the midst of an atmosphere as dense and humid as that of the South of France and England, and the best mode of treating them is no doubt that practised with the Azaleas and Indian Rhododendrons.—*Revue Horticole.*

ORCHID BASKETS.

IT is well known that many kinds of orchids are best cultivated in suspended "baskets," as they are called; and that these are for the most part constructed of fillets of wood. These serve the purpose for

a time, but, as the wood soon decays, they require to be frequently renewed, which is often a matter of

Hybrid Cape and Bedding Pelargoniums

1 Quercifolium roseum
2 Denticulatum superbum
3 radomum variegatum
4 Citriodorum violaceum

5 Odoratissimum punctatum
6 Citriodorum elegantissimum
7 Cleopatra
8 Formosissimum varicum

inconvenience. Wire baskets have been sometimes used, but these, if of iron, are soon liable to rust away in the damp atmosphere of an orchid house, or if of copper are expensive.

"Baskets" formed of terra cotta, or of any other fine earthenware may be advantageously employed, and the annexed figures are given as suggestions of the kind of form they may take for plants of different habit, the more openly constructed being intended for such as the *Stanhopeas*, which push out their flowering stems downwards, through the medium in which they are planted; the other for any kinds which throw their flowering stems erect, or above the surface of the soil. It will be obvious that the patterns may be varied to an indefinite extent.

HYBRID CAPE AND BEDDING PELARGONIUMS.

FLOWER gardening in this country is assuming quite a new character, and instead of the eternal beds of Verbenas and Scarlet Pelargoniums, enquiries are constantly being made for various coloured varieties that are suitable for that purpose. Three years back, our attention was directed to the subject; and the accompanying plate is the result of the progress we have so far made. Some of the varieties are exquisitely beautiful, and perfectly dissimilar from anything in cultivation in the same way; while in the case of P. denticulatum superbum, it will be seen that we have made some little progress towards getting good flowers upon the lovely and Fern-like foliage of the radula and denticulatum species. Beyond this, however, at present we cannot go, the young plants being quite sterile and mule-like. But time will moderate their luxuriance, and then possibly seed may be procured, though in some cases it is found almost impossible to get a plant to produce seed by the pollen of another variety, though it will bear freely by its own. This is more especially the case with some of the Cape species, which require great perseverance and patience to get them to bear seed.

Another distinct and very remarkable variety is P. Sidonia variegatum, a kind which promises to become one of the most desirable acquisitions of the flower garden. The flowers, it will be seen, are almost identical with those of the parent, and are quite as profusely produced. At present it is not our intention to part with this variety, as we wish to make another step a-head before it goes out of our hands; but persons desirous to possess it may forward their orders, which will be executed in strict rotation—possibly in the autumn of 1853. P. quercifolium roseum is a seedling between radula and Unique or quercifolium superbum, raised by Mr. Kempster, gardener to E. Fellows, Esq., Blackheath Park. It is a pure hybrid, and so far quite barren, producing neither pollen itself, nor seed by the pollen of other kinds; but Time, that great ameliorator of all things, may change its nature, and possibly induce fruitfulness; at least we hope so. Like the Uniques it is a very free-blooming kind, producing a truss of flowers at every joint, and a regular succession of them from March until October. It is of free growth, and the trusses are of good size, considerably too large to be represented full size. The foliage is particularly handsome, and much stronger (that is of greater substance) than any variety we know. For bouquets a truss and a leaf are quite sufficient.

P. formosissimum carneum is a hybrid from P. formosissimum of Sweet's Geraniaceæ, with one of the fancy varieties, possibly Jenny Lind, and it will be seen that the flowers are considerably better formed and the foliage stronger than the parent plant, indeed, the foliage itself, without flowers, would make the plant attractive. The flowers are profusely produced, and are very attractive. This plant was also raised by Mr. Kempster, and was shown at Chiswick, in 1851, in the class for "entirely distinct crosses;" but, strange to say, it was not noticed by the censors, though a variety almost identical with it, but not so good, exhibited by Messrs. E. G. Henderson and Son in June last, at the same place, was rewarded with a prize. So much for censorship! Of the preceding varieties P. denticulatum superbum, and the "Rose Unique" have both sweet foliage, and hence are very desirable on that account, but it is to the following variety, P. odoratissimum punctatum that the lover of sweet scents will rush with satisfaction. Most persons know the old Prince of Orange, or its variegated variety; this kind is quite as sweet, and is thus described by the National Floricultural Society, where it was awarded a certificate on June 17th :—" A bedding variety with sweet scented foliage, flowers deep maroon, edged with rosy lilac, lower petals pale rose, with a deep spot." It is a plant of very robust and compact habit, and flowers quite as profusely as any of the fancy varieties. We have it planted out, and bad as the season is, though almost every fancy variety has failed in the open ground, this plant continues to grow and bloom profusely, disregarding both soil and weather. We look upon it as a decided acquisition, and one that must become a decided favourite. It is a cross between the Fancies and sweet scented, and is one of the results of the experiment we commenced two years back to get good flowers with sweet and fancy foliage, and hardy constitutions. This variety we have planted out all the season, and on our soil, which is exceedingly unfavourable, it has continued to bloom profusely up to the present time, with a promise of remaining in the state for some time to come. It is a dwarf and compact grower. Cleopatra is a large blooming kind, and almost clear white, with faint spots on the lower petals, and a decided blotch on the upper ones. It is a perpetual blooming kind, and though a strong grower, does not, when planted out, exceed a foot in height. It also is a sport from the Fancies, with, we imagine, one of the large foliaged Cape kinds. As a pot plant it will be found an exceedingly free, decorative, and constant-blooming variety, and quite worthy of being grown for purposes of competition. We have it planted out, and find it to stand the weather, especially wet, better than any variety in the garden.

Citriodorum violaceum is a new and distinct colour, being a seedling between Fairliæ of Sweet, or what is now better known as Gaines' Delicata, but it is very superior to that variety both in form substance, and marking. The colour is bluish lilac, in habit it is very dwarf, and it blooms most profusely. It will be found exceedingly useful for small beds, and also for pot cultivation. As its name implies it belongs to the sweet-foliaged section, but it is not a strong-growing kind, and hence will require careful management to get a large stock of it.

Citriodorum elegantissimum is another variety of the sweet-foliaged section remarkable for the profuseness with which it produces its very pretty flowers. It is of good constitution and fine habit, and produces flowers with unusual profuseness; indeed, all the bedding varieties of Pelargonium bred through the fancy class are remarkable for the profuseness with which they bloom, and if care is really taken in the selection of parents, a very free-blooming and hardy race will be produced. The whole of the preceding varieties are in the possession of Mr. Ayres, and with those from Mr. Kempster, were raised by him. We believe these varieties will be sent out early in the spring of 1853.

While on the subject of Bedding Pelargoniums, it may not be out of place to offer a few suggestions on their management for bedding purposes; for unless they are prepared, especially the sweet-foliaged varieties, in a special manner, they will not be found so continuously blooming as they otherwise would be. The first requisite, then, is to stop the plants late in the spring, so as to prevent their blooming until they are planted in the open ground, for if you turn out plants which have been

blooming for weeks in the greenhouse or pit, with the expectation that they will continue to bloom for any length of time or with regularity, you will be much disappointed; but turn out young free-growing healthy plants in good soil, and they will not disappoint your expectations. Pelargoniums of this section also require good ground,—that is, it should be well drained, and the soil should be rich and open. If not naturally so, add leaf-mould and gritty sand to the soil, or take out the old soil to the depth of eighteen inches, and replace with prepared compost of loam, leaf-mould, and sand. Through the summer, especially if the weather be very dry, water occasionally with weak manure water, observing, however, at the same time, not to induce very luxuriant growth, or rather growth at the expense of flowers. Few plants are better adapted for cutting, for the decoration of the drawing-room, than these sweet-scented varieties, for the foliage of some of them is exceedingly elegant; and in the cases of

P. denticulatum, radula, and several other varieties, as Blandfordianum and Quercifolium, are almost Fern-like; indeed, so varied and pretty is the foliage of the different species and varieties of the Pelargonium, that by a judicious admixture of the variegated kinds, an exceedingly neat and pretty bouquet may be formed in the winter season, without using any flowers at all, and certainly a much sweeter bouquet than if the flowers were used without the foliage. The use of variegated and fancy foliage in the formation of bouquets, or for mixing with plants for decorative purposes generally, more especially by artificial light, is not sufficiently understood, neither is the use of plants remarkable for their foliage only. But we are progressing; and the gay and tawdry will soon, among persons of taste and refinement, give way to the chaste and beautiful. Annexed is a very suitable stand for showing cut Pelargoniums, and a very fit ornament for the drawing-room.—A.

New Garden Plants.

NYMPHÆA DEVONIENSIS, *Paxton.* Duke of Devonshire's Hybrid Water-Lily. Order Nymphæaceæ (Water-Lily tribe).—One of the very finest of this fine race of aquatic plants now engaging so much attention. It has been raised at Chatsworth by Sir J. Paxton, between *N. rubra* and *N. Lotus.* Both the leaves and flowers are much larger than in the parents; the former have a strongly dentate margin; and are sometimes a foot and a half in diameter; the latter rich crimson, produced without intermission through the whole season, and measuring eight inches in diameter. The colour is not quite so deep as in its parent.

BERBERIS TRIFURCA, *Lindley.* Three-forked Berberis. Order Berberaceæ (Berberid tribe).—A noble evergreen shrub, with pinnated leaves a foot and a half long, with broad and very coriaceous leaflets four or five inches long, deep green, with a few spines at the base, and about three forming a trident quite at the apex. The flowers are not known. It is expected to prove nearly, or quite hardy. Introduced from China by Mr. Fortune, and cultivated by Messrs. Standish and Noble.

GUICHENOTIA MACRANTHA, *Turczaninow.* Large-flowered Guichenotia. Order Byttneriaceæ § Lasiopetaleæ (Byttneriad tribe).—A curious greenhouse evergreen shrub, of hoary aspect, growing two to three feet high, bearing whorls of linear-oblong downy leaves in threes; and from their axils are produced the one to three flowered peduncles. The flowers consist of a somewhat rotate pale purple downy calyx, within which are five small scale-like deep purple petals. It comes from Swan River, and was sent by Mr. Drummond to Kew.

SPHÆRALCEA NUTANS, *Scheidweiler.* Nodding Sphæralcea. Order Malvaceæ (Mallowwort tribe).—A fine shrubby malvaceous greenhouse plant, with large cordate five-lobed leaves, and axillary peduncles longer than the leaves, bearing usually three large nodding crimson flowers, from which the column of yellow anthers project. It is a useful plant, of the same class as the larger Abutilons, and, like them, very showy, where there is space for its developement. It is cultivated by M. Van Houtte, of Ghent, and is well figured in the *Flore des Serres.* Supposed to be a native of Guatemala.

TROPÆOLUM DIGITATUM, *Karsten.* Digitate Indian Cress. Order Tropæolaceæ (Indian Cress tribe).—This is a handsome climbing plant; and as it is not stated to be annual, it is more probably one of the fibrous-rooted perennial kinds. The leaves are peltate, five to seven lobed, the lobes rounded and entire. The flowers have the calyx and spur brick red, inclining to carmine, and running into pale green, the former at its base, the latter at its point; the petals are yellow and ciliate-dentate. It is from the Carracas, and has been raised and flowered by M. Decker, of Jena, from seed sent by Dr. Karsten.

IMPATIENS MACROPHYLLA, *Gardner.* Large-leaved Balsam. Order Balsaminaceæ (Balsam tribe).—This is a coarse-leaved soft-stemmed stove plant, introduced from Ceylon to the Royal Garden at Kew, where it flowered in the early part of the summer after the seeds were sown. It grows two to three feet high, has large ovate-acuminate, deeply serrated, long-stalked leaves, mostly at the top of the stem, and producing from axillary buds, numerous crowded flowers on very short stalks. The flowers are small, but being deep orange-coloured, stained with red, and having a red upper sepal, they are rather pretty. The spur is curiously incurved, spiny, and inflated, and didymous at the apex. The stems are stout, and the leaves ample, with red petioles.

ILEX LEPTACANTHA, *Lindley.*—Slender-spined Holly. Order Aquifoliaceæ (Hollywort tribe).—A hardy evergreen shrub, a good deal like the Nepal *I. dipyrena,* and believed to be a Holly, from its being readily grafted on the common Holly; its flowers and fruit are not known. The leaves are six inches long, by two wide, of a uniform oval figure, bordered with distant slender spiny teeth, and of the texture of Portugal laurel leaves. Introduced by Mr. Fortune from the north of China.

GASTROLOBIUM VELUTINUM, *Lindley.* Velvety Gastrolobe.—Order Fabaceæ, § Papilionaceæ (Leguminous plants).—A very handsome greenhouse shrub, having a remarkably soft velvety surface. The leaves are in whorls of three, sub-sessile, oblong-wedge-shaped, almost bilobed at the apex. The racemes are terminal, elongate, and bear numerous peculiarly rich orange-coloured flowers. It is from Swan River, whence it was sent by Mr. Drummond, and has been raised by Messrs. Henderson, of Pine-apple Place.

CEANOTHUS VERRUCOSUS, *Nuttall.* Warted-stemmed Ceanothus.—Order Rhamnaceæ (Rhamnad tribe).—This fine hardy shrub is in cultivation under the name of *C. integerrimus*, which does not belong to it. It is a stiff branched evergreen, thickly clothed with leaves, which are roundish or roundish-wedge-shaped, and either entire or toothed on the margin. The flowers are pale purplish-blue, produced in small corymbs from the axils of the leaves, and they are abundantly produced in April and May. The stems are remarkable for having two to four ovate brown warty excrescences at the joints.

BRACHYSEMA LANCEOLATUM, *Meisner.* Lance-leaved Brachysema.—Order Fabaceæ, § Papilionaceæ (Leguminous plants.)—A fine evergreen greenhouse shrub, of erect elongate habit, with silky branches and leaves in opposite pairs, varying much in form—ovate to narrow lanceolate. The flowers grow in axils, four to six together, on a sessile sub-compound raceme; and though the corolla is rich scarlet, and of considerable size, yet it is so hidden by the calyx and foliage, that the plant is more botanically interesting than valuable for ornamental purposes. It was sent from Swan River by Mr. Drummond, and has been three or four years in the gardens.

ACACIA CYCNORUM, *Bentham.* Swan River Acacia.—Order Fabaceæ § Mimoseæ (Leguminous plants).—A very handsome Acacia of the pulchella group. It has very hairy branches, without spines; alternate bipinnate leaves, with small, linear-oblong leaflets; and globose heads of deep yellow flowers, on peduncles growing from the axils of the leaves, and rather exceeding them in length. It was raised by Messrs. Lucombe, Pince, and Co., from seed sent by Mr. Drummond from Swan River, where it appears to be common.

ECHEVERIA BRACTEOSA, *Lindley.* Bracteose Echeveria.—Order Crassulaceæ (Houseleek tribe).—A succulent greenhouse plant, with thick glaucous bloom. The leaves grow in rosettes, at the end of a short fleshy stem, and are thick obovate obtuse. The peduncle is leafless, with a few deciduous scales, and terminated in a one-sided raceme of green and red flowers, remarkable for the large fleshy calyx, which is longer than the dull red sepals. It is a Mexican plant. Dr. Klotzsch called it *Pachyphytum bracteosum.*

HEXACENTRIS MYSORENSIS, *Wight.* Mysore Hexacentris.—Order Acanthaceæ (Acanthad tribe).—A very beautiful stove climber, from the Mysore country, introduced by F. Maltby, Esq., and bloomed by Messrs. Veitch, of Exeter. It is a rather tender woody creeper, with opposite oblong-acuminate three-nerved leaves, obtuse at the base, sometimes lobed or hastate. The flowers grow in long pendulous racemes; they are tubular, with a very oblique two-lipped limb, of which the upper lip is obtuse, helmeted, and two-lobed, the lower three-parted with ovate reflexed lobes; the tube is shaggy at the base inside. The flowers are yellow, with the face of the limb marked with rich red-brown blotches. It will become a very favourite stove climber, admirably suited for training on rafters.

COMPARETTIA CRYPTOCERA, *Morren.*—Hidden-horned Comparettia. Order Orchidaceæ (Orchid tribe).—A very pretty stove epiphyte, with elongate compressed pseudo-bulbs, lanceolate ovate leaves, and loose pendulous racemes of flowers longer than the leaves, five to seven flowered; the sepals and petals small pink, the lip much larger, broad, blunt, deeply bilobed, without a crest on its disc, but having a small white tooth at the base. It has been flowered by M. Jacob Makoy. Professor Morren has published a figure in *La Belgique Horticole.* The native country of the plant is not known.

LYCASTE TRICOLOR, *Klotzsch.* Three-coloured Lycaste.—Order Orchidaceæ (Orchid tribe).—A pretty stove perennial, with long ovate compressed pseudo-bulbs, furnished with three to five ribbed leaves a foot and a half long, and producing several flower stalks from the base of the bulbs. The sepals are brown-red, an inch and a half long; the petals rose-coloured, broader; the lip is naked, three lobed towards the inside, rose-coloured darkly spotted. From Guatemala, and introduced to Berlin by M. Warczewitz.

ACINETA WARCZEWITZII, *Klotzsch.*—Warczewitz's Acineta.—Order Orchidaceæ (Orchid tribe).—A stove epiphyte, with ovate-oblong pseudo-bulbs, bearing three or four large leaves at top, and from the base a pendulous many-flowered scape of flowers of a pale waxy yellow colour, the petals and base of the lip dotted with red; the appendage to the lip is dark purple, and quadrangular, its middle lobe golden yellow. Flowers in April. Introduced from Central America to Berlin.

CORDYLINE INDIVISA, *Kunth.* Undivided Cordyline.—Order Liliaceæ (Lilywort tribe).—A noble arborescent plant of yucca-like habit, native of New Zealand, and apparently capable of enduring our winters in the more favoured parts of the country; a plant which has lived out for many years at Exeter, being now twelve to fourteen feet high. The stem is terminated by a tuft of hard, sharp-pointed, sword-shaped leaves, nearly four feet long; and from their centre comes the compound panicle, three or four feet long, covered with large, whitish cup-shaped flowers. It is grown by Messrs. Veitch of Exeter.

AZALEA AMŒNA, *Lindley.* Dwarf crimson Chinese Azalea.—Order Ericaceæ (Heathwort tribe).—A beautiful little dwarf evergreen bush, supposed to be hardy, having stood the winter of 1851-2, at Bagshot, unprotected. It has a very dwarf compact habit, bears small, flat, obovate leaves, blunt at the point, and rosy-crimson, almost regularly five-lobed flowers, nearly bell-shaped, and without calyx, that organ being exchanged or converted into an exterior corolla, so that the flowers have the character which is called " hose in hose," as occurs in some varieties of Primrose. It was found by Mr. Fortune, in a nursery garden at Shanghae, and it is suggested that it may be a Chinese garden variety of some species of Azalea, of which we are as yet unacquainted with its normal state. As a greenhouse shrub it is a charming addition to our gardens, and if it proves hardy, its value will be greatly increased.

THYRSACANTHUS RUTILANS, *Planchon.* Glittering Thyrsacanth.—Order Acanthaceæ (Acanthad tribe).—A very fine stove sub-shrubby plant, with large, subsessile, oblong-lanceolate, acuminate leaves, and terminal or axillary pendent racemes of numerous flowers, which are tubular, slightly ventricose, a couple of inches long, and of a brilliant crimson scarlet. It must be a very fine stove plant. It appears to have been introduced by M. Linden, from Colombia, and is figured in M. Van Houtte's *Flore des Serres.*

SOME FURTHER POINTS IN PEACH CULTURE.

WHAT is more common in gardens than to see hide-bound trees, the stems most disproportionate in size, that part above where they were worked being half as large again as the stock? Can this be remedied? I think so; at least, I have frequently succeeded to my satisfaction, in the following manner:—The first spring, soon after the trees commence growing, take a knife, and run it from the point where it was budded to the ground, cutting into the wood; as soon as the young wood is seen to fill up this incision, make a similar one on either side. By continuing to make two or three incisions in the stem each succeeding year, it will be found that the stock will swell proportionately with the worked part of the stem. These incisions are to be made at the back of the stock. The third season the tree will require the same attention as to stopping and pruning, &c.; and this must be followed up as long as they continue to make strong growth (see p. 125). In a general way this will not be oftener than twice in the season, excepting in case of a very strong tree, which may require it thrice. By the end of the third season the trees will have attained a large size, and their subsequent management any gardener of moderate capacity will understand. Cleanliness, that great preservative of health, is no less necessary to their well-being, than to the general health of the human race. We often hear that the Peach will not succeed in this or that garden. How is it possible that it should succeed, or grow, or even live, where no proper preparation has been made for it? There may be situations where the Peach will not thrive, but they have never come under my notice; and my decided opinion is, that there is no garden, however bad, in which the Peach and Nectarine might not be *well grown,* provided the borders have been all prepared, and the nature and depth of the soil used, having regard to situation and climate, properly taken into account—for, in a damp climate they will not require so great a depth of earth as in a dry, hot one. The great point is to feed the plant according with the climate. As well might we feed the inhabitants of the northern latitudes with the same food as the inhabitants of the Equator, as suppose that the Peach or Nectarine under the burning sun of Persia or America, require the same food as when planted in the wet soil and damp climate of England. In the former cases, should the tree be planted in a rich soil it is of little consequence, from the great demand made upon the foliage, by the intense light and burning heat causing respiration and digestion to go on freely: but, in the latter, should the tree be unfortunate enough to get into a rich or deep soil, the functions of the leaves being performed less freely, the system becomes gorged, sickness commences, canker, gum, blistered leaves, insects, &c., follow, carrying off the tree, branch by branch, until the whole disappears in the vortex of decay.

To prolong the fruit season in large establishments is a consideration of no little importance, as it is to preserve the fruit from the ravages of wasps and other insects in all. Various expedients have been resorted to. That which I have found most suitable, and which, under all circumstances, I strongly recommend, is a wasp-net, which I have direct from the manufacturer, in pieces fifty-one yards long by two and a-half wide, at three shillings per yard. To prolong the Plum season, these nets will be found to answer admirably, admitting, as they do, abundance of light and air, and being, at the same time, a barrier against the encroachments and depredations of all insects. I have found them particularly useful for the Green Gage and Coe's Golden Drop, which latter I have had hang on the trees long after the leaves had fallen; but in this case the nets were occasionally unnailed at the bottom, and the leaves shook out to prevent their rotting the nets. With care these nets will last ten or twelve years, but they must be well dried when put away, and kept in a dry, airy situation.— THOMAS HATCH.

ORNAMENTAL FLOWER STANDS, &c.

SO much attention has been devoted to decorative art, that it is by no means surprising to find it prominent in those departments of social economy with which the culture or enjoyment of flowers

are more especially connected. Flowers, too, and those of the choicest kinds, of all hues, and of the most delicate perfumes, are in these days brought so far within reach of all who find any enjoyment in the refinements and luxuries of civilized life, that not only in the garden and greenhouse, but in the parlour and boudoir, they become almost necessary ornaments.

The accompanying figures show some of the ways in which art and nature, under the form of vases and flowers may be brought into intimate association in the sphere just alluded to. They are from designs by A. Aglio, Esq., jun., and are intended to be constructed in terra cotta, or zinc, on a larger scale, for terrace-gardens, halls, and similar situations, where they are to be filled with ornamental plants in the growing state; or they may be made in porcelain, or any fine material, as stands for cut flowers, or smaller plants suitable for in-door decoration.

The sketch above, with that shown on p. 134, are intended chiefly for the table or boudoir, and are to be constructed of coloured glass, porcelain, or the finer earthen wares, either plain or with the ornamentation coloured. When filled with cut flowers, these should be arranged amongst fine green moss, kept continually damp, and may or may not be covered by a bell-glass. In addition to the central stand, the design at p. 134 has the three supporters continued upwards into a kind of cornucopia to hold smaller flowers, and they may be appropriated each to hold a small plant of some elegant Fern. For these purposes, their size may range from eighteen inches to two feet in diameter. Both designs may be made of larger size,—three to four feet in diameter,—and of zinc or terra cotta, for out-door use, where they may be employed with much appropriateness in detached terrace-gardens, or in situations where vases of summer-flowering plants are required.

The larger design is intended for the double purpose of cultivating a few very choice Ferns in the upright vase, covered by the bell-glass, whilst the stand

in which it is placed is to be kept filled with cut flowers. The supporting figures hold cornucopias, which are intended to take some very choice flower, such as a fine Moss Rose, a Camellia, a fine sprig of Fuchsia, &c. The lower stand may, if preferred, be planted with Lyeopodiums, — *L. denticulatum* being preferable for this purpose. The diameter of the stand may be conveniently from two and a half to three feet, and the diameter of the vase one foot; the height about three feet. It may be made of glass, porcelain, terra cotta, or metal; or the figures alone may be of metal. Colour may be appropriated for the figures and ornamentation.

When vases of this kind are employed for the growth of living plants, the first consideration is proper drainage; there must be no stagnant water. This being the case it would be preferable to use the centre vase for growing plants, and allow this to drain into the lower one, which could be employed for cut flowers. The next point is soil : this should be turfy peat, with plenty of sand intermixed, the mass resting on a thick layer of broken crocks for drainage. Then the plants, if in a living room, must be constantly covered with a bell-glass; and enough water must be given to keep the soil atmosphere moist, but not saturated.

THE GENERA AND SPECIES OF CULTIVATED FERNS.

By Mr. J. HOULSTON, Royal Botanic Garden, Kew; and Mr. T. MOORE, F.L.S., &c.

(Continued from The Gardeners' Magazine of Botany, *p. 332).*

Sub-order—Polypodiaceæ : Tribe—Gleicheniaceæ.

On a review of the whole of the extensive and externally varied group of Ferns, it appears somewhat remarkable that they should nearly all be included under one sub-order, namely, Polypodiaceæ. This arises from the similarity which exists in this large group in respect to the formation of their spore-cases, which are globose or oval, transparent, unilocular, pedicellate, rarely sessile, and furnished with a vertical, usually incomplete, elastic ring, bursting irregularly and transversely. The Gleicheniaceæ are distinguished from these by having their spore-cases globose or pyriform, unilocular, sessile, usually compressed on their interior side, and furnished with a complete, transverse, horizontal, or occasionally oblique ring, opening vertically. Each sorus is composed of a definite number of spore-cases : from two to six, sometimes eight, rarely more ; and they are naked or furnished with indusioid hairs. The character of their fronds is not less remarkable than the peculiarity of the few spore-cases in each sorus ; they are of a rigid, wiry, or sub-shrubby habit, and with one or two exceptions, are always dichotomous,* a peculiarity that distinguishes them from nearly all other Ferns. More than thirty species are described as belonging to this division, and these, on rather slender characters, are distributed among three genera. Their affinity with Polypodiaceæ lies through Trichomaneæ, the spore-cases in this group having a complete ring, though taking a different direction. The Gleicheniaceæ are readily distinguished by their dichotomous fronds, and by the paucity of spore-cases in each sorus.

GLEICHENIA, *Smith.*—Name commemorative of Baron P. F. Von Gleichen, a German botanist.

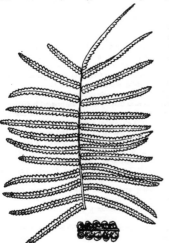

Sori round, solitary, naked and superficial, or immersed in a concave cyst. Veins pinnate or pinnately forked ; venules free, the lower exterior one fertile. Fronds usually rigid, from six inches to one and a half foot high ; pinnæ dichotomously branched, the branches pinnatifid or pinnate, the pinnules or segments small, plane, or revolute and cucullate, or plicate and concave, smooth glaucous, squamose or tomentose. Rhizome creeping.—This exceedingly beautiful genus of tropical or sub-tropical Ferns, is amongst the most difficult to cultivate, appearing to require a closer and somewhat drier atmosphere than is generally afforded to other Ferns ; their slender rhizomes are of a hard dry nature, and usually lose their vitality by transportation ; hence, they are rarely brought to England in a living state. One species, *G. dicarpa,* of which Fig. 82 represents a small portion of a pinna (natural size), with a part of a pinnule (magnified), showing the position of the sori, has been cultivated in the nursery of Messrs. Loddiges, Hackney, for many years, and has been introduced to the Royal Gardens at Kew. It has, likewise, been raised from spores.

1. *G. dicarpa.* R. Brown.—A neat, elegant, evergreen, warm greenhouse Fern, a native of Tasmania. Fronds slender, dichotomous, divaricated, a foot or more high, light green ; branches nearly glabrous, pinnate ; pinnæ pinnatifid ; segments orbicular, arched, with a broad recurved margin. Spore-cases two within the hollow of each segment. Rachis hairy ; lateral adherent to a slender creeping rhizome.

Fig. 82.

* Platyzoma, a genus containing only one species, inhabiting the tropical parts of New Holland, has pinnate fronds.

MERTENSIA, *Willdenow.*—Name commemorative of F. C. Mertens, a French botanist.

Sori round or globose, naked or intermixed with hairs, medial, superficial, with three to eight, or sometimes more, spore-cases in each sorus. Veins simple or pinnately forked; venules direct, free, the exterior one fertile. Fronds rigid, from one to six feet high, many times dichotomously branched; pinnæ pinnatifid, the segments linear, entire, uniform, smooth, glaucous, or villose, rarely dentate.—The species arranged under this genus are more readily recognized from the preceding by their habit than by any technical distinction; they have larger fronds, with plane segments, medial sori, and a more evident venation. Only a solitary species is at present in cultivation, *M. flabellata,* of which Fig. 83 represents a small portion of a pinna (nat. size).

1. *M. flabellata,* Desvaux, (Gleichenia, *R. Brown.*)—An evergreen warm greenhouse Fern, a native of New Holland, Van Diemen's Land, and New Zealand. Fronds rather erect, one and a half to two feet high, lightish green; stipes dichotomous; primary pinnæ opposite, flabelliform; ultimate pinnules lanceolate, deeply pinnatifid, with linear segments slightly serrated on the margin. Spore-cases three to five inserted in each sorus. Fronds lateral, adherent to a creeping rhizome. This species has been in cultivation at Messrs. Loddiges for many years.

Fig. 83.

*Sub-order—*POLYPODIACEÆ: *Tribe—*SCHIZÆACEÆ.

This group, consisting of a few genera widely differing in habit and general appearance from other Ferns, contains about forty species, technically characterized by their spore-cases being oval or oblong, rarely globose, sessile; opening vertically (lengthways) on their exterior side; having a striated (rayed) apex, which is analogous to a transverse ring; and produced on contracted marginal lobules, or special appendices, in the form of either simple, racemose, or paniculate contracted fronds or spikelets. Their nearest affinity is with Osmundaceæ, with which they were formerly united; but Osmundaceæ, as now restricted, differ essentially by having bivalved spore-cases, and materially in habit.

LYGODIUM, *Swartz.*—Name derived from *lygodes,* flexible; alluding to the twining habit of the plant.

Sori on marginal appendices, forming numerous linear spikelets, which are composed of two series of indusiate imbricate cysts, each cyst or cell containing an oval sporangium, which is attached by its interior side, and resupinate. Veins (sterile) forked, free, or (fertile) pinnate; venules arcuate, bearing the spore-cases on their superior sides. Sometimes the segments are contracted and form a dense sporangiferous rachis. Fronds twining, from two to twenty or forty feet high; pinnæ usually conjugate, lobed, palmate, pinnatifid, pinnate or bipinnate. Rhizome decumbent, cæspitose, creeping.—It very rarely occurs that habit stamps a genus with such a permanent feature as that by which the present is distinguished; the permanent twining habit is the natural character that distinguishes the genus. In this particular it is somewhat approached in Pteridæ, by *Platyloma flexuosa,* but that is easily known by being less scandent, and by the pinnæ not being conjugate. There are many species belonging to the genus, chiefly found within or near the tropics, the same species being sometimes common to both hemispheres; one species, *L. palmatum,* extending to the parallel of 41° N. Lat., in the United States. Their twining habit renders the tropical ones well adapted for covering pillars, walls, trellis-work, or for training against the rafters in a moist stove, where they grow freely, and have a beautiful appearance, especially when loaded with fructification. Fig. 84 represents a pinnule of *L. venustum* (nat. size).

Fig. 84.

1. *L. palmatum,* Swartz, (Hydroglossum, *Willdenow*).—A very elegant evergreen warm greenhouse Fern, from North America. Sterile frond glabrous, very slender, about a foot long; pinnæ conjugate, cordate, palmate, membranous, five to seven-lobed, yellowish green above, rather glaucous beneath; lobes oblong, undulated,

round at the apex, deflexed, and entire on the margin. Fertile fronds very slender, two feet or more long, fertile on the upper part only, the fertile pinnæ paniculate, with linear segments. Rachis and stipes light brown; lateral, adherent to a slender creeping rhizome.

2. *L. flexuosum*, Swartz, (Hydroglossum, *Willdenow*).—A beautiful evergreen stove species, a native of the East Indies and China. Fronds twining, from twelve to twenty feet high. Sterile pinnæ conjugate, palmate, five or six lobed, bright shining green; segments lanceolate, nine to eighteen inches long, entire on the margin, and gradually increasing in size upwards. Fertile pinnæ small, conjugately bipartite, and near the apex of the fronds, which are lateral or subterminal, adherent to a cæspitose, decumbent, short rhizome. The plant is known in gardens as *L. circinatum.*

3. *L. articulatum*, A. Richard.—An ornamental evergreen greenhouse Fern, from New Zealand. Fronds glabrous, scandent, four to six feet high; pinnæ conjugate, pinnate; pinnules, lanceolate, yellowish green above, glaucous beneath, obtuse at the apex, the margin entire, cuneate at the base, and articulate with the petiole, which is of a reddish brown colour. Fronds lateral, adherent to a slender creeping rhizome.

4. *L. volubile*, Swartz, (Hydroglossum, *Willdenow*).—An ornamental evergreen stove species, a native of the West Indies. Fronds twining, and minutely pubescent, twenty to thirty feet high; pinnæ conjugate, pinnate; pinnules linear-lanceolate, bright green, four to five inches long, sub-hastate, slightly cordate at the base, finely serrated at the margin, and articulate with the rachis. Fertile pinnæ near the apex of the fronds; lateral, adherent to a cæspitose creeping rhizome. This species is known in cultivation under the name of *L. semi-hastatum.*

5. *L. venustum*, Swartz, (Hydroglossum hirsutum, *Willdenow*).—A very beautiful evergreen stove Fern, a native of the tropics of South America. Fronds twining, from eight to twelve feet high, light green, hairy throughout; pinnæ conjugate, bipinnate; pinnules cordate-palmate, membranous, five to seven-lobed, intermediate one very large, lanceolate, inciso-serrate, acute at the apex, and at the base indistinctly articulated with the petiole. Fructifications copious on the upper part of the fronds, which are lateral, adherent to a short creeping rhizome.

6. *L. scandens*, Swartz, (Hydroglossum, *Willdenow*; L. microphyllum, *of gardens*).—A deciduous stove Fern, from the East Indies and China. Fronds slender, twining, ten to fifteen feet high, minutely pubescent, light green; pinnæ conjugate, tripinnate; pinnules cordate-palmate, five to seven-lobed, intermediate one elongated, linear-lanceolate, and serrate at the margin. Sori abundant on the upper half of the frond, the fertile segments often very small. Fronds lateral, adherent to a slender creeping rhizome.

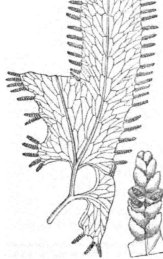

Fig. 85.

L YGODICTYON, *J. Smith.* (Lygodium, sp., *of Authors*; Hydroglossum, *Presl*).—Named from *lygodes*, flexible, and *dictyon*, a net; the plants having a twining habit and a reticulated venation.

Sori on marginal appendices, forming numerous linear spikelets, which are composed of two rows of indusiate imbricate cysts, each cyst or cell containing an oval sporangium, which is attached by its interior side and resupinate. Veins pinnate; venules anastomosing, forming unequal oblong areoles. Fronds twining, scandent; pinnæ conjugate, lobed, or palmate. Rhizome cæspitose.—This genus consists of two or three species, natives of the Islands of the Pacific and Indian Ocean, and South America, which were formerly referred to Lygodium, with which they agree in their twining habit and conjugate pinnæ, and in requiring similar treatment in cultivation; they are only separated on the ground of their reticulated venation. Fig. 85 represents a small portion of *L. heterodoxum* (nat. size), with a spikelet (magn.)

1 *L. heterodoxum*, J. H., (Lygodium, *Kunze*).—An ornamental, evergreen, warm greenhouse Fern, a native of Guatemala and Oaxaca. Fronds slender, twining, from ten to twenty feet high; sterile pinnæ conjugate, palmate, glabrous, rather dull green, five to seven-lobed, cuneate at the base; lobes linear-lanceolate, undulated, four to seven inches long, rather obtuse at the apex, and serrate at the margin. This Fern was introduced to English collections in 1850, from the Continent, and has not yet produced fructification. The fronds are terminal, adherent to a short rhizome, which is somewhat tufted.

S CHIZÆA, *Smith.*—Name derived from *schizo*, to cleave; the fertile fronds being divided into numerous linear segments.

Spore-cases oval, vertical, arranged in a compact row on each side the midrib of the segments, which are linear, unilateral, vertical, and conniving with the opposite ones. Fertile appendices terminal, forming a reflexed pinnate reclinate crest of linear segments, which have an inflexed indusiform margin. 'Fronds simple and linear, or dichotomous, multipartite, or entire and flabellate, from two inches to about a foot high. Rhizome cæspitose or tufted.—Some of the most singular-looking plants among Ferns are found in this genus, of which only a solitary species is known in cultivation. Some of them have their fronds all fertile, and others have a few sterile ones; all are low-growing kinds, scarcely exceeding a foot high. Although there are many known species, and these very extensively distributed in both hemispheres, yet they are almost unknown in cultivation, being very rarely imported. The most northern limit of the genus is New Jersey, in North America, and they extend southward to the Cape of Good Hope and Van Diemen's Land. Fig. 86 represents a whole plant of *S. pusilla* (full size).

Fig. 86.

1. *S. pusilla*, Pursh.—A dwarf hardy or frame species, from North America. Fronds of two kinds; the sterile simple, linear, glaucous, twisted, about an inch long; the fertile erect, filiform, compressed, two or three inches high, with linear-pinnate, reclinate segments on the apex of the frond, in four or five pairs. Fronds terminal, adherent to a tufted rhizome.

NEIMIA, *Swartz.*—Name derived from *aneimon*, naked; in allusion to the fertile portions of the frond, on which the sori are situated, being without a cover.

Sori unilateral on linear segments, forming dense panicles. Spore-cases oval, vertical, naked. Veins forked; venules direct, free. Fronds of two kinds, sterile and fertile, from a few inches to two feet high, smooth or hairy. Fertile fronds stipitate, usually tripartite, decompound with the two opposite branches, contracted, erect, constituting unilateral sporangiferous compound panicles; sterile portion spreading, pinnate, bipinnate or decompound, reclining or semi-erect, and usually much shorter than the fertile appendices. Sterile frond sometimes tripartite, with the two opposite segments small. Rhizome fasciculate, erect or creeping.—Few plants are more striking and

Fig. 87.

attractive, even to a casual observer, or more truly beautiful and interesting to the naturalist, than what are commonly denominated flowering ferns. It is a character possessed by this and an allied genus in common with Osmunda, to have their naked spore-cases borne in clusters or panicles on the apex of the fronds, and, being always contracted, they bear a great resemblance to the inflorescence of phænogamous plants; hence the appellation of flowering ferns. The present genus originally contained nearly fifty species, which are natives principally of South America and the West Indian Islands, one species, however, being detected in Abysainia, one at the Cape of Good Hope, and another in the East Indies; but on account of a free and reticulated venation existing in the group, they have been separated by modern authors, and the species which are retained as Aneimias have a free venation, while those with reticulated veins form the genus Aneimidictyon. Fig. 87 represents the apex of a fertile panicle and a sterile pinule of *A. villosa* (nat size).

1. *A. collina*, Raddi.—An elegant evergreen stove fern, from Brazil. Sterile fronds hairy, lanceolate, pinnate, about a foot long, deep and bright green; pinnæ membranous, oblong, petiolulate, imbricate, round at the apex, upper base round and sub-auriculate, lower truncate-cuneate, and crenate at the margin. Fertile fronds erect, one to one and a half feet high, tripartite; sterile portion lanceolate, eight or ten inches long. The rachis and stipes of both fronds are densely covered throughout with ferruginous hairs; they are terminal and adherent to an erect fasciculate rhizome.

2. *A. tenella*, Swartz.—A dwarf-growing evergreen stove fern, a native of the West Indies and tropics of South America. Sterile fronds slender, hairy, four or five inches long, lightish green, pinnate; pinnæ oblong, deeply pinnatifid, with cuneate segments dentate at the apex. Fertile fronds slender, hairy, erect, tripartite, six to eight inches high; sterile portion spreading, triangularly elongate, pinnate; pinnæ deeply pinnatifid, with cuneate segments dentate at the apex. Fronds lateral, or terminal; adherent to a slender, somewhat creeping rhizome.

3. *A. villosa*, Humboldt. (*A. flexuosa*, *Raddi*, and of *Authors*).—A beautiful evergreen stove Fern from Brazil. Sterile fronds hairy, one foot long, bipinnate, light green; pinnæ oblong, obtuse at the apex, inferior

ones petiolulate, slightly cordate at the base, deeply pinnatifid, with ovate segments, sub-entire at the margin. Fertile fronds erect, hairy, tripartite, one to two feet high; sterile portion spreading, triangularly elongate, eight to ten inches long, bipinnate; pinnæ lanceolate, deeply pinnatifid, with oblong segments, fronds terminal, adherent to a decumbent creeping rhizome, densely covered with articulated hairs.

4. *A. cicutaria*, Kunze.—A low-growing, deciduous stove species, from Jamaica. Sterile fronds slender, triangularly elongate, bipinnate, tripinnate below, light green, six or seven inches long; pinnules obovate-incisodentate, cuneate at the base. Fertile fronds slender, six to nine inches high, tripartite, with the two opposite branches contracted and sporangiferous or triangularly elongate, with two or more pairs of the lower pinnæ opposite or alternate, contracted, and soriferous. Fertile panicle shorter than the sterile portion. Rachis and stipes in both fronds scattered over with hair-like scales. Fronds terminal, adherent to a tufted rhizome.

5. *A. adiantifolia*, Swartz, (A. asplenifolia, *Swartz*).—A beautiful evergreen stove Fern, from the West Indies and South America. Sterile fronds slender, deltoid, light green, one foot long, bi-tri-pinnate, slightly hairy beneath; segments oblong-ovate, dentate at the apex, cuneate at the base. Fertile fronds erect, one to one and half foot long, tripartite; sterile portion deltoid, with the stipes nearly a foot long; lateral, adherent to a scaly creeping rhizome.

NEIMIDICTYON, *J. Smith* (Aneimiæ sp, *Swartz*). — Named from *aneimon*, naked, and *dictyon*, a net; alluding to the naked inflorescence, and the reticulated venation.

Sori unilateral on linear segments, forming dense panicles, spore-cases oval, vertical, naked. Veins forked; venules anastomosing, forming unequal oblong areoles. Fronds sterile and fertile, sub-glabrous or hairy, from

Fig. 88.

one to two feet high. Fertile fronds usually tripartite, with the two opposite branches contracted, erect, constituting unilateral sporangiferous compound panicles, the sterile portion spreading, semi-erect, and usually shorter than the fertile appendices. Sterile frond pinnate, or sometimes tripartite, with the two opposite segments or inferior pinnæ small, and pinnatifid or pinnate. Rhizome fasciculate, erect.—The analogy existing between this genus and Aneimia is very close. The character of venation alone is regarded by some as insufficient for generic definition, while by others it is considered of paramount importance. We have in our progress already pointed out that, in our opinion, a free state of venation, and a partial anastomosing of the veins, cannot with propriety be made the ground of generic separation, unless combined with other permanent marks, since both forms are sometimes met with in the same frond; but we have not been able, in any instance, to detect a free, and a *regularly reticulated* venation on the same plant, consequently we are disposed—at least for the present—to retain genera which are founded on the reticulated venation. The following list shows the genera which have hitherto been established on the character of the reticulated venation, along with the genera from which they have been separated, and to which they must revert, if the constancy of reticulated venation is ever found to fail:—

* Syngramma	from	Gymnogramma.	* Synaphlebium	from	Lindsæa.
* Hewardia	„	Adiantum.	* Cionidium†	„	Deparia.
Litobrochia	„	Pteris.	Lygodictyon	„	Lygodium.
* Schizoloma	„	Isoloma.	Aneimidictyon	„	Aneimia.

Those which are marked with an asterisk are not at present in cultivation. Fig. 88 represents a sterile pinna, and a portion of a fertile panicle of *Aneimidictyon Phyllitidis* (nat. size).

1. *A. Phyllitidis*, J. Smith, (Aneimia, *Swartz*).—A beautiful, evergreen, stove fern, from the West Indies and tropics of South America. Sterile fronds pinnate, light green, one to one and half foot long; pinnæ glabrous, oblong-lanceolate, acute at the apex, somewhat round or obtusely cuneate at the base, crenate-serrate at the margin. Fertile fronds erect, tripartite, one to two feet high; sterile portion spreading, and from eight inches to a foot long. Rachis and stipes slightly hairy. Fronds terminal, adherent to a fasciculate-erect rhizome.

2. *A. Haenkei*, Presl (Aneimia longifolia, *Raddi*).—An ornamental evergreen stove fern, from Brazil. Sterile fronds very hairy, pinnate, about a foot long, deep green; pinnæ oblong, membranous, petiolulate, obtuse at the apex, superior base round and sub-auriculate, inferior truncate-cuneate, crenulate on the margin. Fertile fronds erect, tripartite, one and a half to two feet high, very hairy; sterile portion spreading, pinnate, eight to ten inches long; pinnæ oblong, obtuse at the apex, upper base rounded and sub-auriculate, lower truncate-cuneate. Fronds terminal, adherent to a fasciculate erect rhizome.

3. *A. fraxinifolia*, J. H., (Aneimia densa, *Link* in part).—An ornamental evergreen stove fern, from Brazil.

† Cionidium Moorii, T. M. MS.—Deparia Moorii, *Hook*, in *Journ. of Bot.* iv. 55.

Sterile fronds hairy, pinnate, deep green, one foot long; pinnæ oblong-lanceolate, petiolulate, acute at the apex, and slightly cordate at the base. Fertile fronds hairy, tripartite, one to one and half foot high; sterile portion spreading, pinnate, eight or ten inches long. Frond terminal, adherent to a fasciculate-erect rhizome.

MOHRIA, *Swartz.*—Name commemorative of Mohr, a German cryptogamist.

Sori marginal, attached on or near the apices of the venules, with the margin of the segments inflexed. Spore-cases ovate-globose, rarely globose, sessile, naked, vertical. Veins forked direct, free. Fronds of two kinds, sterile and fertile; the fertile erect, uniform, contracted, from six inches to one foot high, bi-tripinnatifid, usually constituting a rachiform unilateral sporangiferous panicle; the sterile spreading, reclining or semi-erect, bi-tripinnatifid, pinnæ entire, laciniate or multifid, with segments linear and dichotomous. Rhizome cæspitose, creeping.—One solitary species constitutes this genus, which has a considerable affinity to Aneimia, though readily distinguished from it by having distinct fertile fronds, which are less contracted, and by not being tripartite. Fig. 89 represents a portion of the sterile, and a pinnule of the fertile frond of *M. thurifraga* (nat. size) with a small portion (magn.) showing the venation.

1. *M. thurifraga*, Swartz.—A very elegant evergreen, warm greenhouse Fern, from the Cape of Good Hope, Madagascar, and the Mauritius. Fronds of two kinds, sterile and fertile. Fertile fronds lanceolate, erect, sub-tripinnate, from eight inches to a foot high, scaly beneath; pinnules sub-cordate, with two or three lobed segments. Sterile fronds lanceolate, semi-erect, six to nine inches long, yellowish green,

Fig. 89.

tripinnatifid; pinnules sub-cordate, round at the apex, inciso-serrate, with linear and dichotomous segments. Stipes and rachis scaly, of a light brown; lateral, adherent to a short cæspitose creeping rhizome, forming thick tufts.

Sub-order—POLYPODIACEÆ: *Tribe*—OSMUNDACEÆ.

As this group originally stood, it contained a very heterogeneous mass of species, widely differing in habit and venation, and in the structure of the sori; but being divested of those forms whose spore-cases have a radiated apex, it is now reduced to two genera, containing about a dozen species, which have a great uniformity of habit, and are recognized by their spore-cases being sub-globose, pedicellate, reticulated, unilocular, opening by a vertical fissure (bivalved), with an oblique gibbose pellucid apex, and destitute of a ring. They are borne either on the same or on separate contracted fronds. Their spore-cases dividing vertically into two halves, and being destitute of the radiate apex, are the primary characters that distinguish them from Schizæaceæ.

OSMUNDA, *Linnæus.*—Name of uncertain derivation.

Sori naked, and densely clustered on contracted fronds, or on some portion of the segments only, which are contracted, rachiform, simple, or paniculate. Spore-cases large, sub-globose, pedicellate, bivalved. Veins forked; venules direct, free. Fronds from one to ten or more feet high, pinnate or bipinnate. Rhizome thick, caudiciform, or tufted.—All the cultivated species of Osmunda are perfectly hardy, and are natives of North America, one of them being likewise indigenous to Britain. The genus contains but few species, chiefly inhabitants of temperate climes; only one or two are recorded as being found within the tropics. They are the most ornamental of all our hardy Ferns; but not being easily propagated, are not very common in collections. The sub-globose, pedicellate, bivalved spore-cases readily distinguish them from all other kinds except Todea, from which they are chiefly known by their fertile portions being so contracted as to have no evident venules. Fig. 90 represents a portion of the fertile frond, and a pinnule of the sterile one, of *O. interrupta* (nat. size).

Fig. 90.

1. *O. interrupta*, Michaux.—A very ornamental hardy deciduous Fern, from North America. Fronds of two kinds; the sterile glabrous, lanceolate, pinnate, one to two feet long, light green, with lanceolate pinnæ, of which the inferior are petiolulate, deeply pinnatifid, with oblong-obtuse segments, entire at the margin; the fertile ones erect, lanceolate, one and a half to two feet high, pinnate, their pinnæ lanceolate, the inferior sterile, petiolulate, the intermediate contracted and sporangiferous, the upper sterile at the apex. Fronds terminal, adherent to a stocky crown.

2. *O. cinnamomea*, Linnæus.—A beautiful hardy deciduous species, from North America. Fronds of two kinds; the sterile lanceolate, subbipinnate, one to one and a half foot long, pale green, with lanceolate, sub-petiolate pinnæ, deeply pinnatifid, with ovate-obtuse segments, entire at the margin; the fertile ones erect, contracted, bipinnate, one and a half foot high, of a rusty brown colour, and very woolly. Fronds terminal, adherent around a stocky crown.

3. *O. regalis*, Linnæus.—A beautiful, hardy, deciduous Fern, indigenous to Britain, and found generally throughout Europe, Asia, Africa, and North America. Frond glabrous, bipinnate, four to ten feet high, rather glaucous; pinnules oblong, nearly entire, obtuse at the apex, dilated and somewhat subauricled at the base, crenulate on the margin, and articulated with the rachis. Sori paniculate, on the apex of the frond. Fronds nearly all fertile; terminal, adherent to a caudiciform rhizome, often forming very large tufts.

O. regalis β spectabilis (O. spectabilis, *Willdenow*).—An ornamental hardy deciduous Fern, from North America. Frond slender, glabrous, ovate-lanceolate, bipinnate, two foot high; pinnules oblong, petiolulate, obtuse at the apex, obliquely-truncate at the base, crenulate-serrate on the margin. Sori paniculate on the apex of the fronds, which are terminal, adherent to a caudiciform rhizome.

TODEA, *Willdenow*.—Name commemorative of Henry Julius Tode, of Mecklenburg, an experienced mycologist.

Sori oblong, simple or forked, and subsequently confluent. Spore-cases naked, subglobose, bivalved, produced on evident venules, and but few to each sorus. Veins simple, or forked; venules direct, free. Fronds bipinnatifid, from one to three feet high; pinnæ coriaceous, and serrated, or membranous pellucid and multifid. Rhizome thick, caudiciform.—A very limited genus, the species having an aspect widely different from that of Osmunda, although the spore-cases are of a precisely similar description. They are natives of New Holland, New Zealand, and the Cape of Good Hope, and are rare in gardens, being very seldom imported, and not easily propagated. They are distinguished from Osmunda by their spore-cases being produced on evident venules, and the fertile portions of the fronds being, if at all, only slightly contracted. Fig. 91 represents a pinna of *T. africana* (med. size).

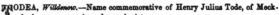

1. *T. africana*, Willdenow (Osmunda totta, *Swartz.*; Osmunda barbara, *Thunberg*).—An evergreen warm greenhouse Fern, a native of the Cape of Good Hope, and New Holland. Fronds glabrous, lanceolate, subbipinnate, two to three feet high, darkish green; pinnules subcoriaceous, lanceolate, repand, decurrent at the base, forming a winged rachis, obtuse at the apex, and serrate at the margin. Sori confined to the inferior pinnules, on the lower half of the fronds, which are terminal, adherent, dilated at the base, where is formed an erect caudiciform rhizome.

2. *T. pellucida*, Carmichael (T. hymenophylloides, *Richard*).—A very elegant evergreen warm greenhouse species, from New Zealand. Fronds membranous, ovate-lanceolate, subtripinnate, one to two feet long, olive green; pinnules oblong, deeply pinnatifid, decurrent at the base, forming a winged rachis; segments linear, repand, with a single vein. Spore-cases small, abundant on the inferior pinnules. Rachis and midrib of pinnæ hairy. Fronds terminal, adherent, dilated at the base, there forming an erect caudiciform rhizome.

Fig. 91.

Order—MARATTIACEÆ.

This very distinct and well-marked natural group contains but few genera, and probably not more than twenty species. Their aspect and habit is so peculiarly characteristic, and so widely different from those of other Ferns, that they may be recognized in almost any stage of their development, even in the absence of fructification. They have large sessile or pedicellate spore-cases, which are either horny, opaque, distinct and unilocular, or laterally and oppositely connate, so becoming multilocular; round oblong or linear, biserial or bivalved, opening by pores or vertical slits in the interior side. The plants are usually large and robust, inhabiting tropical or subtropical regions; and under cultivation are only seen in their natural character, when a liberal allowance of pot and head room, and a rather high temperature, with abundance of moisture, is supplied to them.

MARATTIA, *Smith.*—Name commemorative of J. T. Maratti, of Vallombrosa, in Tuscany, a writer on Ferns. Sori linear, submarginal, consisting of a transverse row of large oblong opaque multilocular spore-cases, one on each vein; each spore-case sessile, distinct, solitary, subterminal, longitudinally bivalved; each valve laterally connate, and containing from six to twelve cells, opening by a vertical slit internally. Veins forked; venules direct, free. Fronds stipitate, glabrous or muricate, from four to eight feet long, bi-tri-pinnate. Rachis sometimes winged. Rhizome large, fleshy, sub-globose, or caudiciform and erect.—The most prominent feature by which this genus may be recognized from all others, except Angiopteris and Eupodium, is its large robust-growing fronds, swollen at the base of the pinnæ and stipes, where they have an indistinct articulation; but it is so closely allied to the genera above mentioned, that it can only be distinguished from them when in fructification, the technical distinctions between these genera being based upon the position or formation of the spore-cases. The marks which characterize Marattia are, that the spore-cases are oblong, sessile, and multilocular. Fig. 92 represents a pinnule of *M. cicutæfolia* (mod. size) with a spore-case (magn).

1. *M. elegans,* Endlicher.—An ornamental, evergreen, warm greenhouse Fern, a native of Ascension and Norfolk Islands, and New Zealand. Fronds glabrous, bi-tripinnate, six to nine feet high, darkish green; pinnules lanceolate petiolulate, coriaceous, serrate at the apex, unequal or obliquely truncate at the base, slightly serrate at the margin, and articulate with the rachis. Midrib of pinnæ marginate or slightly winged. Stipes three to four feet long, very stout, rough towards the base, and clothed with woolly scales, especially when young. Base of the pinnæ and stipes swollen, and indistinctly articulated.

M. elegans β erecta.—An evergreen stove Fern, from Ascension Island. Fronds glabrous, dark green, three to four feet long, bipinnate; pinnules lanceolate, coriaceous, petiolulate, truncate at the base, serrate at the margin. Stipes rounded, muricate. Fronds terminal, indistinctly articulated with a thick, fleshy, foliaceous, erect caudiciform rhizome, attaining the height of a foot or more.

2. *M. cicutæfolia,* Kaulfuss.—A robust-growing evergreen stove Fern, from Brazil. Fronds glabrous, bi-tripinnate, from four to six feet high, bright green; pinnules lanceolate, petiolulate, articulate, serrate at the apex, unequal or obliquely truncate at the base, and deeply serrated with large triangular teeth on the margin, the apex often irregularly lobed, deeply pinnatifid, and leafy. Stipes rounded, muricate, scaly while young,

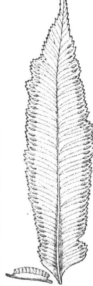

Fig. 92.

and much swollen at the base. Midrib of pinnæ marginate or slightly winged, swollen at the base, and indistinctly articulated with the rachis.

3. *M. alata,* Smith.—A very beautiful evergreen stove Fern, from Jamaica. Fronds rather erect, tripinnate, light green, six or eight feet high, and scaly beneath; ultimate pinnules small, oblong-ovate, cuneate at the base, deeply and sharply serrate at the apex. Midrib of pinnæ and pinnules winged throughout. Stipes covered throughout with light brown soft scales. Fronds terminal, swollen at the base, and indistinctly articulated with a fleshy and globose rhizome. This species has been recently introduced to the Royal Botanic Garden, Kew.

EUPODIUM, *J. Smith* (Marattia, *sp.* of *Authors*).—Name derived from the Greek *eu*, well, and *pous*, a foot; alluding to the very evident foot-stalk that sustains each spore-case.

Spore-cases large, oblong, multilocular, seated on a slender pedicel, becoming longitudinally bivalved; each valve laterally connate, containing five to eight cells; each cell opening by a vertical slit on the inside. Sporangiferous receptacle medial. Veins simple or forked, free. Fronds tripinnate, three to four feet long. Rhizome thick, fleshy, subglobose, or by age becoming rather erect.—This genus contains a solitary species,

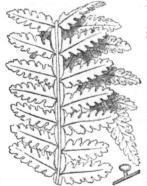

Fig. 93.

native of South America, which has been separated from Marattia in consequence of its spore-cases being stipitate; it is of a rather fragile nature, and not very common in cultivation. Fig. 93 represents a small portion of *E. Kaulfussii* (nat. size), with a spore-case (magn.)

Aneimia cicutaria

1. *E. Kaulfussii*, J. Smith (Marattia alata, *Raddi*; M. Kaulfussii, *Kunze*; M. lævis, *Kaulfuss*).—An ornamental evergreen stove Fern, from Brazil. Fronds glabrous, triangular, three-branched, grass green, from three to four feet high; branches tripinnate; ultimate pinnules ovate or oblong obtuse, sessile membranous, pinnatifid, obliquely truncate at the base, and obtusely lobed at the margin. Midrib of pinnæ and pinnules winged throughout. Stipes roundish, about half the length of the frond, and, as well as the pinnæ, swollen at the base and indistinctly articulated.

ANGIOPTERIS, *Hoffman.*—Named from *aggeion*, a vessel, and *pteris*, a fern; alluding to the formation of the sori.

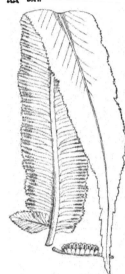

Sori linear, continuous, compound, submarginal. Spore-cases obovate sessile emarginate, laterally confluent, and definitely arranged in two opposite series; each series containing from five to seven distinct entire cells; each cell opening by a vertical slit internally. Sporangiferous receptacle medial. Veins simple or forked, free. Fronds large, stipitate, bi-tripinnate, from six to ten feet long. Rhizome large, fleshy, subglobose.—Only a solitary species of this genus is at present in cultivation; it is one of the most robust-growing of herbaceous Ferns, and so precisely coincides with Marattia, in aspect, habit, and venation, and in the circumscription of the fronds, that it cannot be determined with certainty even by the best pteridologists, except by the aid of the fructification. The geographical distribution of plants is frequently found to be a valuable auxiliary in the determination of genera or species; and so in the present instance, whilst Angiopteris is confined to the East Indies, no species of Marattia, according to Dr. Wallich, has been detected there; though one if not two species are found in the islands of Mauritius and Bourbon. The genus is readily known when in fructification by the spore-cases being definitely disposed in two opposite rows, each row laterally confluent, each spore-case distinct, and opening with a vertical slit on the inside. Fig. 94 represents a pinnule of *A. evecta* (med. size), and a sorus (magn.)

1. *A. longifolia*, Greville et Hooker? (A. evecta, *Hort.*)—An ornamental evergreen stove Fern, from Ceylon. Fronds glabrous, bi-tripinnate, from six to ten feet high, deep olive green; pinnules lanceolate-petiolate, five to ten inches long, coriaceous, shining, serrate at the apex, roundish or obliquely truncate at the base, and finely crenate-serrate at the margin. Stipes terete, three to four feet long, very stout, and scattered over with woolly scales, especially when young. Both stipes, pinnæ, and pinnules are swollen at the base, and indistinctly articulated. Midrib of pinnæ marginate, or slightly winged. This plant was introduced to Kew in 1845, and has been recently imported, by Messrs. Rollisson of Tooting, from Java.

Fig. 94.

DANÆA, *Smith.*—Name commemorative of Pierre M. Dana, a writer on the plants of Piedmont.

Spore-cases linear, biserial, multilocular, each cell opening by a circular pore. Sporangiferous receptacle occupying nearly the whole length of the venules. Veins forked; venules direct, parallel, arcuate on their apices, where they anastomose with a cartilaginous margin. Fronds of two kinds, sterile and fertile, simple or pinnate, from one to three feet long; pinnæ lanceolate, entire or serrate on the margin. Fertile fronds usually contracted, and densely sporangiferous throughout the under surface. Rhizome thick, fleshy, decumbent, and creeping.—Two or three minor characteristics exhibited by this genus serve to distinguish it from the other portion of Marattiaceæ, namely, the curved venules anastomosing with the cartilaginous margin, and the decumbent rhizome. The essential character, however, consists in the

Fig. 95.

compact linear spore-cases opening by two rows of pores. It is one of the most distinct of genera, and contains but a few species, which are natives of the West India Islands, and South America; they are very scarce in cultivation, though oftentimes introduced, being difficult to establish. Fig. 95 represents a pinna of a sterile and fertile frond of *D. nodosa* (nat. size), with part of a spore-case (magn.)

1. *D. nodosa*, Smith.—An evergreen stove Fern, from Jamaica. Fronds glabrous, somewhat triangular, two to three feet high, pinnate, deep shining green; pinnæ oblong-lanceolate, petiolate, coriaceous, unequal or cuneate at the base, subentire at the margin. Rachis winged, knotty. Stipes half the length of the frond, swollen at the base, and covered with small scales. Fronds lateral, indistinctly articulated with a thick decumbent rhizome. This plant is very scarce in cultivation, and has not yet produced fructification.

Order—OPHIOGLOSSACEÆ.

According to the strict principles of the classification of cryptogamous plants, this small group is excluded from among true Ferns, in consequence of having a straight vernation. It contains three genera, and about twenty species, which are very widely distributed throughout both hemispheres. They are of a rather succulent nature, with thick roots, the fronds usually bipartite, their spore-cases large, roundish or subglobose, sessile, opaque, unilocular, without a ring or cellular reticulation, bivalved, and opening by a transverse fissure.

BOTRYCHIUM, *Swartz.*—Name derived from *botrys*, a bunch; alluding to the form of the fertile portion of the frond, which somewhat resembles a cluster.

Spore-cases sessile globose, distinct and unilocular, bivalved, of a leathery texture, opening transversely. Fronds usually two-branched; fertile branch erect, contracted, constituting a compound sporangiferous unilateral panicle. Veins simple or forked, radiating; venules direct, free. Fronds solitary, stipitate, from a few inches to two feet high, bi- or tripartite; sterile branch spreading, pinnate or bi-tripinnate, and shorter than the fertile one. Stipes covered at the base with membranous scales. Rhizome fasciculate.—In aspect and habit the species of this genus have a great similarity to Aneimia, sterile and fertile branches being united on the same frond. About ten or twelve species of Botrychium are described: these are all terrestrial, and are chiefly found inhabiting extra-tropical countries, one species being indigenous to Britain. They are known by their compound solitary fronds, which are rather fleshy, and by their spore-cases being without a ring, or reticulation. Fig. 96 represents a frond of *B. lunarioides*, of very small size.

1. *B. Lunaria*, Swartz.—A hardy deciduous species, indigenous to Britain, and found throughout Europe and North America. Fronds solitary, glabrous, bi- or tripartite, three to ten inches high, glaucous green. Sterile branch pinnate; pinnæ lunate or flabelliform, crenate on the margin. Fertile branch erect, contracted, bipinnatifid, with the spore-cases crowded on the margin. Fronds terminal, with membranous sheaths at their base, in which they are inclosed during the state of hybernation.

2. *B. lunarioides*, Swartz.—A half-hardy, or frame species, from North America. Fronds solitary, glabrous, one to one and a half feet high, dull green. Sterile portion bipartite, branches bipinnatifid, with oblong or flabellate segments, crenate on the margin. Fertile branch erect, paniculate, and much longer than the sterile one; spore-cases crowded on the margin. Fronds divided below the middle of the stipes.

3. *B. dissectum*, Muhlenberg.—A half-hardy or frame species, from North America. Fronds solitary, glabrous, about a foot high, reddish-green. Sterile portion tripartite, branches bi-tri-pinnatifid, ultimate divisions small, flabellate-multipartite, with linear dentate or bidentate segments. Fertile branch erect, paniculate, longer than the sterile one; spore-cases crowded. Fronds divided below the middle of the stipes.

Fig. 96.

Begonia prestoniensis

PHIOGLOSSUM, *Linnæus.*—Name derived from *ophis*, a serpent, and *glossa*, a tongue; from the spike of fructification somewhat resembling the tongue of a serpent.

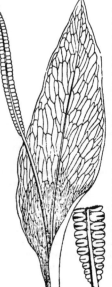

Spore-cases sessile, roundish, coriaceous, unilocular, opaque, bivalved, opening transversely, arranged in two parallel rows, forming a simple, compact, pedicellate, connate spike. Sterile portion spreading, ovate-lanceolate, and usually shorter than the fertile portion. Venation uniform. reticulated, forming elongated areoles. Fronds stipitate, simple, from a few inches to about a foot high, ovate-lanceolate, or linear and forked.— All the exotic species belonging to this genus, which is rather extensive, remain to be introduced; they are terrestrial or epiphytal, and have a very extensive geographical range, one species only being found in Britain. Fig. 97 represents a frond of *O. vulgatum* (nat. size), with a fertile portion (magn.).

1. *O. vulgatum*, Linnæus.—A deciduous hardy species, indigenous to Britain, also common in Europe, and said to be found in Africa and North America. Fronds simple, glabrous, solitary, from three inches to a foot long, of a deep green; sterile portion entire, ovate-lanceolate, obtuse; fertile linear, pedicellate, erect, forming a cauline spike. Fronds terminal. Rhizome with thick roots.

The cultivation of the Ophioglossum has been often thought to be difficult. The plant has, indeed, a peculiar mode of growth; one or more of the stiff coarse fibres, which appear like a spreading tuft of roots, becoming a runner, and organizing a bud at its extremity, from which a young plant is produced. These root-fibres, with their matured buds, should be taken up just as the foliage is decaying, and so carefully that they may not be at all broken; and they may then be transplanted with success. They like a close, heavy, loamy soil, rather damp than otherwise, and potted in rich soil, and kept in a cold close frame. We have had them succeed well in the atmosphere of London. In the out-door fernery they must be planted in a similar soil, and the situation must be one that is not liable to become much affected by drought.

The Botrychiums are very similar to the Ophioglossums in their habit of growth; and we have succeeded in cultivating them on a similar plant. Only, instead of a heavy loamy soil, we find them flourish best in soft, unctuous, peaty soil, not too retentive of moisture. They do not like to be kept quite so moist as the Ophioglossums.

Fig. 97.

BEGONIA PRESTONIENSIS.*

THE original species of Begonia which have found their way into our gardens, furnish a group of plants which have generally had many admirers, on account either of the brilliant colour and profusion of their flowers, or their singular and elegant foliage, or of some peculiar and grotesque habit of growth; or perhaps, above all, by reason of the facility with which they are cultivated in a moderately warm temperature. Latterly the skill of cultivators has called into existence some hybrid forms, which, uniting the desirable qualities of more than one species, are so much more desirable, in an ornamental point of view, than either parent, and indicate the probability of Begonias soon becoming as popular as Achimenas and Gloxinias have already become. Our present subject is one of these hybrids, and one which justifies such anticipations. It was raised in the garden of E. L. Betts, Esq., of Preston Hall, near Aylesford, in Kent; and Mr. T. Frost, Mr. Betts's gardener, states that it was obtained by crossing *B. cinnabarina* with *B. nitida*,† which latter has imparted to it

* B. (Diploclinium) *prestoniensis* (hyb: ♀ cinnabarina, ♂ nitida); stems branched flexuose; leaves obliquely ovate-acuminate, sinuate-lobed, doubly serrate, with scattered hairs on the upper surface and on the ribs beneath; stipules triangular-lanceolate; flowers in trichotomous axillary cymes, pedicles longer than the leaves, bracts ovate, sharply toothed; male flowers four-petalled, female five-petalled; ovary roundish triquetrous, two of the angles very narrowly winged, the third with a large triangular projecting wing; placentas "double." (! ♀ rubra, ♂ cinnabarina.)—M.

† It has been suggested to us, that this Begonia is not a seedling from *cinnabarina*, but from *rubra*, fertilized with that species; and this origin appears by no means improbable. It is possible the raiser's memoranda may have been in confusion.

a free-flowering and shrubby habit, whilst it retains nearly the foliage and blossoms of the tuberous annual-stemmed female parent. This combination has produced what is probably the handsomest Begonia to be found in cultivation: certainly it is a most beautiful and brilliant thing. We owe to Messrs. Lucombe, Pince, and Co., of Exeter, (who possess, we believe the entire stock,) the opportunity of figuring it, from fine flowering branches communicated a few weeks since. It appears to bloom chiefly in autumn, and continues some time in beauty. The original plant was exhibited last October, at the meeting of the Horticultural Society, in Regent Street, and it was then greatly admired.

The stems of *Begonia prestoniensis* are round, smooth, flexuose, and branched, tinged, in the younger parts, with red. On these the leaves are borne alternately on hairy petioles which are about an inch long, and have triangular-lanceolate stipules at their base. The leaves are obliquely ovate-acuminate, slightly sinuate-lobed and 'doubly serrated with rose-coloured cuspidate teeth. The upper surface is scattered over with short hairs, which occur more numerously on the ribs beneath. The flowers, of a brilliant orange-scarlet, and sweet-scented, come in trichotomous cymes from the axils of the leaves, the peduncles being longer than the leaves, and furnished at its forkings, and at the base of the pedicels, with roundish-ovate, sharply and finely-toothed bracts, which, as well as the peduncles, pedicels, and ovaries, are coloured red. The male flowers consist of four spreading petals, the two outer of which are oblong-obovate, much larger than (more than twice the size of) the obovate wedge-shaped inner petals, and of a dense tuft of orange-coloured stamens. They are deep orange-red, and measure an inch and a half in diameter. The female flowers are smaller than the males, of the same colour, and have five petals, three of which are smaller than the others. The ovary is roundish-triquetrous, having two of its angles very narrowly winged; the other angle bears a large and somewhat triangular wing. The placentas are double, not irregularly lobed, as in *B. cinnabarina*; it is therefore a Diploclinium, not a Platyclinium.* Messrs. Lucombe & Co. speak of the plant as of a neat and dwarf habit, and very profuse in flowering, which the specimen exhibited last year in Regent Street evidenced; they also state that it requires only greenhouse treatment, and is as fragrant as any of the tea-scented Roses.

Most of the Begonias thrive best in a shady house, kept at a temperature intermediate between that of a stove and greenhouse; and we imagine the present to be no exception, though, from the season of its blooming, it would doubtless flower readily in a warm greenhouse. They prefer a rather light soil, composed of equal parts sandy loam and leaf-mould, with sand added, and plenty of drainage. They may be grown to perfection in a pit, kept rather close and shaded, and at a temperature of from 55° to 60°. Cuttings, when these are afforded, offer the best mode of propagation. They grow readily planted in rather sandy soil, and placed in such a pit as that just mentioned. To grow a specimen, a healthy free-rooted cutting should be selected, and kept shifted on as it advances; and the points of all its shoots should be continually nipped off as soon as they have formed three or four leaves. As the Begonias grow in such a situation through the winter, a cutting selected then, and grown on in this way until the next autumn, would form a large full-branched mass, and might be expected to bloom finely, if stopping the shoots were desisted from shortly after midsummer. As soon as the flowers were beginning to develope, it might be removed to a close warm greenhouse; but there must be no sudden transition from hot to cold, or from shade to full sunlight, or from moisture to drought, or the blossom-buds would probably be cast off.—T. M.

New Garden Plants.

LONICERA FRAGRANTISSIMA. *Lindley.* Most fragrant Honeysuckle.—Order Caprifoliaceæ (Caprifoil tribe).—A hardy sub-evergreen shrub, with oblong acute leaves, and white flowers exceedingly fragrant, combining the richness of the perfume of Orange blossoms with the delicious sweetness of Honeysuckle. A native of China. The flowers appear in spring with the earliest development of the leaves.

LOASA BICOLOR, *Klotzsch.* Two-coloured Loasa.—Order Loasaceæ (Loasad tribe).—An annual, with twice

* See *Gard. Mag. Bot.,* ii. 153.

pinnately cut leaves, and white flowers with a crown of scarlet scales. It was brought to Berlin from Central America, by M. Warczewitz.

CHIONANTHUS RETUSUS, *Lindley.* Retuse-leaved Chionanthus.—Order Oleaceæ (Olivewort tribe).—A hardy deciduous shrub, introduced from China by Mr. Fortune. The leaves are long-stalked, obovate, notched out at the end, downy beneath. The flowers come in slender, terminal, somewhat whorled, panicles, and are pure white of no beauty, but deliciously fragrant. It was found by Mr. Fortune in a garden near Foo-chow-foo, on the river Min.

RYTIDOPHYLLUM HUMBOLDTII, *Klotzsch.* Humboldt's Rytidophyllum.—Order Gesneraceæ (Gesnerad tribe).— A half shrubby stove plant, growing three feet high, with oblique oblong leaves and few-flowered corymbs of flowers, two inches long, greenish, spotted with purple. From Central America, and introduced by M. Warczewitz, who called it *Gesnera Humboldtii.*

RYTIDOPHYLLUM TIGRIDIA, *Klotzsch.* Spotted Rytidophyllum.—Order Gesneraceæ (Gesnerad tribe).—A climbing half-shrubby stove plant, with oblique elliptic leaves, and bell-shaped pendulous flowers, three inches long, greenish, spotted with purple. This comes from Venezuela, and was introduced by M. Moritz. It is the *Gloxinia Tigridia* of Ohlendorff.

CESTRUM WARCZEWITZII, *Klotzsch.* Warczewitz's Cestrum.—Order Solanaceæ (Nightshade tribe).—A handsome greenhouse shrub allied to *C. aurantiacum.* The leaves are oval, shining above, and tapering to each end. The flowers are light orange-yellow, their tube about twice as long as the calyx. It is a native of Central America, near the volcano of Casthago, and was called *Habrothamnus aureus* by M. Warczewitz.

BEGONIA PUNCTATA, *Link, Klotzsch, and Otto.* Dotted Begonia.—Order Begoniaceæ (Begoniad tribe).—A handsome stemless, herbaceous, hothouse perennial, with large cordate leaves cut into about seven toothed palmate lobes, the stalks furrowed, and furnished, just below the blade, with a purple ramentaceous collar. The flowers are in panicles, bright rose-colour, with deep red spots outside. It is a native of Mexico, and is cultivated in the Berlin gardens.

HUNTLEYA CERINA, *Lindley.* Waxy Huntleya.—Order Orchidaceæ (Orchid tribe).—A curious and very beautiful stove orchid, introduced from Central America, and recently flowered by S. Rucker, Esq. The flowers rise singly from the base of the leaves; they are very fleshy, nearly circular, concave, and about three inches across yellowish white and waxy; the lip is more yellow, and has a semicircular ruff of plaits and folds. The column is deep violet near the base.

MAXILLARIA ELONGATA, *Lindley.* Elongated Maxillaria.—Order Orchidaceæ (Orchid tribe).—A terrestrial hothouse Orchid, with elongate pseudo-bulbs, bearing a couple of lanceolate leaves, and producing dense oblong racemes of pale yellow and brown flowers, which do not possess much beauty. It is from Central America, and has been introduced by Mr. Skinner.

BURLINGTONIA DECORA, *Lemaire.* Neat Burlingtonia.—Order Orchidaceæ (Orchid tribe); Syn. *B. amœna,* Planchon.—A beautiful little Brazilian epiphyte, with compressed ovate one-leaved pseudo bulbs, and loose racemes of three to five flowers, of which the sepals and petals are small, connivent, rose-coloured, spotted with red, and the lip broad, flat, two-lobed, and pure white, with a lacerated pinnate, red and speckled appendage on each side of the base. It was introduced from St. Paul's, in Brazil, by M. Libon, the collector for M. de Jonghe, and flowered in May in 1851, with M. Makoy.

MAXILLARIA REVOLUTA, *Klotzsch.* Revolute Maxillaria.—Order Orchidaceæ (Orchid tribe).—A very pretty stove perennial, with oblong pseudo-bulbs an inch long, terminated by one linear ligulate leathery leaf, and producing one-flowered peduncles. The flowers are golden yellow, the points of the petals being recurved. It has been flowered at Frankfort, but its native country is not known.

SCELOCHILUS OTTONIS, *Klotzsch.* Otto's Scelochilus.—Order Orchidaceæ (Orchid tribe).—A neat bulbless stove epiphyte, with oblong coriaceous leaves, and radical, somewhat branched racemes of flowers, which are small, yellow, with a few red streaks. A native of Caraccas, and introduced a few years since to the Botanic Garden at Berlin, where it flowers in April.

MORMODES FLAVIDUM, *Klotzsch.* Yellowish Mormodes.—Order Orchidaceæ (Orchid tribe).—A terrestrial stove Orchid, with long cylindrical pseudo-bulbs, bearing leaves at its joints. The racemes are few flowered; the sepals are linear-lanceolate, greenish-yellow, the lip obovate, yellowish-white, bent inwards, with a small point, almost entire, with both edges curved back. Introduced to Berlin from Central America.

ONCIDIUM CUCULLATUM, *Lindley.* Hooded Oncid.—Order Orchidaceæ (Orchid tribe).—A very pretty stove epiphyte, with long oval pseudo-bulbs, bearing a pair of oblong-lanceolate leaves, and a simple, scarcely panicled raceme of small but pretty flowers; the sepals and petals are dull rose, and the lip violet, covered over with crimson spots. It is from Central America, and was introduced by Mr. Linden. It was flowered in February last at the Fence, Macclesfield.

BESCHORNERIA YUCCOIDES, *Lindley.* Yucca-like Beschorneria. Order Amaryllidaceæ (Amaryllid tribe). A fine half-hardy perennial from Mexico. It has thick, rigid, broad-lanceolate radical leaves, and produces a scape six or seven feet high, bearing a somewhat panicled raceme of green tube-like flowers, seated among deep red bracts. It has been flowered by the Hon. W. F. Strangways, in his garden at Abbotsbury.

ODONTOGLOSSUM PESCATOREI, *Linden.* Pescatore's Odontoglot.—Order Orchidaceæ (Orchid tribe).—One of the most beautiful of this fine genus of Orchids. It has ovate two-leaved pseudo-bulbs. The leaves are strap shaped, shorter than the panicle, which is loose, many-flowered, and erect. The flowers are large, with ovate oblong sepals, white, with a delicate rosy central bar; the petals more ovate and wavy, pure white; the lip heart-shaped, oblong, cuspidate, with a stain of yellow near the base, and a pair of broad, deep, lacerated appendages. The panicle is two feet high and branched. It has been introduced by M. Linden, from New Grenada, and flowers in April. It is beautifully figured in *Paxton's Flower Garden.*

MECONOPSIS WALLICHII, *Hooker.* Dr. Wallich's Meconopsis.—Order Papaveraceæ (Poppy tribe).—A handsome perennial from Sikkim Himalaya, raised in the Royal Gardens at Kew. It grows two to three feet high, and is everywhere hairy, with long ferruginous setæ. The root-leaves are large, lyrate-pinnatifid, those of the stem sessile, oblong pinnatifid. The flowers are large, of a pale blue colour, with a broad ring of orange-coloured anthers surrounding the style. It was introduced by Dr. Hooker, and flowered in June, 1852.

ABELIA TRIFLORA, *R. Brown.* Three-flowered Abelia.—Order Caprifoliaceæ (Caprifoil tribe).—A beautiful Indian shrub, growing about three feet high, with slender grayish branches, dark green ovate-lanceolate acute leaves, fringed with long hairs, and pinkish flowers growing in clusters of three at the end of shoots; they are pale yellow before expansion, but when open, are white, with the rounded segments of the limb tinged with rose. The flowers are remarkable for the long hairs—as long as the tube of the corolla, which cover the five narrow reddish sepals. It flowered at Glasnevin last June, under the care of Mr. Moore, and had been raised five years previously from seeds sent by Major Madden from Simlah. It is hardy in Ireland, but will probably require some protection in this country.

MORMODES IGNEUM, *Lindley.* Fiery Mormodes.—Order Orchidaceæ (Orchid tribe).—A fine stove epiphyte from Central America, introduced by M. Warczewitz. It has a long many-flowered raceme of large fleshy blossoms, of which the sepals and petals are flat, linear-lanceolate, and chocolate-coloured, and the lip rolled back and angular-looking, and of a "rich fiery orange brown." It was flowered by S. Rucker, Esq., of Wandsworth, in January last.

POSOQUERIA REVOLUTA, *Nees von Esenbeck.* Revolute-leaved Posoqueria.—Order Cinchonaceæ (Cinchonad tribe).—A handsome hothouse shrub, with ovate-oblong evergreen leaves. The flowers grow five or six together at the end of the shoots, and are white, with a slender tube four inches long, suddenly expanding into a five-lobed limb. It has been introduced by Messrs. Veitch, and flowers in spring.

DIPLACUS GLUTINOSUS GRANDIFLORUS. Large-flowered glutinous Diplacus.—Order Scrophulariaceæ (Linariad tribe).—This very pretty Diplacus has been figured in *Paxton's Flower Garden,* under the name above quoted, and is, along with *D. puniceus,* ranked as a variety of *glutinosus.* There is, however, this difference between them, besides size and colour, that whereas, in *D. puniceus* as in *D. glutinosus,* the tube of the corolla is very slightly widened towards the mouth, and the limb is spreading, in the plant under notice that part of the corolla above the calyx is widened very rapidly into a broad funnel-shaped mouth, the limb, at the same time, being much less spreading. The plant is a shrub, with erect branching stems, clothed with a short viscid glandular pubescence. The leaves are opposite, oblong-lanceolate, narrowed towards the base, where they are slightly connate, the margins revolute, serrulate in their upper half, the upper surface dark shining green, paler beneath. The flowers are solitary from the axils of the leaves, the pedicels densely glandular-pubescent much shorter than the calyx (usually about one-third its length), the calyx is elongate (1¼ inches), its tube pentagonal, slightly swollen about the centre, and terminating in five unequal acuminate teeth, the upper of which is about twice the length of the lower, the surface glandular, here and there a little hairy, the margins of the teeth being fringed with an entangled mass of curved hairs, so that the mouth appears woolly. The corolla is large, and of a peculiar delicate tint, between nankin and salmon-colour, that part of the tube included in the calyx being very narrow and cylindrical, about a line in diameter and an inch long, the upper part widening rapidly for about an inch, where it is fully seven-eighths in diameter; the limb is about half an inch long, the lobes broad, oblique, the two upper larger, and all cleft down the centre nearly their whole depth, so that the limb becomes almost ten-lobed. It was raised from Californian seeds, imported last year, and sold by Mr. Duncan Hairs, a seedsman, of London. Our plants, at Chelsea, flowered sparingly in the autumn of 1851, and more abundantly during the present year. It has been exhibited from several collections during the present summer.

THE END.

INDEX OF CONTENTS.

Lightning Source UK Ltd.
Milton Keynes UK
UKHW010710140219

337321UK00011B/769/P